English literary hands from Chaucer to Dryden

English literary hands from Chaucer to Dryden

Anthony G. Petti

Harvard University Press

Cambridge, Massachusetts

1977

September 1978

Library of Congress Catalog Card Number 77–74782

ISBN 0–674–25666–2

Printed in Great Britain

Preface

This book has a double purpose: to act as a guide to the handwriting of literary texts in England from the late 14th century to the end of the 17th century, and to provide a comprehensive set of examples from the hands of the leading authors in the period. Surprisingly, these two functions have not been previously combined; neither have they been adequately carried out individually. Few works on palaeography span the medieval and Renaissance periods, and those which do (like L. C. Hector's invaluable book) are chiefly concerned with documents; while the study of 17th-century handwriting has been largely ignored. There are some distinguished books on English literary autographs, most notably by W. W. Greg and Peter Croft; but Greg covers only the period 1550–1650 and Croft confines himself to poets and even excludes those whose English autograph poetry no longer survives.

It is hoped that, apart from being of general and intrinsic interest, this book will be especially useful to students of literary history at a time when more than ever before they are both encouraged and enabled to look beyond the printed word to the manuscript source, and when, with the aid of palaeographical methods, the possibilities of finding new holograph material are considerable. With literary students in mind, the introduction includes sections on the nature and range of literary manuscripts, methods of editing them, principles of textual emendation and the techniques for identifying hands. But the introduction also tries to cover, in basic terms, most of the common aspects of palaeography relevant to the period, among them, writing materials, the different scripts, abbreviation and punctuation; and it provides a guide to terminology. The sequence of material presented is that which has been found most convenient both for teaching and learning about the subject.

A particularly strong endeavour has been to make the text as comprehensive as possible within a reasonably compact space. It contains sixty-seven illustrations drawn from twenty-one libraries or archives in Great Britain, the United States and Spain. They relate to the work of close on sixty authors, and include a wide range of poetry, prose and drama. Accompanying the plates are transcriptions, a discussion of the handwriting, and an indication of the sources and availability of other manuscript material.

Writing a palaeography book is a slow, painful process, bringing with it a profound understanding of why such works are uncommon and their commentaries often slender. Handwriting is many thousands of years old, but the study of palaeography is still young and its practitioners comparatively few. Further, what resources there are seem to have been directed mainly towards the earlier centuries, almost as if post-14th-century palaeography were not only too modern but somewhat unnecessary as well, though this attitude is gradually changing.

Under the circumstances, I am all the more grateful for what I learned from my palaeography teachers at University College London, most notably the late Winifred Husbands, and for the help and encouragement I received from my former colleagues, Mr John Dodgson and Professor T. J. Brown.

Special acknowledgement should be made to my former teacher and colleague, Professor Arthur Brown, now of the Department of English, Monash University, from whom the idea for this book originated, and who was to have been co-author but for other pressing commitments. His assistance was most useful in the early stages of the book.

I have a debt of gratitude to all the librarians and archivists I dealt with, for they were unfailingly kind and ready to assist, and I should like to mention in particular Mr Joseph Scott, Librarian of University College London, the staff of Cambridge University Library, and Miss Joan Gibbs, the Librarian of the outstanding palaeography library in the Senate House, University of London. I wish also to express my thanks to Clare Hall, Cambridge and University College London for giving me an affiliation with them during my sabbatical, and to the University of Calgary for providing that sabbatical. I am especially indebted to the Canada Council for awarding me a Leave Fellowship with which to complete the project.

The last paragraph is reserved for those who have suffered through various stages of the book, including Dr David Atkinson, who as my research assistant checked some of my transcriptions, Mrs Betty O'Keeffe, who combined skilful typing with an uncanny palaeographical gift of being able to decipher my handwriting and typing, Mrs Marianne Wahl for copying out most of the illustrations in the introduction, and my wife, who read through and checked my manuscript, to the possible detriment of her eyesight, but never at the expense of her boundless patience.

Acknowledgements

For permission to publish illustrations and transcriptions grateful acknowledgement is made to the following:

The British Library Board   nos. 4, 10–2, 14–5, 17, 19–22, 24, 26, 28, 30–3, 36–7, 40, 44–9, 53, 55–6, 60, 64, 66–7.
Controller of H.M. Stationery Office   nos. 1, 25, 27, 34, 37, 50–1.
Master and Fellows, Balliol College, Oxford   no. 62.
Bodleian Library, Oxford   nos. 23, 61.
Trustees of Bunyan Meeting, Bedford   no. 65.
Cambridge University Library   nos. 8–9.
Master and Fellows, Corpus Christi College, Cambridge   no. 16.
Corpus Christi College, Valencia   no. 18.
Governors of Dulwich College   nos. 39, 41–3.
Folger Shakespeare Library, Washington, D.C.   no. 35.
Henry E. Huntington Library, California   nos. 3, 7, 52.
Director, University of London Library   no. 5.
Master and Fellows, Magdalene College, Cambridge   no. 63.
Master and Fellows, Peterhouse, Cambridge   no. 2.
Rector of Stonyhurst College, Lancashire   no. 29.
Master and Fellows, Trinity College, Cambridge   nos. 54, 59.
University College London   nos. 6, 38.
Trustees of Dr Williams's Library, London   nos. 57–8.
Warden and Fellows, Winchester College, Hampshire   no. 13.

Contents

Abbreviations

A	*Anglia*, 1877–
BC	*The Book Collector*, 1952–
B.L.	The British Library (formerly the British Museum)
CBEL, i	*The new Cambridge bibliography of English literature*, vol. i, 1974
Croft	P. J. Croft, *Autograph poetry in the English language*, 2 vols., 1973
C.U.L.	Cambridge University Library
DDC	W. W. Greg, *Dramatic documents from the Elizabethan playhouses*, 1931, Commentary
DDR	W. W. Greg, *Dramatic documents from the Elizabethan playhouses*, 1931, Reproductions
ECH	C. Johnson and H. Jenkinson, *English court hand, 1066–1500*, 1915
E.E.T.S., e.s.	Early English Text Society, extra series, 1867–1920
E.E.T.S., o.s.	Early English Text Society, original series, 1864–
EL	Ellesmere manuscripts, Huntington Library
ELBSH	*The English library before 1700*, ed. F. Wormald and E. C. Wright, 1958
EPA	D. J. N. Flower and A. N. L. Munby, *English poetical autographs from Sir Thomas Wyat to Rupert Brooke*, 1938
EVH	C. E. Wright, *English vernacular hands from the twelfth to the fifteenth centuries*, 1960
F.&W.	A. Fairbank and B. Wolpe, *Renaissance handwriting*, 1960
FRHL	G. F. Warner, *Facsimiles of royal, historical, literary and other autographs*, 1899
FTTC	W. W. Greg, *Facsimiles of twelve early English manuscripts in the library of Trinity College Cambridge*, 1913
Greg	W. W. Greg, *English literary autographs, 1550–1650*, 2 vols., 1925–32
HA	Hastings Manuscripts, Huntington Library
Hector	L. C. Hector, *The handwriting of English documents*, 1966
H.L.	Henry E. Huntington Library, San Marino, California
HLB	*The Huntington Library Bulletin*
HMC	The Historical Manuscripts Commission
Lib.	*The Library*, 1899– (incorporated with *Transactions of the Bibliographical Society*, 1920–)
Lieftinck, 1954	B. Bischoff, G. I. Lieftinck, G. Battelli, *Nomenclature des écritures livresques du IXe au XVIe siècle*, 1954
Lieftinck, 1964	G. I. Lieftinck, *Manuscrits datés conservés dans les Pays-Bas*, i, 1964
MEV	Carleton Brown and R. H. Robbins, *The index of Middle English verse*, 1943
MLR	*Modern Language Review*, 1905–
Morton	A. Morton, *Men of Letters*, Public Record Office Museum Pamphlet no. 6, 1974
MP	*Modern Philology*, 1903–
MVS	Carleton Brown and R. H. Robbins, *Supplement to the index of Middle English Verse*, 1965
N&Q	*Notes and Queries*, 1849–
Parkes	M. B. Parkes, *English cursive book hands 1250–1500*, 1969
PBSA	*Publications of the Bibliographical Society of America*, 1964–
PMLA	*Publications of the Modern Language Association of America*, 1886–
P.R.O.	Public Record Office, London
RES	*The Review of English Studies*, 1925–
R.O.	Record Office
S.P.	State Papers, Public Record Office, London
Spec.	*Speculum, a journal of mediaeval studies*, 1926–
TOEM	W. Skeat, *Twelve facsimiles of old English manuscripts*, 1892
TLS	*The Times Literary Supplement*
U.C.L.	University College London
U.L.L.	University of London Library
V.&A.	The Victoria and Albert Museum, London
YWES	*The Year's Work in English Studies*, 1919–

Introduction

1. The survival of medieval and Renaissance literary manuscripts

Time and the elements have not been particularly kind or discriminating in their treatment of literary manuscripts. The combination of time, light and air has caused parchment to yellow and wrinkle, paper to brown and crumble, ink to corrode or fade. Fire has destroyed many famous collections including, in 1731, some of the Cottonian Library, the source for so many important English manuscripts, among them *Beowulf*, which also sustained damage. Earth has played its part either by a violent quake such as destroyed the library of the King of Portugal in the 18th century, or by a more gradual process of burial amidst dust and rubble. Water has taken its toll by flood, as in Florence recently, and by seeping damp, which has attacked so many of the collections in old family houses. The smaller members of the animal kingdom have done their share, especially the bookworm and the rodent, who have between them devoured a considerable amount of ancient literature.

All these depredations have usually been abetted by man himself. In the name of religion or for political expediency, manuscripts and books have been burned or defaced, or have been destroyed in the course of war. More usually, through simple neglect or in a primitive form of recycling, paper and parchment have been converted to other uses irrespective of what was written on them. Sometimes this process of conversion contributed to the life of other books and manuscripts, in reinforced bindings, fly leaves and repairs, as in the case of Malory's *Morte Darthur* (no. 13), patched up with a piece of vellum cut from an indulgence granted by Innocent VIII. Less worthy uses included scouring candlesticks, polishing boots, providing wrapping for grocers and soapsellers and toilet paper for the jakes.[1] Perhaps the most notorious example of recycling is provided by Betsy the Cook, a depressingly archetypal figure who, placing food for the body above that for the mind, tore her way through many manuscript volumes of plays to provide linings for her pies.[2]

It is clear, too, that continuous use often has caused complete disintegration or at least serious damage, among famous English manuscripts so endangered being *The Booke of Sir Thomas Moore* (nos. 36, 40) and Milton's *Minor Poems* (no. 59), though they have now been carefully restored. But acts of restoration have not always been so beneficial, and many 19th-century repairs, with their drastic cropping, unsuitable glues, reinforcing tapes and ink restoratives, actually hastened the process of obliteration.

The preservation of manuscripts has also been subject to the strictures of convention and what Herbert Read calls 'the sieve of taste'. In the Middle Ages, works of devotion, especially if written in Latin and illuminated, were highly prized, a good example being the bible which its scribe, a German nun, was able to barter for a farm.[3] They were also likely to be housed in the library of a religious institution or a noble patron. Small-scale secular works were not usually so fortunate unless they catered for the tastes of the court. The Renaissance, in its concern to revive Classical literature and learning, tended to neglect works of the near past, and still considered some forms of literature too ephemeral to be worth preserving, including popular drama and much poetry.

With the dawn of the Renaissance in England also came one of the most disruptive influences on early manuscripts: the breaking up and dispersal of monastic libraries, though, as already implied, it is doubtful whether they possessed all that many literary manuscripts in the vernacular.[4] Nevertheless, the wilful destruction inflicted on the contents of these libraries was considerable, as Bishop John Bale, formerly a Carmelite monk, often testified. In a letter to Archbishop Parker, July 1560, he refers to the 'tyme of the lamentable spoyle of the lybraryes of Englande' when he found manuscripts 'in stacyoners and boke bynders, store howses, some in grosers, sopesellars, taylers, and other occupyers shoppes, some in shyppes ready to be carryed over the sea into Flaunders to be solde'.[5]

Yet another product of the Renaissance, the printing press, did not simply reduce the circulation of manuscript copies; it gave a primacy to the printed word which made the preservation of the authorial manuscript behind the book unnecessary.[6] Even literary figures preoccupied with posthumous fame did not apparently place value on preserving their holograph manuscripts after publication, much less their earlier drafts, and neither, generally speaking, did anyone else, other than close friends, for the cult of collecting literary autographs did not begin in earnest until the end of the 18th century. Account must also be taken of unpublished manuscripts which, like some of Keats's sonnets, were destroyed by their authors in partial fulfilment of the principle of art for art's sake or, more usually, with the just or mistaken notion of the worthlessness of what they had written.

It should therefore be understandable why there is a dearth of literary holographs even of major English authors from the earliest times to the end of the Renaissance period and beyond. For Chaucer a strong probability exists of two holograph items (nos. 1 and 2), neither of them of his poetry, but there is nothing, for example, for the *Gawain* poet, Langland, Gower, Lydgate or Malory. In the Renaissance the situation is better, but there are still large gaps, with many writers represented only by their correspondence. For instance, no poetical autographs have survived for such major authors as Surrey, Spenser, Marvell and Vaughan, while Sidney, Donne and Dryden are each, as yet, represented by one minor poem. The dramatists are worse off: Marlowe has only a signature, and for Beaumont, Ford, Webster and Tourneur, to name but a few, no handwriting whatsoever is known to exist. Shakespeare is better served than most other dramatists, in that six signatures are extant, one of them with two short preliminary words, and three pages of fairly plausible ascription in an otherwise indifferent and unperformed play.

It is impossible to gauge with even moderate accuracy the extent of loss of medieval and Renaissance manuscripts, but to judge from extant catalogues from monastic and private libraries,[7] wills, accounts, registers, diaries and literary references, it is considerable in all the main genres.[8] R. W. Chambers claims that if the lost poetry of the medieval period had been preserved, the history of medieval literature, at least prior to Chaucer, would appear in a different light,[9] and while his assertion has not always been fully accepted, there is agreement that much written poetry has perished as well as that in the oral tradition.[10] It is clear, too, that much unprinted poetry of the Renaissance has been lost, particularly that written in the shorter verse forms, for example, sonnets, lyrics, the briefer ballads, and many of those poems which it was unwise to keep or which quickly lost their relevance, such as obscene verse and topical political lampoons. In many cases, the loss is undoubtedly greater to the palaeographer or the social historian than it is to the literary critic. A particularly heavy toll has been taken of drama. It is obvious that not only single plays of the medieval period have disappeared but also complete cycles. The manuscript holdings for Renaissance drama are in a poorer state: there are references to over three thousand plays in the Elizabethan and Jacobean period, but only a handful of manuscript copies survive,[11] and a mere fraction is extant in print. The survival rate for prose literature is on the whole much higher. Nevertheless it has sustained considerable losses in narratives and romances. Even didactic and religious works have suffered depredations, and the reverence accorded them by monastic institutions is offset by the Henrician and Elizabethan measures against 'popish' literature, and the Marian ones against Protestant writings.

Ascertaining how many copies of a given work have been lost is an almost insoluble problem, especially for the medieval period. Though manuscripts could not compete with the printed book in numbers of copies circulated, many works retained great popularity for a considerable time, in some cases, centuries, so that by the end of the 15th century, hundreds of copies are likely to have been made of those in greatest demand, and the longer the work, seemingly the more numerous the copies. The *Prick of Conscience* and Love's *Mirror of Christ* survive in over a hundred examples, the *Canterbury Tales* in over eighty; *Piers Plowman* and Gower's *Confessio Amantis* have about fifty each, and Lydgate's *Life of Our Lady* forty-two. What proportion this represents of the total number will never be known, but it cannot represent anything like a full roll-call. The loss is obviously far greater among the romances, for even of the extant ones, eighty-four in all between 1100 and 1500, forty per cent exist only in single copies made in the 15th century, and many of these have lost and torn pages.[12]

The survivors of the diverse onslaughts against manuscripts have often had a chequered career, but are now, for the most part, safely and comfortably housed, in some cases many thousands of miles from their original homes, and often additionally protected from too frequent use by provision of facsimiles and microfilm. Their survival is due in great part to the rescue attempts of a few far-sighted scholars and antiquarians of the 16th and 17th century. Prominent among the earliest of these were John Bale, himself an avid collector,[13] and John Leland, the King's Antiquarian, both of whom made valiant though not consistently successful attempts to save the monastic manuscripts from wafting[14] into oblivion by having them collected up and housed in the Royal library, which had started modestly in the reign of Edward IV. But Henry VIII and his Commissioners were more interested in gathering up the other treasures from the suppressed houses. Neither did Elizabeth add much to the Royal collection, and its first substantial enlargement did not occur until the Earl of Arundel's manuscripts were added in the reign of James I, as also were such presentation copies of literary manuscripts as Jonson's holograph *Masque of Queenes* (no. 46). Another concerned scholar was the mathematician John Dee, who anticipated the idea of a historical manuscripts commission. The most effective of the earliest antiquarians were, however, Archbishop Parker, Sir Thomas Bodley and Sir Robert Cotton. The first two of these were to refurbish the decaying

university libraries of Oxford and Cambridge; the library of the third would provide part of the foundation for the British Museum manuscript collection.

The universities of Oxford and Cambridge had never been heavily endowed with manuscripts. In 1424, for example, Cambridge possessed 122 books. In 1530 it had between five and six hundred, but by 1574 this number had fallen to 175 volumes, of which 120 were manuscripts.[15] Parker, whose special interest was Anglo-Saxon manuscripts, salvaged what manuscripts he could and either gave or bequeathed them to Cambridge and its colleges. To the main university library he gave twenty-five manuscripts in 1574, and at his death, a year later, left nearly 500 to Corpus Christi College.[16] Bodley, returning to Oxford towards the end of Elizabeth's reign after a political career, found that the ancient library, which had included 264 volumes donated by Duke Humphrey of Gloucester in the previous century, had been devastated by the Commissioners of Edward VI, and the room bereft even of the readers' desks. By his efforts the library was refounded, and at its opening in 1602 contained about 2,000 volumes, of which just under 300 were manuscripts. Many donations of manuscripts to these universities followed these early and crucial benefactions, including, among important sources of English literary works, the Rawlinson and the Douce collections.[17]

Cotton, who with Parker and Camden founded a Society of Antiquaries which lasted until 1604, was active both in stimulating others to conserve literary and historical manuscripts and collecting them himself.[18] Several unique works were acquired by him, including the four poems by the *Gawain* poet (no. 4). His collection was augmented by his son and grandson until it contained almost a thousand volumes. In 1700 it passed into the hands of public trustees and, having sustained the fire which seriously damaged a hundred manuscripts and partly scorched a hundred others while at Ashburnham House, it was eventually transferred in 1753 to the British Museum, which had been established that year by Act of Parliament. There it joined two other important private collections, that of Robert Harley, Earl of Oxford, and his son Edward, and of Sir Hans Sloane. The Old Royal Library, now much enlarged, was transferred from St James's Palace to the Museum in 1757 to make up the fourth in the basic collection.[19] Thereafter there was a steady flow of additions, by purchase or bequest, including the Lansdowne, Egerton and Stowe collections, to make the Museum, among other things, the largest and most important library of English vernacular manuscripts.

The 18th and 19th centuries saw the growth of large private collections, the like of which will never be seen in England again. This development coincided with renewed interest in medieval and Renaissance literature, the strongest focus of attention being Shakespeare and his contemporary dramatists. The most outstanding of all these collections was that of Sir Thomas Phillipps of Middle Hill in Worcestershire, who had a special talent for buying all the best manuscripts that came on the market in London, and did so steadily for almost fifty years starting from 1823.[20] Extremely varied in its scope, it was nevertheless rich in English literary and historical manuscripts, though a few of them have sometimes come under suspicion as forgeries. No sooner was the staggering collection assembled and catalogued than it began to be sold off piecemeal. Sales started in 1886 and continued for several decades, and so widespread were the buyers that there is scarcely a manuscript library of note which does not possess at least one with a Phillipps catalogue mark. The Gower and

Hoccleve manuscripts reproduced in this volume, for example, were both from the Phillipps collection, but the first is now at University College London, and the second in the Huntington Library.[21]

As the acquisition of literary manuscripts became more prestigious and their sale more lucrative, literary forgery became almost fashionable, especially when, with palaeography still in its infancy, deception was especially easy. Then, as now, forgers acted mainly for gain, but the two most prominent forgers of Shakespeareana of the late 18th and 19th centuries seem to have been motivated by conceit, though the earlier and less skilful of the two, William Henry Ireland (no. 38), at first set out to please his father by satisfying his craving for new Shakespearean documents. He soon appears to have gloried in hoaxing the eminent scholars, critics and actors of his day, until his bubble was punctured by the shrewd Edmund Malone. The second forger, John Payne Collier (no. 39), was infinitely more experienced and less ambitious, stopping far short of forging whole plays as Ireland did. He was also better placed to carry out his deception, having complete access to virtually all the main sources of literary documents, including those in the British Museum and at Dulwich College, which, founded by the actor Edward Alleyn, was, and probably still is, the most important source of Elizabethan dramatic documents other than the plays themselves.[22] It was thus easy for Collier to make interpolations and additions and then proclaim them to the world as his discoveries. The full extent of his forgery is difficult to assess but it is sufficient to make most historians of Elizabethan and Jacobean drama jittery whenever they deal with a document that passed through his hands. The best forgers are, of course, those who are never discovered, but although they may still exist for medieval and Renaissance manuscripts, their chances of success are now extremely limited not only by increased skill in detection but also by the awkward question of provenance.

With the 20th century came a vast increase in the exodus of literary manuscripts to the United States. The demand arose not only from such well established American universities as Harvard and Yale, but also from many of the newer ones, most notably, of recent years, the University of Texas at Austin. Leading the field were wealthy private institutions such as the Pierpont Morgan Library, New York, the Rosenbach Foundation, and the Newberry Library, Chicago, all of which have impressive collections. But the most important of these private institutions are the Folger Shakespeare Library, Washington, D.C. and the Henry E. Huntington Library, San Marino, California. The Folger, as its full name implies, was dedicated to gathering all the materials it could acquire relating to Shakespeare and his fellow dramatists, but it also concerned itself with literature in general of the Renaissance and medieval period, so that it has, for example, an impressive collection of manuscript poetry and a number of important literary autographs. Some of its sources of material have been large collections of family papers, including the Loseley manuscripts, which encompass such items as papers of the Master of the Revels and letters of John Donne. The Huntington Library is especially rich in medieval and Renaissance material though it has far less relating to Elizabethan and Jacobean drama. Among its prize acquisitions are the Ellesmere manuscripts, which were purchased with the Bridgewater Library in 1917, and include the beautiful Ellesmere Chaucer (no. 3). Another fine private collection deserving mention is that of James Osborn, which contains a wide range of rare works and a number of

holograph manuscripts, most of them deposited in Yale University Library.[23]

The process of acquisition and migration of manuscripts of early English literature has now slowed down considerably, though the pattern for private collections continues to be one of shrinkage in England and growth in the United States and Canada. Perhaps the present attitude towards rare literary manuscripts is best summed up by the case of the Donne holograph poem which fetched the phenomenal sum of £23,000, the bid of a foreign buyer, but permission to export it was denied, and the manuscript now resides in the Bodleian Library.

In his quest for literary material the student has the aid of innumerable library guides and catalogues, and a fair number of general indexes of manuscripts according to genre. All the major manuscript libraries of Great Britain have been catalogued, albeit in many cases imperfectly, with many in need of updating.[24] Thus there is ample guidance for the British Library, the Oxford and Cambridge libraries, and the main university and cathedral and diocesan collections. Nearly all the private collections of any consequence have been itemized and in many cases calendared by the Historical Manuscripts Commission, which began its work towards the end of the last century and now has an impressive list of volumes to its credit, including the invaluable calendars of the Hatfield House manuscripts. The Public Record Office is well stocked with guides, calendars and indexes, and the National Register of Archives (Chancery Lane, London) has compiled a vast catalogue of all the archive collections of Great Britain, which it updates by a yearly publication of accessions and migrations. Though the likelihood of discovering major literary works in archives is not very great, there is always the possibility of finding small items and important related material in the form of correspondence and similar records of biographical and bibliographical significance.

In terms of a comprehensive catalogue of specifically medieval and Renaissance literary works, the United States and Canada are admirably dealt with by the monumental *Census* by S. De Ricci and W. J. Wilson, 1935–7, with a Supplement by C. U. Faye and W. H. Bond, 1962, providing extensive itemization of the contents of each manuscript collection, library by library, in each state and province. For Great Britain N. Ker has undertaken a detailed and methodical survey, *Medieval manuscripts in British libraries*, of which volume 1: London, appeared in 1969.

Also catering for the medieval period, though in a more general way and including literary commentary, is *A manual of writings in Middle English* by J. E. Wells, 1916, which has been followed by a series of supplements.

Turning to catalogues of literary manuscripts by genre, one of the most valuable is the *Index of Middle English verse* by Carleton Brown and R. H. Robbins, 1943, with Supplement, 1965. This contains around six thousand entries each with a brief description and location and short bibliography. One of the most comprehensive aids to medieval manuscript location, it is hard to see how it will be quickly superseded. Also useful for poetry is M. Crum's *First-line index of manuscript poetry in the Bodleian Library*, 1969, and it is to be hoped that a similar index can eventually be provided for all Renaissance manuscript verse. For drama, the work by Harbage and Schoenbaum referred to in note 11 is helpful and can be supplemented for the Renaissance period by W. W. Greg's *Dramatic documents from the Elizabethan playhouses*, 1931. Finding appropriate catalogues for prose is more problematical, especially since there are innumerable categories. Among the most recent of useful aids for devotional writings is *Check-list for Middle English writings of spiritual guidance*, by P. S. Jolliffe, 1974.

Aids of this kind are still very inadequate, however, and insufficient research projects are devoted to collecting and collating manuscript sources. It would be invaluable if a project similar to Ker's catalogue of medieval manuscripts were undertaken for those of the Renaissance, and also a check-list of the contents of the numerous Renaissance commonplace books scattered throughout the libraries of Great Britain and the United States. Further, it would be helpful if bibliographies of Renaissance authors uniformly provided lists of early manuscript copies of their works and, when appropriate, had a separate section on holograph material.

In one sense, inadequate or inaccurate cataloguing can prove a boon to the alert researcher, since it increases the chances of making a discovery through correct identification, as has been brilliantly demonstrated by Walter Oakeshott in the case of the Malory manuscript (no. 13) and the Ralegh notebook (no. 47). Opportunities are also greater than ever before for discovering holograph material, and the last ten years have brought to light several poetry holographs, for example, those of Sidney, Donne and Herrick, identified by Peter Croft, and one by Dryden, found by A. M. Crinò among the Lansdowne manuscripts. It surely will not be too long before poetic autographs by such important writers as Spenser, Marvell and Vaughan will appear, and perhaps the dramatists will also find fuller representation. As recent examples have shown, holographs are not confined to known literary sources of manuscripts. They are to be found scribbled in printed books, in correspondence, among despatches, interpolated in accounts, in diaries and commonplace books, in short in every conceivable type of manuscript, book or other record either here or in North America, or on the Continent of Europe, bearing in mind that a Thomas More holograph (no. 18) was found recently in Valencia. Obviously, the search has to be backed by a well-informed idea of likely sources and location, some knowledge of palaeography and, for preference, a basis of comparison on which to establish an incontrovertible identification. It is one of the endeavours of this book to be of assistance in the quest.

2. Writing materials

a. Parchment and vellum.
Man has availed himself of diverse materials upon which to scratch or write his messages and ideas, including stone, wax, bone, wood and various metals. But for use with ink, three surfaces have predominated: papyrus, parchment and paper, each gradually superseding its predecessor. Parchment in one form or another was used from earliest times but did not come into its own until papyrus was in short supply. During one such shortage in Pergamum in the 2nd century B.C., caused by an Egyptian embargo, its king, Cleomenes II, revived the use of skins but had them prepared in a new way by being dressed and rubbed. The resultant material grew very popular and was named after the city, hence the word parchment. When by the 3rd century A.D. the export of papyrus was severely restricted, parchment became the chief writing surface and remained so until well into the 15th century. Unlike its predecessor it was extremely hard-wearing, stood up well to sponging and scraping, and was capable of being used at least

twice. Above all, it took the ink well, its surface remaining firm beneath the pen and absorbing neither too little nor too much ink.

Parchment (also called membrane) was made from the skins of sheep or goats, with sheep-skin being prevalent in England. For important manuscripts, lambs or kids were used, or, more commonly, calves, hence the name vellum (through Old French from Latin, *vellis*, a calf). Calf was especially prized because it combined quality with strength and size. The highest grade of skin was taken from unborn or stillborn calves, lambs and kids, and was therefore known as uterine or abortive vellum, or as 'virgin parchment'[25] (the skin being free from hair or other blemishes). It has however been suggested that rabbit skin was often used as a substitute,[26] and as one writer drily observes, there are innumerable little bibles of the 13th century said to be written on uterine vellum, which would each have required the skins of about fifty stillborn calves, implying an incredibly high infant mortality rate among cattle.[27]

It is also as well to bear in mind that the terms parchment and vellum were sometimes loosely used, and the former might serve for both, as when Horatio (*Hamlet*, v. i) observes that parchment is made from calf-skin as well as from sheep-skin. Also, there is a tendency, still prevalent today, to distinguish between the two by degree of quality and refinement rather than by the animal of origin.[28]

Distinguishing vellum from parchment in the strict sense of the terms is usually extremely difficult, in any case, and some codicologists have abandoned the attempt as pointless. While it is true to say that vellum can sometimes be distinguished from parchment because of its relative smoothness, polish and thinness and the absence of the points caused by hair or wool, parchment was often so well prepared that it met these criteria. More especially, the membranes of both were usually so thoroughly scraped that only the reticular tissue remained, making laboratory tests unavailing.[29] Sometimes the class of document provides the clue. Important liturgical books, for example, were usually on vellum, and even after the invention of printing there are cases of the most vital parts of a service book (e.g. the canon of the mass in a missal) being on vellum, while the rest is on paper.[30] On the whole, it appears that until paper came into its own, the more prominent, well prepared and carefully written manuscripts containing even vernacular literature, especially the illuminated ones, were on vellum.[31]

The quality of parchment varied considerably from country to country and centre to centre. A lot obviously depended in the first place on the quality, breed and type of animal used. England was well stocked with sheep of good quality, and their skins were much in demand at home and abroad. On the other hand, continental processes were often much better. At one time, for example, Flemish and Norman parchment were held in high regard, while Burgundian was considered of poor quality, often being spotted, stained and mottled.[32] Consistently prized was the Italian parchment with its whiteness and fine texture. One of the most celebrated of Italian centres for parchment-making was Bologna and its methods were frequently imitated.[33]

A fair number of accounts survive of the different local methods of parchment-making, including an English one which involved, at a late stage of the proceedings, spraying the flesh side with mouthfuls of 'good ale'.[34] However, the general principle was to procure an unblemished skin, wash it in warm water and then soak it in a lime solution for several days. This prepared the skin for removing the hair or wool and the grease. The thickness was reduced by extra washing, scraping with a semicircular knife (*lunellarium*) and by rubbing. Next, it was dried stretched out on the ground or, more commonly, on hoops. The further processing, usually performed by the scribe, was smoothing the skin with a knife or plane, pumicing, and rubbing it with powdered chalk to whiten it, a process called pouncing.[35] It was also possible to buy parchment already prepared.[36] Despite these preparations there is generally a difference in appearance, especially in the lower grades, between the flesh side, which is white and smooth, and the hair side, which is harder, rougher, and browner or more yellow, so that the one was sometimes referred to as the white side (*pars alba*) and the other as the dark side (*pars nigra*).[37] In the finest vellum this difference was virtually non-existent, both sides having received equal care in preparation.[38]

b. **Paper.** Though parchment possessed the virtues of durability and of resistance under varying conditions of humidity and heat, it was expensive and bulky when used in any quantity, both of which factors made it unfeasible for publication on the scale possible with printing. So it was that paper, though a less resilient and sturdy substance and more easily torn, came to oust parchment, and still remains in its eminent position despite its own rising cost and the encroachment of other media of communication.

Paper was invented by the Chinese as early as the 6th century B.C., but it made its progress very slowly into Europe, arriving by two main routes, one through Central Asia to Greece and thence to Venice and on to Germany, the other by way of the Arabs, who learnt of it from their Chinese prisoners in the 8th century and brought it with them into Spain during the Moorish invasion. The earliest mills were set up in Spain *c.* 1151, followed by one in France, at Valenciennes in 1189, and in Italy at Fabriano in 1270, from which mill probably originated the idea of a watermark. Germany then entered the field with mills at Ravensburg (1290) and Kaufbeuren (1312).

Paper-making arrived very late in England, and the first known paper mill was that set up at Stevenage in Hertfordshire in the 1490s by John Tate, a mercer of London. It also took a long time to become firmly established. Tate's efforts were not a financial success, and the next recorded mill was not until 1548 when a German set up one at Dartford. A further surge of interest arose in the third quarter of the 16th century when, for example, the Stationers' Company petitioned unsuccessfully for the sole right of manufacturing paper. There were apparently no more concerted attempts at paper-making until 1641, but even then, because old rags, the main ingredient for paper, were a source of contagion, the industry suffered another setback. However, the next major attempt, in 1678, with the aid of Huguenot immigrants, set the industry finally on its feet, and by 1700 there were about a hundred mills in England.[39]

The main difficulty about establishing paper-making in England seems to have been that the financial returns were so poor, and it was economically preferable to import paper than to buy it at home. In any case, the home product could not easily compete with its foreign rivals in quality either. So it is that from about the beginning of the 14th century until well into the 17th, paper used in England was mainly imported, the chief sources of supply being France and Italy. A typical price was about £400 for just under 1,730 reams, with customs duty of a little over £10.[40]

Paper seems not to have been used in any quantity in England before the 14th century. The earliest document on paper in the Public Record Office is apparently a roll dated 1303,[41] and among the other early paper documents are the Red-Book at King's Lynn, Norfolk, beginning 1307–8, and records of the hustings court, Lyme Regis, Dorset, 1309.[42] It is unlikely that as a general rule paper was used for other than relatively unimportant documents and for literary jottings until the end of the 14th century.

No literary manuscript either entirely or in part on paper is known before 1400.[43] One of the earliest is a copy of *The Prick of Conscience*, written out by John Farnelay in 1405.[44] As the 15th century progresses so vellum and parchment gradually give way to paper for manuscripts in general, though some manuscripts actually alternate parchment and paper. Of the *Canterbury Tales* manuscripts, dating mainly from the early 15th century, over a third are on paper.[45] For an equivalent set of manuscripts from the middle of the 15th century the proportion of those on paper could be expected to be a little over half. The earliest illustrations written on paper in this book are the second of the Lydgate manuscripts (no. 9), the *Westron wynde* lyric (no. 11), the *Morte Darthur* (no. 13) and, the earliest that can be dated with certainty, the Paston letter, 1453 (no. 10). Virtually all the Paston letters, even the earliest ones, are on paper, but then it is only to be expected that private correspondence would be among the first classes of documents to make use of paper. The latest on parchment or vellum in this book are the Skelton illustrations, one of which (no. 16) is written in the flyleaf of a 13th-century chronicle, so does not strictly speaking count, and the other two (nos. 14 and 15) are both from a vellum manuscript dated 1509. By the 16th century, parchment is very uncommon for general literary use, and vellum so rare as to be confined usually to special presentation copies, as is indeed the case with the Skelton examples cited.[46] Even for governmental and legal use, paper came rapidly to rival parchment during the reign of the Tudors, though for such documents as Chancery enrolments, plea rolls and deeds, parchment was retained well into the 19th century.[47] Parchment was also retained for important classes of ecclesiastical documents.[48]

The chief ingredients in the making of paper were linen rags. These were pulped with the aid of the mill, and then poured into moulds consisting of rectangular wooden frames with brass wires forming a sieve, through which the water drained away. Around the mould was a wooden removable frame called a deckle which acted as a kind of ledge to preserve the required thickness of the paper during the draining process. So it was that the edges of the paper were often irregular because of the fibres that got lodged between the deckle and the frame. Running from top to bottom were, at regular intervals, strong supporting wires called chain-lines, and wired in with them was usually the maker's emblem, the watermark, first used in 1285 in Italy.[49] It is possible to see on early paper the graining following the pattern of the horizontal wires, and by holding the paper up to the light to observe the chain-lines and watermarks, which show up as apparently translucent because the fibres tended to gather a little more thickly around them during the drying process, causing a sharper contrast of light and dark then elsewhere on the sheet. Very early paper was coarse, fibrous and spongy.[50] But by the 15th century, when effective use of water mills ground the fibres to a very fine paste, the texture improved considerably, with a firmer and finer surface being acquired. It was also well sized to make the pen run

5

smoothly over it and prevent the ink from being too readily absorbed.

c. **The manuscript book.** Though parchment and paper were obtainable in single sheets and were often used that way,[51] as for instance in deeds or in correspondence, it was usual in literary manuscripts for the quire to be the main unit of both parchment and paper, especially in the medieval period. The number of leaves in a quire could vary considerably. Ten leaves were common in Italy, twelve were quite frequent in the major European universities, and sixteen, eighteen, twenty or even twenty-four were not unusual, especially with paper, since it was thinner and more manageable than parchment.[52] However, the standard quire was a quaternion (*quaternio*), comprising four sheets folded in two (*bifolia*) to give eight leaves (*folia*) or sixteen pages (*paginae*).[53] It is probable that the sheets were always folded individually for parchment, but they may sometimes have been folded together for paper. Be that as it may, the sheets were then so ordered that the outer one formed folios one and eight (pages one, two, fifteen, sixteen), the next, folios two and seven (pages three, four, thirteen, fourteen) and so on. This is referred to as the *bifolia* method of quiring and could be used for all multiples of two. A further refinement for parchment was to ensure that hair-side was placed against hair-side and flesh against flesh to avoid a contrast in colour on facing pages. This could be achieved by placing the outer sheet flesh-side down, the next on top of it hair-side down, the third flesh-side and the fourth hair-side, the process of alternation continuing to the last leaf. This not only ensured the matching of faces, but also, in the quaternion, that the outer and centre pages would be the whiter, being all flesh. This practice seems to have been employed after the 8th century for most manuscripts,[54] either by design, in the bifolia system of quiring, or by inevitability, if the alternative method of quiring was employed.[55]

The alternative method, which became quite common for paper, the printed book being based on it, is known as the 'multifolded' or 'undivided sheet' system,[56] employed for four or multiples of four leaves. For a quaternion two large sheets would be laid on top of one another and then folded over twice, usually first along the width and then the length. A gathering of twelves could be effected by folding a large sheet once across its width, then folding it in three and finally in half. The difference in method of folding has been used to explain the fact that Oxford manuscripts are long and narrow, and those of Paris squarish.[57]

The multifolded way obviously requires the use of much larger sheets than the *bifolia* for a manuscript of equivalent size. This did not, apparently, present any difficulty for parchment, since an average sheep-skin measured three by four feet,[58] and manufacturing paper in large sizes presented no problem. There seems to have been a surprising degree of standardization about the size of sheets used, whether of parchment or paper. For a parchment *bifolia*, about ten by eighteen inches was common, and for paper, about twelve inches by sixteen inches.[59] As printing took over, it established a pattern for the paper book with regard to format which the manuscript book seems to have followed, making bibliographical terminology useful if not necessary, and the position of the watermark and chain-lines pertinent.

In the early medieval period the quires were normally made up in the scriptorium, or by the scribe himself. As paper came into use the practice of buying blank quires in bulk was adopted, and eventually whole blank books of paper.[60]

Before writing commenced, in the more formal manuscripts, a frame was provided for the writing area of each page and the lines ruled. At first the frame was open at the top, but by the 13th century it was entirely closed in. The ruling was made by stylus, called dry point, in the early medieval period. In the 12th century dry point was replaced by lead, which continued until the beginning of the 15th century, when it was superseded by ink (invariably used in the examples in this book), though both lead and dry point seem to have come back into use in the late 15th and 16th centuries, if ruling was used at all. Guidelines for the rules were made, in the earlier period, at least, by means of a sharp metal instrument such as an awl, a pair of dividers, or perhaps a spiked wheel, with the aid of a ruler, a process known as pricking. The prick-marks, which might be pointed, circular or triangular, according to the instrument used, were made at the extreme edges of the parchment or paper, so as not to be easily visible when the manuscript was cropped and bound, and usually penetrated the whole quire, in some cases, several quires at once, to ensure consistent alignment. The pricking and probably the ruling were usually done before folding, but in the 12th and early 13th century, and later often for already made up paper quires, they were done after folding, a practice detectable from prick-marks in the inner margins. Pricking does not seem so common from the middle of the 15th century, about which time ruling came to be confined simply to a frame, as in the York Plays (no. 12) and the *Morte Darthur* (no. 13), the Skelton examples (nos. 14–16) being the last instances in the volume of visible rules for individual lines.[61] Even using frames had become unfashionable in literary manuscripts by the 16th century. They do not occur, for example, in Ascham's translation of *Oecumenius* (no. 23) and Jonson's *Masque of Queenes* (no. 46), and it is to be noted that lines are absent in some early and mid-15th century examples, including the Hoccleve (no. 7) and the second Lydgate (no. 9). But it is not to be supposed that the Renaissance dispensed with ruling altogether. Lead and dry point were still occasionally used, and one Spanish writer describes an ingenious frame consisting of a board of beech or walnut, with lute strings glued into regular grooves, which by being rubbed on to the paper with a cloth, could rule a whole page in one go. This method was not only quicker, it also ensured a greater uniformity in the length of lines than is observable in many of the early illustrations here (e.g. *Gawain*, no. 4, and Lydgate, no. 8). The same writer refers to a ruled undersheet called a *false ruler*, which must have been employed in the case where meticulously straight lines of writing appear without any visible means of support.[62]

Ruled or not, the sheets of the quire were usually separated for writing. In a bifolium quire, the scribe would work through, page by page, completing both sides of the left half of the first sheet, and then moving on to the left side of the second sheet. But in the multifolded quire, the sheet, after pricking and ruling, would be unfolded again and the pages written out in a sequence similar to that for printing an octavo book.[63] To ensure the correct sequence of quires the method employed up to the 12th century was to number them in roman numerals or, less usually, to letter them. This procedure gave place to the catchword, whereby the first word of a quire was written at the bottom of the last leaf of the preceding quire. From the 14th century it was common to number the leaves of the first half of the quire, to ensure that the pages of the quire were in the right order, an early form of signatures adopted by the printed book. These signatures were at first roman numerals in red, blue or green ink. By the

15th century they were written in black ink and gradually changed to arabic numerals.[64]

All the quires of a given work might be done by one scribe or shared out among a group. In the case of the Malory manuscript (no. 13), two scribes were at work, the senior one sometimes beginning a new page and then leaving his colleague to carry on. Sometimes the copying was done from separated quires (*pecie*) which were farmed out to professional scribes, a system often used for textbooks in the university.[65] In the scriptorium, there was usually a strict division of labour: the scribe would be responsible for copying out what was in front of him or dictated to him.[66] The task of illuminating fell to a separate individual, as did that of the corrector. For the small-scale literary works written out by an isolated scribe, conditions would of course be quite different, and he would be expected to be his own general factotum.

A completed manuscript might remain unbound for quite a while and would sometimes share the same volume with other works, as in the case with the second Lydgate manuscript (no. 9). The bound volume was often foliated, albeit unsystematically, in roman numerals, which, as in the case of signatures, gave way to arabic numerals in the 15th century.[67] Pagination, however, is not common until the 16th century, when printed books adopted the practice. Medieval bindings were usually of vellum or leather secured over wooden boards, with bands across the back which were intertwined with the threads from the sewn gatherings. While not quite so sumptuous, Renaissance bindings were more elegant and made in a larger variety of materials, though leather is commonest. The Renaissance also saw a major advance in decoration with gold tooling, which was practised in Italy in the 15th century and introduced into England just before the middle of the 16th century.[68]

By the Renaissance, too, the formal processes of the scriptorium were rapidly disappearing, and literary works are to be found in many formats, from the odd scrap of paper to the ready-made commonplace book. The ritual of bookmaking was now within the province of print.

d. **Pen and ink.** The main implement for writing with ink in the period covered by this book was the quill pen, though, in the Renaissance if not earlier, for large thick script like heavy *black letter* a metal pen was used, made of iron, brass or steel.[69] The quill made its appearance around the 6th century A.D., displaced the reed pen (*calamus* or *arundo*) about the time of the Norman Conquest, and remained dominant until well into the 19th century, when metal pens or nibs superseded it.[70] For general purposes the most common quill was taken from the goose, preferably of the domestic variety, alternatives being feathers of the swan and raven, with vulture preferred for large script, and crow for fine or very small work.[71] The ideal goose quill was white, rounded, unflecked, transparent and with little fat, selected from the third or fourth feather of the wing or the pinion.[72] Most authorities held that the left wing should be used because the curve of the feather would better fit the right hand (by the same token, presumably, a left-handed scribe would select from the right wing).[73] Cutting the quill was effected by means of a long thin well-tempered steel knife. The fatty tissue was gently scraped away, the tip was sliced off and then long curving cuts made to shape the end like the top of a hawk's beak. The point was slit down the middle. For the *gothic* hands (including *secretary*) the nib would be cut at an angle, with the right-hand tongue shorter than the left; for *italic* and the *round hand* it would end in a small rounded

point. It was also customary to make a longer slit in the nib for a rounded point than for a slanted one to ensure that the ink would flow more easily.[74] To preserve a good point fairly frequent trimming with a knife was required, and when not in use the nib was kept in water. The recommended way of holding the pen, at least in the 16th century, was with the finger and thumb, using the third finger as a rest.[75] In the medieval period it was common not to rest the arm on the table and the writing desks were sloped to make this difficult in any case, while in the Renaissance the arm was usually rested lightly on the table with the wrist free. The angle of the pen was fairly upright to the paper for the *gothic* hands and at roughly an angle of 45° for the *italic* and *round* hands.[76]

Ink was usually black in the medieval and Renaissance periods and was basically made in two different ways. The first was by mixing a form of carbon with gum and water. The carbon constituent would be most commonly soot or lampblack, or even, as a special ingredient, charcoal made from shoots of vine. The resultant liquid gave a deep black and lustrous colour to the writing (hence the name *atramentum*), which survived the test of light and time well. It was also easy to eradicate with a sponge, being soluble. On the other hand, this solubility made it a prey to damage by water, and since the carbon did not integrate easily with the writing surface, especially in the case of parchment, it was liable to crack off, a misfortune which seems partly to have befallen the *Gawain* manuscript (no. 4). It is perhaps for these reasons that the carbon-based ink was not used in documents intended to have legal validity, even though from about the 15th century it was sometimes added to the other forms of black ink to intensify the colour.[77] It seems to have been quite generally used for literary manuscripts in the medieval period, and although it begins to fall off by the 15th century it is still to be found in the Renaissance, sometimes being referred to as 'speciall blacke yncke' by contrast to the other variety, termed 'common yncke'.[78]

The alternative to the carbonaceous black ink was made from galls (the round excrescences produced by the gall-fly on branches of oak trees) and iron sulphate (usually known as copperas or Roman vitriol), the reaction of the tannic acid in the galls with the iron salt causing a blackish compound to form. The method was known in Classical times, but did not come into widespread use until about the 11th century.[79] The usual English recipe was to take three ounces of dry and quite firm gall nuts, break them up and soak them in a quart of wine or of rainwater and leave them out in the sun for a couple of days, then stir in two ounces of iron sulphate and leave in the sun for another day. Finally an ounce of gum Arabic was added, the resultant mixture also being left in the sun for a day. Strained and placed in a well-stoppered lead container, the liquid would be serviceable for a considerable time. For extra lustre it was recommended that a slice of pomegranate be added and the mixture simmered on a slow fire.[80]

The proportions of five parts of gall to three of iron sulphate and two of gum are fairly constant among the English recipes of the 16th century, though one of them gives five, two and two.[81] Italian and Spanish proportions are three, two, one in thirty parts of water.[82] A Spanish recipe further suggests that rainwater should be used as the base for writing on paper and wine for parchment. To make ink flow better, vinegar or wine was usually added. A quick recipe for ink was to burn wool, beat the remains to a fine powder and mix it with water or vinegar.[83]

Iron gall ink was preferred to carbon ink because although it did not have the same degree of lustre it made a more lasting impression on the writing surface, tending to bite or burn its way into the paper (hence the name *incausta*), but this very advantage could lead to corrosion through acidity, especially in the case of thin paper. Further, although initially it became quite dark through oxidation, it eventually faded, sometimes to a quite light brown shade. It is therefore quite easy to distinguish the manuscripts in which carbonaceous ink has been used or at least those in which iron-gall ink has had carbon added.[84]

Coloured inks were known in ancient times and were especially employed in illumination together with silver and gold paint. The commonest was red, used for rubrics (from *ruber* 'red') and quite often for rules, marginalia, headings and colophons. A good example of the range of colours possible is provided by the Ellesmere Chaucer (no. 3) and nearly all the earlier medieval manuscripts represented here contain more than one colour. Though the range of inks was much diminished in the Renaissance, when manuscripts become more utilitarian, red is still quite common, and recipes exist for making a diversity of colours. A small late 16th-century commonplace book belonging to a Norfolk family contains recipes for seven colours besides black: white, from diluted ceruce or white lead; blue from turnsole (a violet-blue plant) mixed with ceruce, water and gum; yellow from masicot (protoxide of lead) tempered and ground with the fingers; green from verdigris mixed with gum water; tawny from senna and gum water; russet from brasil wood shavings placed in a shell with white of egg, left for twelve hours and tempered with alum or gum; and red from white of eggs well beaten, left overnight and then mixed in with vermilion.[85]

It seems that ink was supposed usually to dry by itself in the medieval and Renaissance period. There appears to be no specific mention of the materials used at other times for this process: chalk, sand or blotting-paper. Indeed it is likely that blotting-paper would have taken off much of the surface of the ink, as it apparently did in the early 19th century, to judge from a House of Lords report (1836) complaining about the ink used for the new-fangled steel pens.[86]

3. The terminology of handwriting

a. **General.** Palaeographical terms have never been fully codified. As a result, although there is much common ground, there is also considerable variety, not to say confusion, in the description of styles of writing, components of letters, types of abbreviation and even punctuation. That this should be so is understandable. Palaeography is still an evolving science requiring a modification of classifications as new discoveries are made. Further, there is a lack of standardization among countries, though the situation is now improving. The later periods in particular have been poorly served, because Greek and Latin palaeography has been the centre of attention, and it is only recently that serious attempts have been made even to name the basic hands used, for example, in the 15th century. The writing-masters of the medieval and Renaissance period provide a great deal of help in terminology, but they themselves are very inconsistent, and, in general, the everyday writers seem to have paid as little attention to them in the 16th and 17th centuries as composers did to musical theorists. It should also be noted that the analytical approach to the description of letters has often been a haphazard and impressionistic affair in dealing with English literary manuscripts, certainly not keeping pace with developments in literary analysis.

The confusion and conflict of jurisdiction applies to the very word *palaeography* itself, which means literally 'ancient handwriting' (from Greek *palaios*, 'ancient', *graphein* 'to write'). It is now usually accepted as the umbrella term covering all forms of writing and writing materials until the end of the 17th century, but *epigraphy* (*epi*, upon) which deals with inscriptions carved, scratched or engraved on hard materials (e.g. stone, metal, clay, wood) has often been a schismatic, while a rival claimant to the throne has been *diplomatic* (from Greek, *diploma*), strictly speaking the study of documents, charters and similar materials. This is to say nothing of *codicology*, the study and collation of manuscripts, especially with a view to discovering their relationships and the scriptoria that produced them.

It therefore seems appropriate to provide a basic guide to the terms used in this book to describe the act of writing, individual letters, styles of writing and classes of script, not only for the benefit of the general reader, but also perhaps as an encouragement to the student in need of a simple palaeographical vocabulary. It should be added that in selecting the terms the principles of 'highest common factor' in usage and directness of description have been followed where possible, with special regard to the period covered by this book.

b. **The action of the pen.** A mark made by the pen in any direction on the writing surface is a *stroke*. The action of raising the pen from the paper between strokes is known as a *pen lift*. A stroke which moves only in one direction is a *single movement*. If it changes direction sharply without pen lift it is a *broken stroke*. Direction is indicated by such terms as *upstroke* (usually thin), *downstroke* (somewhat thicker), *right-handed* (to the right), *left-handed* (to the left), and, for curved strokes, *clockwise* and *counter-clockwise*. An ornamental stroke, usually curved or wavy, is called a *flourish* or, when shaped like a corkscrew, a *curlicue*. When a stroke has no apparent function it is *otiose*, the most common application being to a mark which normally indicates abbreviation but is superfluous in context.

The characters or letters formed by the pen are often referred to as *graphs*. The distinctive way in which the graphs are written, including the cut of the nib and the manner of holding the pen, is known as the duct (or *ductus*).[87] Handwriting which conforms to an established style of writing is said to be in a given *script* or *hand*, though *hand* also refers to the writing of an individual.[88] If a manuscript is entirely in the hand of its author it is said to be *holograph* or *autograph*. Since *autograph* can also relate solely to the signature, *holograph*, even if it is unfashionable, has been preferred in this book to avoid ambiguity.

c. **The letters.** Letters are basically divided into two main categories: the *capitals* or *majuscules*, and the *small letters* or *minuscules*. The terms *upper case* and *lower case* respectively are also used, though they relate strictly speaking to printing, since they derive from the lay-out of the type cases for compositing. It should be noted that the two categories originally represented two different scripts, as in Roman times, and that the distinction can be based on shape or size or both; but the difference caused by function is not a consistent one until the 18th century. In some cases, for example, a capital will appear in the middle of a word for no apparent reason in the medieval and Renaissance periods.

A useful point of reference in describing a letter is the base-line of the line of writing, providing four categories:

linear letters, minuscules written on the line and projecting only a small way above it (e.g. modern, *a, c, e*); *supralinear letters,* those which extend well above the line (e.g. modern, *d, b, h*); *infralinear,* which descend well below (modern, *g, j, p*) and *double-length* letters which go well above and below (modern handwritten *f*).[89] Some palaeographers use a series of four imaginary equidistant parallel lines for their descriptions, the base-line being second from the bottom.[90] This is especially useful in scripts which endeavour to observe exact proportions, as when linear letters have to be of uniform height between lines two and three, and the heads of the supralinear and double-length letters have to touch the top of the fourth or uppermost line. Another point of reference for the letter is its position in the word, the three basic terms being *initial* or *final position* for the beginning or end of a word, and *medial* for any other location.

For describing the components of a letter geometry plays a useful part. Straight lines can be referred to as *horizontal, vertical* or *perpendicular,* and *oblique,* though the shortest vertical stroke actually forming part of a letter is known as a *minim* (most common in *i, m, n, u*). The curved parts of a letter include *circles, arcs, ovals, ellipses* and *cusps* (the point at which two curved lines meet). Angles are useful, particularly the *right angle* and the *oblique;* and the smallest geometrical sign, the *dot,* is much in evidence for decorating rounded capitals in many medieval and Renaissance hands.

The most common terminology for components of letters is that used for parts of the body (as is customary with pieces of type). Thus the main part of the letter is the *body,* the top is the *head,* and the bottom the *foot* or *feet.* Lines extending from the body are *arms* if they point upwards (as in *v*) and *legs* if they point downwards (as in *n*), though the neutral term of *limbs* can be used. The individual arms and legs are referred to as *left* or *right* or, in the case of three limbs (as in *m*) *middle.* Pursuing the body metaphors, the part just below the head where a letter branches to the left or right can be called the *shoulder* (as in *r*). The upright support to a letter is the *back, backbone* or *shank* (as in *b, d*), more commonly known as the *shaft* for double-length letters (as in *f*), the *stem* for linear letters (*a, r*), and the *column* in the case of capitals (H, which has a *left* and *right column*). The lower rounded part of a letter is sometimes called the *belly* (as in open *b*). The whole of the rounded part (e.g. in *a, b, d*) is known, with some anatomical dislocation, as the *lobe,* though *bowl* is a common alternative. If a letter has two roughly equal circular parts it is *double-lobed* or *twin-bowled* or has *two compartments,* usually divided into *upper* and *lower* (as in *B, g*). Yet another anatomical term is the *eye,* which forms the top of *e,* though this is also known as the *lobe;* and the part of the letter which hangs below the line, usually in the form of a curve, is the *tail,* which moves to the left or right or crosses over itself.

Supralinear strokes are called *ascenders,* and infralinear ones, *descenders,* both normally tending to be straight and vertical, but these terms are sometimes used interchangeably with *upstroke* and *downstroke.* A horizontal stroke touching or intersecting a stem is a *cross-stroke;* at or near the top of the stem, a *head-stroke;* joining two stems a *cross-bar,* though this term is often used for the other two also. In scripts where the letters are joined, linking or ornamental *loops* are often to be found on ascenders and descenders. Letters can terminate in a variety of ways: in an angular or rounded *hook;* or in a curl, known as a *finial;* or in a heavily inked thickened end, a technique known as *clubbing.* In the most formal scripts, short cross-strokes called *serifs* are used to finish off the ends of letters, a practice derived from carving on stone, where such forms as *incised, curved, horizontal* and *slabbed* were employed, especially for Roman capitals. Serifs are generally paired as *head* and *foot* serifs, but also sometimes appear on cross-strokes, a variant being the long thin vertical line occasionally placed on the extremity of a final letter in the medieval period, which is referred to in this book as *pendant hair-line.* Another term which should be mentioned, if only for its Shakespearean connotations, is the *spur,* a single or double stroke, straight or curved, above and to the right of a letter, sometimes connected to it and joining it to the preceding letter (e.g. nos. 30, 36).[91]

The running of two or more letters together to form one graph is known as a *ligature,* frequently found in this period in combinations with *s.* When the letters so joined form one vowel sound they are known as a *digraph,* the most common being *æ* and *œ.* When two rounded letters coalesce so that their adjacent arcs form a curved *x,* the process is called *biting* (cf. *ba, de, do* in no. 6), and is usually found only in the most formal scripts.[92] The stroke which connects one part of a letter with another (e.g. a loop connecting the two arcs of *o*) can be known as a *tie* to distinguish it from a *link,* which joins two letters. Ties and links are usually horizontal or diagonal.[93]

When no term is apparently available to describe parts of a letter, it is best to use a form of description which is as clear and direct as possible, and it is often helpful to draw analogies with modern letters or numerals, preferably in their standard printed form. Finally, it is immeasurably useful here, as in the case of scripts, to provide illustrations wherever possible.

d. **Scripts.** There are two main categories of script in the period: *book (libraria)* and *documentary (documentaria),* though some palaeographers prefer the terms *business* or *charter* to documentary. The distinction between book and documentary is made more on the basis of contents than of script, since the same was sometimes used for both. In earlier book hands the main part was written in *text (textura* or *textualis,* from *textus,* 'woven', since the writing gave this effect). The commentary, translation and headings (or capitularies) were usually written in a *glossing* hand (*glossularis*); and informal annotations in *note* hand (*notularis*).[94]

Within the book and documentary categories there is a variety of distinctive scripts (to be dealt with in the next section) but all those between the 12th and the 16th centuries are placed under the general heading of *gothic* scripts, originally a term of abuse applied by the humanists to what they considered a barbarous hand. There has also been a convention of labelling all documentary and informal book hands in the same period as *court hand* regardless of what script they are in, a practice begun by Andrew Wright and continued by Charles Johnson and Hilary Jenkinson.[95] As clear-cut nomenclature evolves for the different documentary scripts, so *court hand* is reverting to its original specific meaning as pertaining to the higher courts of law and royal departments (*manus curialis*).

When in 15th- and 16th-century handwriting a *textura* script is amalgamated with a freer and more flowing one, the resultant script is known as *bastard (bastarda).* Since this term, though used by the writing-masters, seems to imply doubtful lineage rather than legitimate union, some palaeographers prefer to use *hybrid (hybrida).*[96] A script which resembles *textura* but is an amalgamation of diverse scripts can be called *quasi-text* or *fere-textura*, and it is further suggested that *quasi* or *fere* be applied in conjunction with other scripts as well.[97] When a script does not conform to any system it is best to use *unclassified book* or *unclassified documentary hand*[98] accompanied by one of the grading terms suggested below and a short descriptive statement.

From about the beginning of the 13th century different levels of formality began to appear in scripts, which are usually indicated by grading terms based on such criteria as the amount of care taken, how *cursive* the writing is (i.e. to what extent the letters are joined together without pen lift) and, in some of the later hands, the degree of slope. The most formal grade is known as *set* (*formata*).[99] This is carefully written, often with *calligraphic* decoration. Its letters are clearly formed in accordance with an accepted style, and until the later periods, are upright and unlinked. In legal scripts the most formal variety is also sometimes termed the *engrossed*. The lowest grade, extremely cursive, swiftly written, and either sloped or sprawling, has been known by many names, including *free*, *current*, *running* and *cursive*, or in Latin, *currens*;[100] but since the English terms have been used in a diversity of ways by palaeographers, it is suggested *rapid* be used instead, retaining *currens* as the Latin alternative. For a middle grade, semi-cursive and a compromise between care and speed, *facile* is proposed, with the Latin equivalent *facilis*, a term borrowed from the early 17th-century writing-master, Martin Billingsley.[101] For intermediate grades the three basic terms can be combined, for example, *set/facile* (*formata/facilis*) or *facile/rapid* (*facilis/currens*).[102] In labelling the different scripts it is advisable that the terminology should not be polyglot. Thus *set secretary* is preferable to *secretary formata*.

4. The succession of literary scripts
a. **General.** Handwriting in western Europe has a cyclic history, a characteristic it shares in varying degrees with the arts in general. From the time the Roman alphabet first came into use, it has moved through a period of fairly swift development to a state of perfected simplicity combining art and utility, and has then suffered a gradual decline, being made to bear either an intolerable weight of embellishment or to suffer the maltreatment of inexpert writers anxious to drag it through the rush of everyday business. Whenever grotesquery or illegibility have threatened to destroy it, a revival has occurred, usually led by men of letters, based on a fundamental return to the perfected Roman alphabet. Each of the major cycles seems to have taken roughly 500 years from the reforms of the Carolingian period to those of the humanists of the 14th and 15th centuries down to the calligraphers of the late 19th and 20th centuries. There have, of course, been continual minor reforms, and from the medieval period to the present day there has been an army of writing-masters, many of whom have had some effect, usually for the better. However, it is possible to overestimate their influence, and frequently their books tell us how they wanted people to write rather than how they actually did write.

In talking of the succession of scripts it is as well to remember that there are remarkably few precise dates to denote the inauguration of a particular style of handwriting, and that there is often considerable overlap. The rate of change is conditioned by the degree of conservatism of the scribe, the scriptorium, the region and the country, and more especially, the degree of isolation. Again, it should be noted that while genealogical trees for scripts are useful, they can

be misleading, in that every script, no matter how distinctive, tends to be an amalgam from diverse sources, even though one influence may predominate.

b. **English handwriting to the time of Chaucer.**[103] The alphabets of western Europe derive from the Roman alphabet which, in its turn, originates from the type of Greek script used by the Euboeans and adopted by the Etruscans. To begin with, there were basically twenty letters in the Roman alphabet: all that are presently in English excluding the consonants *J*, *K*, *Y*, *Z*, and with *V* used only as the capital form of *u*. By the late Roman period all twenty-six letters were in use, with *j* being a variant of *i*. The earliest Roman script, to judge from inscriptions, was entirely of capitals, the most formal variety of which was known as square capitals (*capitalis quadrata*), especially suitable for carving on stone, and seen in perfected form in the famous example of Trajan's column, erected A.D. 114. Square capitals provide a good illustration of the cyclic history of Western handwriting and of its Roman origins, since they have virtually the same form as modern block capitals (figure 1).[104]

ABCDEFGHIL MNOPQRSTVX

1. Square capitals

Though possessing great geometric beauty, square capitals were laborious to write, and for more general purposes the less formal *rustic* or *negligent capitals* (*capitalis rustica*) were used, being more swiftly and easily formed and, written with a reed pen, especially suitable for papyrus and parchment. They were somewhat narrower than square capitals, angular and with free use of broken strokes and long foot-serifs, particularly noticeable on *E* and *F* (which are thereby easily confused), and *I*, *P*, *T* (looking like *I*). *A* often lacked a cross-bar, while the cross-stroke on *E* usually fully intersected the stem (figure 2).

ABCDEFGHIL MNOPQRSTVX

2. Rustic capitals

In addition to the capitals there was a cursive script in use from quite early times, as evidenced by the Pompeii inscriptions. A simple elongated script basically dependent on straight lines, it was particularly useful for writing on wax tablets. It was inelegant and often so lacking in definition that its graphs were sometimes confused with one another, but it survived in a normalized form for a long time as a documentary hand in Italy and France. It had considerable influence on the development of other Roman scripts, as well as providing early models for minuscules, including *d*, *f*, *h*, *m*, *n*, *r*, and long *s*, as can be seen in a selection from the Pompeii examples (figure 3).

ΛbⅭdЄϜGⱧіΚL ΜΝΟΡᴧⴖſΤⵡⵝⵞⵙ

3. Roman cursive

Until about the 5th century A.D. capitals served for book hand, but thereafter were reserved mainly for headings and display. The new book script was *uncial*, developed by the law and school books and influenced by cursive. It is thought to derive its Latin name, *uncialis*, from the fact that its letters were sometimes nearly an inch high (figuring in St Jerome's attack on the vanity of elaborate gold and silver letters on purple parchment), though other suggested derivations include *uncia*, 'the twelfth part', there being about twelve words per line in this script, and, with less likelihood, *uncinatus*, 'shaped like a hook'. *Uncial* was still a majuscule script, and several of its letters (e.g. *B, C, N, O, R, S*) were almost the same as the capitals. However, in some respects it might be considered a transitional script from capitals to minuscules. Most of the letters are rounded, and while they are contained within parallel lines there is no longer a complete commitment to making the bodies the same height as the columns, and there are infralinear tails. Thus alongside the capitals are anticipations of minuscule graphs, exemplified in *e, h, m, p, q, u,* and *d* with the angled back (to be known as *uncial d*) which is frequently to reappear, if not in its own right, at least as an alternative form (figure 4).

aBCoEFGhILm NOpqR s TUX

4. Roman uncial

A further step towards minuscule was the development of a more cursive script than *uncial*, known as *half-uncial* (*semiuncialis*) examples of which can be found as early as the 5th century in Italy and France. Its main differences from *uncial* are *a* with a rounded bowl, *b* with a single bowl, *d* with an upright stem, *f* with an infralinear stem, *g* with a flat-topped open head, *r* with a stem and right shoulder like its modern counterpart, long-stemmed *s* and *t* with a curved shank. Of the capital forms only *N* now remains (figure 5).

abcdefShil mNopqrrcux

5. Half-uncial

While the Roman capitals continued to be used as the norm for display matter and remained somewhat static, the other Roman scripts were developed and modified with the formation of national hands as the Roman empire broke up and the countries of Europe assumed or resumed their own identities. The Roman cursive played an important part in

the growth of the three main continental scripts: the *Beneventan* of southern Italy, which reached its height in the hands of the 12th-century scribes of Monte Cassino (formerly known as *Lombardic* because of its early use in Northern Italy); *the Visigothic* script of Spain; and the *Merovingian, Frankish* or *Pre-Carolingian* for France, with the scripts of *Luxeuil* and *Corbie* as its leading examples.

Discounting the period of Roman occupation, from which no examples survive, England had from its early days of Christianity two main book hand scripts, both brought by the missionaries, one from the north, the other from the south. The first of these was the *uncial* in its Roman form, fostered by the arrival of St Augustine in Kent in 597 and the development of a school of writing at Canterbury and other monastic centres. The second script is based on the Roman *half-uncial* as adopted and developed by the Irish after their conversion by St Patrick in the 5th century. Known as *Irish insular* script it is seen in its perfected form in the Book of Kells (*c.* 8th century). The *Irish insular* script became established with the coming of St Columba (d. 597) to Iona and St Aidan to Lindisfarne (*c.* 635), where the community established one of the most celebrated schools of writing, of which the Lindisfarne Gospels (*c.* 700), one of the Cotton manuscripts in the British Library, is a famous example.

As sometimes happens in the history of handwriting, the two scripts were caught up in a quasi-nationalistic and religious controversy, which in its extreme form became a North–South or an Irish–Italian feud. Both vied for official recognition as the liturgical book hand, but although the Council of Whitby, 663 favoured the Roman liturgy, the *insular* script seems to have gained acceptance. As a result, though *uncial* continued to be employed in the 7th and 8th centuries it was superseded by *insular* script. But it never entirely lost its footing, and the Norman Conquest in a sense effected a compromise in that it resulted in the introduction of a reformed Roman script but one partly influenced by *insular* nevertheless.

A somewhat confusing variety of names has been applied to *insular* script in England, including *Irish, scriptura Scottica, scriptura Saxonica* and *Hiberno-Saxon*, though the commonest is *Anglo-Saxon*. Like its Irish parent, the *insular* or *Anglo-Saxon* script had two main forms. The first and earlier, termed *half-uncial* or *majuscule*, is a rounded, rather fat hand with spade-like serifs. Its letters are similar to the Roman *half-uncial* (figure 5), including the flat-topped *g* and *t* looking like a capital with a curved shank, but it takes from its Irish parent *a* which resembles *o* and *c* run-together, *uncial d, n* like the capital with the diagonal almost touching the ground (though two-minim *n* is more common), and capital form of *r* and *s* (figure 6).

œbcoeFShil mnHopqRSτuⴕ

6. Anglo-Saxon majuscule (insular half-uncial)

By about the 7th century a more cursive, thinner and more angular script developed which with its full range of linear, supralinear and infralinear letters is genuinely minuscule and is known as *insular* or *Anglo-Saxon minuscule*. This was to become the predominant script for vernacular manuscripts until well into the 11th century. It is very similar to its counterpart the

Irish minuscule and has obvious descent from the Roman *half-uncial*. Especially to be noted are its single-bowled *a* with a straight stem, the long-stemmed, right-shouldered *r*, long forked *s* and small *y* with *v*-shaped head (figure 7).

abcdefɜhil
mnopqrɼⲧuꭓy

7. Anglo-Saxon or insular minuscule

For vernacular use graphs were added for those sounds which had no equivalent in Latin. One source for these graphs was the runic alphabet, the sacred inscriptional writing of the Germanic peoples still current in the late Anglo-Saxon period, and based mainly on the straight line to assist carving on wood and soft materials. The runic graph *thorn*, þ, so named because of its physical resemblance, was borrowed for the *th* sound equivalent to the Greek *theta*, but used for voiced *th* also. Used both as a minuscule and, in larger form, as a capital, it survived as a separate graph from the 8th to the end of the 15th century. It underwent many alterations however. The top of the shaft gradually disappeared, the body became rounded and open at the top so that it resembled a *y*, which had to be dotted to avoid confusion. By the 16th century the *y* had completely assumed the role of *thorn* (cf. Wyatt, no. 19) and retained it until well into the 17th century (cf. Herbert, no. 57). From the 8th to the 13th century Old Icelandic *eth* was used as an alternative to *thorn*. It comprised an *uncial d* with a crossed stem (sometimes used as an ordinary *d*), with Ð for the capital form. Though *thorn* and *eth* were interchangeable, it was normal practice by the 11th century to use *thorn* initially and *eth* medially and finally.

Another borrowed rune was ƿ, *wyn* (Old English for 'joy'), employed from the beginning of the 8th to the 13th century to do service as *w*, since the sound of the Greek digamma was not represented in Latin. It tended to be confused with *y* and with *thorn*, though the closed bowl and the absence of shaft above the body afforded sufficient distinction when the graphs were properly formed. Prior to the introduction of *wyn* Anglo-Saxon manuscripts had employed double *u* (hence the name) and this form was reintroduced by the Normans. There is also a case of the sound but not the form of a runic letter being used in the digraph *æ* borrowed from Latin to represent the back vowel sound of *aesc* or *ash* (from its runic resemblance to an ash tree). Also to be noted is the graph ȝ, *yogh* ('yoke', possibly because placed on its side, it resembled the yoke for oxen). This was simply the flat-topped *g* of the minuscule, used for a variety of palatal and spirant sounds (cf. *Gawain*, no. 4) and retained until the beginning of the 15th century.

The *Anglo-Saxon minuscule* in its four centuries of use was not, of course, entirely standardized for every region or for every purpose. A difference can be seen among the separate kingdoms of the heptarchy, with Northumbrian noticeably spiky, the Mercian compact and elegant, and the Wessex hands rough and somewhat straggling, though the differences tended to disappear as the kingdoms became unified. It is also observable that the hands used for charters are a little

more cursive than the book hands, though the script is basically the same.

In the 8th century a major European reform in handwriting occurred under the general patronage of Charlemagne (742–814) and with the encouragement of such clerics as Alcuin of York, abbot of the influential monastery of St Martin of Tours, 796–804.[105] The reform was not a sudden, inspirational or rigorous one, but was none the less effective and of incalculable influence. It resulted in the attainment of an international script easy both to write and to read, combining the clarity of *uncial* and *half-uncial* with something of the swiftness of the cursive. It derived its models from diverse sources, so that not only the old scripts but the more recent French, Beneventan and English scripts contributed to a none the less completely integrated and classically simple script known as the *Carolingian minuscule* (*Carolina*). Among its *uncial* antecedents are *a* with a small bowl and high stem (to avoid confusion between open *a* and *u* as in other minuscule scripts), occasional *d* with angled back and *t* with a capital cross-bar and curved shank. The *half-uncials* include upright-stemmed *d*, compact *r* and long *s* with shoulder serif. From French *Pre-Caroline* script comes *g* with a small, closed bowl and headstroke from the right (figure 8).

abcdefɜhil
mnopqrſⲧuꭓ

8. Carolingian minuscule

Perfected by the early 9th century, the *Carolingian minuscule* took a little time to spread through western Europe, the usual pattern with handwriting as with many other movements in European art being to begin in Italy or France and then spread slowly North. It first made its presence felt in England in the 10th century and was in general use by the following century, being virtually the only script for Latin manuscripts, with Roman capitals and uncials used for display and versals.

Just as the adoption of *Carolingian minuscule* was an international phenomenon, so was its gradual alteration from a rounded to a highly angular hand, at least for countries north of the Alps. The earliest examples of this change of shape derive from Northern France and are widespread elsewhere by the end of the 12th century. The angularity was to remain in what was essentially a parallel movement in gothic architecture and to a lesser extent music, until the end of the 15th century and beyond.

Several reasons have been given from time to time for the change from roundness to angularity, and it is probable that both general and particular circumstances account for it. First of all there is a pendulum of taste which swings from plain to fancy and in this case from round to angular and back to round again. It has affected objects as diverse as medieval churches and modern automobiles. The particular circumstances are said to have involved the desire to save writing space, thereby cramping and elongating the letters, and the use of an oblique nib (with the shorter side to the left). The resultant script is known as *gothic* (*gothica*), a general title given to all post-12th-century medieval hands. In its primitive form, it still showed an affinity to *Carolingian* in type of graph, though not shape, with the addition of an alternative *r* resembling an arabic *2* at first used mainly after *o*, and a compressed form of *S* used as an alternative to long *s*, usually in final position (figure 9).

abcddefghilm nopqrzsstuxyz

9. Early gothic text

With the establishing of the *gothic* script, Roman capitals gave place to *uncials*, which were adapted to the angularity of the *minuscule* by elongation, broken strokes, reinforcing lines and in the later, more cursive hands, further adornments like cusps, spurs and lozenges.

By the late 12th century there came a gradual parting of the ways between formal book hand, now known as *text* (*textura*), and documentary hands, and together with it the growth of a hierarchy of scripts adapted to purpose and degree of urgency. These developments are understandable, especially since *text* was an elaborate and extremely laborious script, and even within book hands less formal and more swiftly written hands were used for glosses and notes. By the end of the 13th century the cursive hands evolved for documentary began to be adopted for literary purposes too, and were fully developed by the time of Chaucer.

c. From Chaucer to Skelton.[106] By Chaucer's time all twenty-six letters of the English alphabet had long been in use, the last to arrive being *k* (for which *c* or *ch* had served), *z*, which was still uncommon, and *j*, developed from a tailed *i*.

The role of *j* was secondary to *i*, which served both for vowel and consonant in all but final position, a situation which held good until the late 17th century. Until the same period, *u* and *v* were used interchangeably for vowel and consonant, *v* normally appearing initially and in capitals and *u* medially. Among the other capitals it should be noted that *I* and *J* are virtually indistinguishable, though the assumption is that *I* is usually intended by analogy with the minuscules, and *ff* generally serves for *F* until the reintroduction of Roman capitals.

In the period of roughly 150 years from the beginning of the *Canterbury Tales* (*c*. 1387) to the death of Skelton, the main scripts for English literary works are *text*, the two cursives termed *anglicana* and *secretary*, and amalgams of *text* and cursive known as *hybrid* or *bastard* script.

i. *Text*. Being a very formal and conservative script, *gothic text* changed very little from the time of its perfection in the 13th century to its slow demise in the early 16th century, though the degree of embellishment, thickness and angle did vary from time to time. There were four basic accepted styles of *text* or *textura* in the period: *prescissa* or *sine pedibus* (*cut short* or *without feet*); *quadrata* (*square*); *semiquadrata* (*half-square*); and *rotunda* (*round*).[107]

Prescissa is of English origin and dates from the beginning of the 13th century. Its most striking characteristic is that, as its alternative name suggests, the feet of the minims and many of the uprights seem to have been amputated, with the ends squared off (figure 10a). *Quadrata*, also known with more descriptive accuracy as *fracta* or *fractura* (*broken*), is without curves (to that extent, 'squared') and with lozenged serifs at an oblique angle at the head and feet of most uprights (figure 10b and no. 13). *Semiquadrata* or *semifractus* usually has the lozenge serifs at the head but not at the feet, which generally end in a slight angle, hook or curl (figure 10c and no. 6). *Rotunda*, which was often used as a general duty book hand, is the least formal, and derives its name mainly from the fact that it contains neither breaking nor serifs (figure 10d and no. 8).

a

abcdefghilmnopqrzsstux

b

abcdefghilmnopqrzsstux

c

abcdefghilmnopqrzsstux

d

abcdefghilmnopqrstux

10. Text hands: a. *prescissa*; b. *quadrata*; c. *semiquadrata*; d. *rotunda*

It should be noted that, as in most scripts, there are sometimes deviations from the norm in *textura* and inconsistencies in the treatment of minims so that the difference is often blurred, for example, between *quadrata* and *semiquadrata*, and between *semiquadrata* and *rotunda*. In such cases the total impression of the hand has to be the deciding factor in identifying it.

ii. *Anglicana*.[108] The chief literary cursive hand at the time of Chaucer was *anglicana*, formerly known by palaeographers as *court hand*. Though it was probably imported in its earliest form from France, it has recently been given the name *anglicana* because of its widespread and distinctively English use. It first appeared in England in the 12th century as a correspondence hand, was in general use by the end of the 13th century, predominated until close on the middle of the 15th century, and survived in a degenerate cursive form until the 16th century. Among the changes it underwent was the addition for a brief period of long, often threadlike forks during the late 13th century, the altering of the pen angle from oblique to almost upright position at the beginning of the 14th century, resulting in a greater uniformity in thickness of the pen strokes, and the introduction, at approximately the same time, of a reversed and circular *e*. Nevertheless, throughout the period there were basic letter forms which remained fairly constant and made the script readily distinguishable. These include a double-lobed *a* extending above the level of the other linear letters, *d* with a looped stem, a two-compartment figure *8* form of *g*, long forked *r*, and *w* either like a circle enclosing a *2* or *3*, or, more usually, like two looped *l*'s and 3 (figure 11).

11. Anglicana: *a*. late 13th century; *b*. late 14th century

In the 14th century sigma form of *s* (as in figure 11*b*) becomes common both in initial and final position with long *s* usually medial, and towards the end of that century the shaft of *t* tends to rise above the head-stroke. As in *textura* the *2* form of *r* was used after *o* and sometimes after *p*, occasionally with a tag attached to its base.

Among the many modifications of *anglicana* in the 14th century was the development of a *formata* grade, based partly on *textura* from which it acquired a squatter and squarer appearance, some broken strokes and hooked serifs. It employed thicker and more angled penstrokes than for normal *anglicana* (termed *anglicana facilis* in this book), and its

ascenders were somewhat taller and usually arched. The graphs were not otherwise different except that a diamond-shaped form of small capital *S* was used in final position and the use of the circular *e* was usually limited to a type of ligatured *re*. At its best, as in nos. 3 and 5, it was a comely though rather congested script, and it is understandable that it held sway as a formal book hand for most of the first half of the 15th century (figure 12).

12. Anglicana formata, end 14th century

iii. *Secretary*.[109] No sooner was *anglicana* at its height than it was challenged by another cursive script as the general-purpose documentary and book hand below the class of *formata*. The new script has only recently been given a separate name, being known as *secretary*, partly because it is the main antecedent to 16th-century *secretary*, while its continental counterpart is called *cursiva*. Though the earliest forms of *secretary* seem to have originated in Italy, it was a direct importation from France during the reign of the Francophile, Richard II, and is found in Chancery warrants in the 1370s. It steadily grew in popularity and was widespread by the middle of the 15th century. It is a much more angular hand than *anglicana*, which looks quite rounded by comparison, being written with an angled nib with a studied contrast of thick and thin strokes. With the angularity came broken strokes, the use of horns or cusps on the heads and sides of bowls and lobes, long, tapering shifts and often something of a general splayed appearance. It is a much more variable hand than *anglicana* with respect to size, slope and range of graphs. However, among the letters which immediately distinguish it from *anglicana* are single-lobed *a* with a pointed head; single compartment *g* with a pointed head and a small tail; short, right-shouldered and *v* forms of *r*; final *s* looking like a small *B* or *c* and *3* run together; and *w* usually resembling double *v*. It should be noted that of these graphs *g* seems to vary the most; in the 15th century its head comes to resemble *u* or *v* with the right limb often higher than the left, and it acquires a very pronounced headstroke (figure 13).

13. 15th-century secretary

Though more angular than *anglicana*, *secretary* could be written rather more swiftly, and effected a greater

14

cursiveness by a large number of diagonal links, some of which are so faint as to be almost invisible. It never attained a *formata* grade which could rival *anglicana formata*, but none the less achieved a degree of elegance combined with compactness to provide a very serviceable quasi-formal book hand (e.g. Hoccleve, no. 7).

As often happens when two or more distinctive scripts are current, *secretary* and *anglicana* often borrowed from one another both in features of general style and in use of graphs. *Anglicana*, for example, assumed some of the angularity of *secretary* during the course of the 15th century, and employed such distinctive *secretary* graphs as tailed *g*, two forms of *r*, and final *s* (e.g. no. 9). *Secretary* too, borrowed liberally from *Anglicana*, especially in its early phase.

iv. *Hybrid*.[110] Both scripts combined with *textura* to form what are now known chiefly as *hybrid* scripts, though the term *bastard* (*bastarda*) is still prevalent, being derived from the practitioners themselves. The basic idea behind the mixture was to effect a union of the best features of text and cursive, combining the beauty and formality of one with the smoothness and ease of the other, at the same time producing graphs which were clearer than in either script. On the whole, from *textura* was derived a rigorous adherence to parallel lines for linear letters, a fairly regular size to the bodies, and a consistent use of serifs. While the general appearance was thereby *textura*, the graphs were cursive in origin, and although their loops, links, ascenders and descenders were curtailed, they were still in evidence.

Hybrid anglicana developed in the middle of the 14th century, and was perfected by the beginning of the 15th century. Its basic difference from *anglicana* was that it was slightly larger, more liberally spaced and often employed the *quadrata* or *semiquadrata* system of serifs. Somewhat easier to write than *textura formata*, it occurs in *de luxe* manuscripts and is used for display purposes in others where *anglicana formata* is the basic script—there are traces of it, for example, in the Ellesmere Chaucer illustration, no. 3, 11.29 ff. In their simplest form the graphs were as in figure 14.

14. Hybrid anglicana, early 15th century

Attempts by 15th-century scriveners to upgrade *secretary* resulted in several forms of *hybrid secretary* both in England and on the Continent, one French and German variety being known as *brevitura*. The earliest native attempt at *hybrid* was along the lines of *hybrid anglicana* and actually included *anglicana* graphs alongside its own. Its system of serifs was also influenced by *quadrata*. Like *hybrid anglicana* it, too, was used for important manuscripts and for display in texts otherwise written in a near-*formata secretary* (e.g. no. 7, 1.10). Sometimes the degree of formality is so slight that the borderline between the hybrid and the cursive script is quite slender (e.g. no. 12). However, the norm in the earlier 15th century was as in figure 15.

15. Hybrid secretary, early 15th century

By the middle of the 15th century, forms of *hybrid secretary* developed in France gradually superseded native ones, understandably so, because of their greater elegance and calligraphic expertise. The principal influence was the *lettre bastarde*, which was to be preserved in 16th-century *bastard secretary*. One of its basic differences is the use mainly of arched curves rather than broken strokes in the lobes. The finest variety, developed at the Court of Burgundy, is known as *lettre bourguinonne* (*Burgundian script*), the main characteristics being a slight slope to the right, long finely tapered shafts, hairline links between minims and *quadrata* serifs (Skelton, nos. 14–16, figure 16).[111]

16. Lettre bourguinonne, late 15th century

d. **From More to Shakespeare.** With the advent of printing in England, a few years before the birth of More, and with changes in taste brought about by humanism, gothic *text* gradually fell into disuse in literary manuscripts, but it did not entirely disappear, being especially popular for display, and was still being taught by the writing-masters towards the end of the 16th century. Elaborate specimens are provided in the main Elizabethan copybooks, for example, de Beauchesne and Baildon, *A booke containing divers sortes of hands*, 1570, and the anonymous *A newe booke of copies*, 1574. The text hands they show are still basically the old *textura quadrata*, but de Beauchesne's version is embellished with scroll-work and the *Newe booke* specimen is decorated in French style with threadlike forks and hairline terminals (figure 17).

The *hybrid secretary* hand was far more popular than *textura* and occurs quite frequently in the more formal manuscripts. It was of special service in works divided into text, translation and commentary and therefore requiring differentiation and levels of formality of script.[112] Though based on the *lettre bourguinonne*, it had become squarer, clearer and more upright, with fewer serifs on the minims, but a long foot serif on *t*, and with shorter though still tapering shafts. Known in England as *bastard secretary*, the title given it in de Beauchesne, it had acquired international fame as *bastarde angloise*. The English copybook examples are much the same as one another, the following in a Dutch book

The texte hande.

Aa a Bb Cc Dd Ee Ff Gg Hh Ii Kk Ll Mm
Nn Oo Pp Qq Rr Ss Tt Uu ww Xx Yy Zz Cc

17. Textura quadrata, 1574

by Hondius, *Theatrum artis scribendi*, 1594 (engraved by an Englishman) is bolder and wider, but otherwise a fair representation of what is certainly a very elegant and strikingly legible script (figure 18).

The basic concern, however, in English handwriting in the 16th century was for acquiring a generally acceptable, all-purpose hand combining aesthetic appeal and clarity with smoothness and facility in execution, and the scene comes to be dominated by two cursives, one a development of the traditional gothic script, known as *secretary*, the other a drastic return to Roman simplicity, commonly called *italic*. They reached parity of esteem by the end of the century, formed a brief alliance and then gothicism was driven out of circulation, though it still found a refuge in the departments and higher courts of law.

i. *Secretary*. Every country of northern Europe had in general use a cursive derived from 15th-century *secretary*. The English variety was in fact called *secretary hand* by Elizabethan writing-masters, including de Beauchesne and Martin Billingsley (*The pen's excellencie*, 1618), probably because it was the script employed by the amanuensis. To indicate phases of its development and to distinguish it from 15th-century *secretary* it is convenient to apply the qualifying terms, *early Tudor, mid-Tudor* and *Elizabethan*.[113]

Early Tudor secretary could be said to cover about fifty years, from roughly the accession of Henry VII in 1485 until the later years of the reign of Henry VIII. It appears to derive its general style mainly from a broad, fairly open and somewhat splayed version of *secretary* in use from about the middle of the 15th century, with admixture from the more cursive form of *anglicana* as used in correspondence, from which it obtained its boldness and relative roundness, for there is a return to an

almost straight, upright and slightly blunt nib.[114]

Most of its graphs are from 15th-century *secretary*, including the pointed single-lobed *a*, the uncial *d* (sometimes indented), tailed *g* with a wide *u* shaped top and long headstroke and *w* in its simple double *v* form. There are several letters, however, which although probably taken from immediate *secretary* models, go back to *anglicana*, among them the open-bodied looped *d*, reversed circular *e*, the broad-bodied *h* and the sigma *s*, though now in a much smaller form and with a high, often curved ascender. Other letters are traditional, for example *c*, with a straight top and curved stem, and *z* form of *r*, used exclusively. Marked developments are the use of looped and curved links as frequently appear on *f*, *h* and *y* (no. 17 and figure 19).

There is a remarkable uniformity of style in the use of this hand, as can be seen from examples as diverse as parish records, a poetry commonplace book of Thomas Wyatt (no. 19), and the letters of Henry VIII and Katherine of Aragon.[115]

The next phase, *mid-Tudor secretary*, is a short one not easily determinable in chronology or exact style, but seems to extend from the mid-1530s to about the beginning of Elizabeth's reign. It is best defined as an intermediate stage in which there is a gradual narrowing and angularity, with more definition in thickness between upstroke and downstroke, as the pen becomes more angled, and increased cursiveness, especially noticeable in *d*, where the body is losing its definition, and *e* in which the eye is sometimes almost split from the body, so fine is the connecting stroke. The stem of *c* is now straight, as part of the process towards the *r* form; the tail of *g* now crosses over the head to link with the succeeding letter, *p* has acquired an introductory *2*, *r* is developing a twin-stemmed variety, and long *s* has many

La Bastarde Angloise.

Like as the cutting of vines and other plants
is cause of much better & more plentie of y
fruit: so the punishment of euill men, cause
good men to flourish in a common welth.

18. Hybrid secretary, 1594

16

19. Early Tudor secretary, c. 1520

more ligatures than the *st sh* combinations (cf. no. 20 and figure 20).[116]

20. Mid-Tudor secretary, c. 1540–50

By about 1560, if not a little earlier, *Elizabethan secretary* had evolved, though it was to acquire calligraphic features and typical idiosyncrasies in the hands of the later Elizabethan writing-masters, and, more especially, was to be recognized in three distinct grades of set, facile and fast, with their varying degrees of slope.[117] It was now a compact hand, written with a very fine nib held at a slightly oblique angle. It was almost entirely cursive except in its set form, and could obviously be written at great speed. One of the first expert practitioners was Ascham, who even as early as the mid-1550s was writing a fully fledged, compact but fairly rapid form (no. 24).

The most formal *Elizabethan secretary* was the *engrossing hand*, a kind of deluxe set script, often used for documents. It owed much of its regularity to *textura*, and the most common variety depended heavily on the linking diagonal. The typical set *secretary* letters it contained are the *r* form of *c* with a foot serif, uncial *d*, Greek *e*, *g* in its hybrid form, twin-stemmed *r* and *textura* *r* with a foot serif, and *x* looking like *v* with an enclosing tail. In the following example, which opens in *hybrid secretary*, loops have been employed on

ascenders and ligatures to counteract the general angularity (figure 21). A small version of the engrossing hand was also current, being known in England as a *glozing hand* and on the Continent as *anglicana*.[118]

Elizabethan *secretary* in general use had a far wider range of minuscule forms than the engrossed, even in its most formal hands, a fact insufficiently recognized by the writing-masters, whose lists of alphabets are therefore somewhat limiting and misleading, being prescriptive rather than descriptive. For example, *a* was very often open, and by the end of the century had acquired a large variety of spurs. In the case of *e*, several types co-existed, including Greek *e*, open reversed *e*, and two-stroke *e*. For *h* there seem to be innumerable variants from a simple double-looped shaft to an elaborately looped body. For *r*, in addition to the *2* and twin-stemmed forms there is the left-shouldered version, *v* form and Roman *r* with a foot-serif. There are many varieties of long *s*, mainly dependent on the ligature with the succeeding letter, and it is to be noted that sigma *s* is much more common than the French *c+3* form, though the copybooks would seem to indicate otherwise (figure 22).

22. Elizabethan secretary, late 16th century

Capitals tended on the whole to be based on the 15th-century *hybrid secretary* forms. In the set hands they appear with all the traditional embellishments, but in the lower grades, the more basic and cursive forms were employed, including a circular form of *C* with a horizontal cross-stroke, and *E* resembling a modern *C* with *2* set within it. The capital form of F is still double *f* (figure 23).[119]

21. Engrossing Elizabethan secretary, 1574

23. Secretary and hybrid secretary capitals, late 16th century

The growth of *secretary* was furthered by being taught in the schools, and it was found suitable for general use, including the transaction of business and correspondence, and for literary purposes, being apparently the hand most frequently used by Spenser and Shakespeare. It was also capable of considerable misuse, and a number of literary hands at the end of the century lapsed into illegibility when written at speed, with the minims tending to merge, and the linear letters, only partly formed and open at the top, having little or no differentiation, the most notorious example being provided by Thomas Heywood (no. 55). It is perhaps significant that the Heywood illustration occurs in the dying days of *secretary* as a script in its own right.

ii. *Italic*. The major handwriting reform of the Renaissance was the introduction of an entirely new style of handwriting. This was as far-reaching in its way as the Carolingian reform and closely related to it, since the *Carolingian minuscule*, together with Roman capitals, was to be the formative influence. The impetus for the reform started in 14th-century Florence and is usually ascribed to the efforts of Petrarch (1330–1406) succeeded by Coluccio Salutati (1330–1406), the Chancellor of Florence. Dissatisfaction with the current gothic book hands, which sorely strained the eyesight, coincided with the revival of interest in the Classics, the texts of which were found to be written mainly in *Carolingian minuscule*. The result was an attempt to restore gothic script to something of the simplicity of its ancestor (usually termed *fere-humanistica* or *gothica-humanistica*) and then to create a completely new script modelled almost entirely on *Carolingian*. The new script was aptly named *littera antiqua*, but was also known as *romana*, *rotunda* or *tonda*. Among its chief exponents were Niccolò Niccoli (1363–1437) and Poggio Bracciolini (1380–1459) who established links with England.[120]

Littera antiqua was used in three basic grades, *formata* in which the letters were perfectly upright, exactly proportioned and usually unlinked, though the script was so compact that they seemed to be joined. The next grade was called *cursiva*, and though still upright its letters were mainly linked. The third grade, *currens*, had a slight slope and had distinctive diagonal links. Though the hand formed the basis for roman

type, it did not survive for long as a book hand because it was rather laborious to write and could not compete with a larger more cursive form that had developed. It still appears in the 16th century and More (no. 18) provides a good example of a fairly rapid cursive variety mixed with *secretary*.

By the middle of the 15th century a humanistic cursive had evolved which was to lay the foundation for modern handwriting. It owed much of its advancement to being adopted by the Papal chancery under Pope Eugenius IV (1431–47) thereafter being known as *cancellaresca corsiva* (*cursive chancery* or *letera da brevi*), since it was used for Papal briefs. It assumed widespread popularity in Italy by the 16th century and was extensively taught by Italian writing-masters, including Ludovico degli Arrighi, who was the first to print examples of it (*La operina da imparare di scrivere littera cancellarescha*, 1522). Arrighi taught that the bodies of the letters should be of uniform height and oblong rather than square in shape. Ascenders and descenders were also to be of the same height and to have the same rate of curve (figure 24).[121]

Larger and more rounded varieties of *cancellaresca* are also to be found in 16th-century copybooks, and Ascham provides a good example of a round *formata* grade (no. 23).

A a b c d e e f g g h i k l m n o p q r s s t u x y z

A A B B C c D D E E F F G G H H J J K L L M M N N O P P Q Q R R S S T T U V V X X Y Z & e R & R l

Ludouicus vicentinus scribebat Roma' anno salutis M DXXIII

24. Cancellaresca corsiva, 1523

18

There was also a *hybrid cancellaresca* (*bastarda*), which was bold, clear, almost upright, with unlinked letters and often with consistent use of short *s*.[122]

Many forms of humanistic cursive evolved in the late 15th and early 16th centuries, including a large number of business hands for the different Italian cities, for example, the *merchantile* scripts of Rome, Milan, Florence, Venice and Genoa.[123] But all varieties of the cursive were known under the general heading of *italic* or *Italian*, since they originated in Italy. They were also sometimes referred to as *roman*, but strictly speaking this applied to the set *littera antiqua*, and the typeface made from it, just as *italic* referred also to the sloped typeface derived from the cursive. While the hands used by the Italian humanists in the 15th century can be conveniently termed *humanistic* it is preferable to use *italic* for the later period since it has much more general application and is the term used by the contemporary writing-masters.[124]

Italic was a little slow coming to northern Europe, though it was encouraged and practised by the Northern humanists. Examples of *littera antiqua* had reached England around the middle of the 15th century, and towards the end of the century the cursive was introduced, probably through the influence of Petrus Carmelianus of Brescia, who arrived in England around 1480 and became Latin secretary to Henry VII.[125]

Royal patronage gave the cursive additional prestige, and the royal children were taught to write the hand, among the prominent tutors being Sir John Cheke and Roger Ascham (*vide* no. 23). Cheke was an extremely influential figure in the propagation of the script, though his particular form of hand, seen in the Ascham example, seems to die out by the middle of the 16th century. A notably popular form was a squarish version especially in the early 16th century, seemingly based on a form of *hybrid*, and having no equivalent in the copy-book of the Italian writing-masters, Arrighi, Palatino and Tagliente. In its basic form it looks much as in the Leland example, no. 21, which is large, with mainly straight strokes except in the shafts and tails, without serifs, and containing the minimum of adornment. Nicholas Udall's hand is somewhat similar at the same period (1530–45), a formal version of it was taught to Edward VI (presumably by Ascham), and traces of it are still to be seen at the end of the century, as in the hand of Lady Arbella Stuart (1602).[126]

A *hybrid* form of *cancellaresca* was common for the most formal book and letter hand. It was practised by Queen Elizabeth from her early youth and a version of it is included by de Beauchesne in his 1570 copybook.[127] But the most popular formal *italic* of the later 16th century is a fairly large rounded version of *cancellaresca* with curved and clubbed heads on the ascenders and therefore known as *testeggiata* (*headed*). The limb of *h* also usually ended in a curled club (figure 25).[128]

The *testeggiata* style was to remain popular as a formal hand until well into the middle of the 17th century, outstripping rather more fanciful varieties such as *piacevole* (*pleasing*), with curled finials, and *lettre pattée* (*with paws*), though both styles are illustrated by the writing-masters (figure 26).[129]

26. *a.* Piacevole; *b.* Pattée, 1574

For general correspondence, more utilitarian styles were in use in England, as in the angular, economical hand of the 17th Earl of Oxford (no. 28), and the extremely looped sprawling hand of Philip Sidney (no. 27), though he had apparently been taught to write *cancellaresca* and *testeggiata* as a boy.

It is clear that the nobility followed the example of royalty in learning the *italic* hand, and in their wake came the gentry and the rising middle class by the end of the century. Generally speaking, the nobility used *italic* for their own correspondence hands, while their secretaries would employ the more traditional *secretary*. They also usually signed their names in *italic* from about the middle of the 16th century, the last signature by a nobleman in *secretary* in this book being Surrey's (no. 20, 1545). It is very likely that most educated men in the period were able to write both scripts with equal facility, as in the Spenser, Ascham and Chettle illustrations, in which Ascham and Chettle show that they signed their names in either script. In most literary manuscripts and in correspondence there was a division of labour whereby *italic* would be employed for Latin, and *secretary* for the vernacular, as in the examples from More, Ascham and Kyd, who uses *italic* for Latin quotations in an otherwise *secretary* hand. The practice was also adopted of using *italic* for proper names

25. Testeggiata italic, 1571

(though not always consistently), for display, and for speech headings and stage directions in plays written in *secretary* or, by the early 17th century, in the newly employed *mixed hand*.

e. From Donne to Dryden. The 17th century in England witnessed the extinction of *secretary* as a literary hand in its own right by about the end of the third decade. It was to survive for much longer in diluted form by admixture with *italic*. The resulting combination is normally known as *mixed hand*, though it does not appear to have been sanctioned by any of the writing-masters.

i. *Mixed*. The mingling of scripts is a common palaeographical phenomenon, being often the way in which new scripts are created. The interchange of *secretary* and *italic* graphs was not an entirely new occurrence at the end of the 16th century, and this book contains examples which date from as early as the 1530s, when More uses a few *secretary* letters in a mainly *italic* script and Wyatt does almost exactly the reverse (nos. 18, 19).

However, it is true to say that mixing does not appear with any noticeable frequency until almost the end of the century, when it is used by an impressive array of literary figures including Bacon, Ralegh and Ben Jonson, the earliest clear example in the text being Bacon's, dated 1604 (no. 45). The mixture is probably partly due to the fact that by this time both hands were employed with such frequency by any given writer that the graphs were interchanged almost involuntarily. It seems likely, too, that the interchangeability was the greater because both scripts could be written in much the same size and with the same degree of cursiveness, though *italic* had lagged behind *secretary* a little in this respect till the end of the century. It should be noted that there does not appear to be a specific system of exchange of graphs, and sometimes a large number of different forms from both scripts can be found side by side and in any position in a given hand.

The earliest *mixed* hands seem to be mainly *secretary* with a few *italic* letters, usually capitals, which were much more simply written, and with minuscules *f*, *r*, long and short *s* prominent. Then follow *e*, *h* and *c*, usually as alternatives. By the end of the first decade of the 17th century there is a much more genuine equality of letter forms, though the general style and look of the hand, at first glance at least, is suggestive of *italic*. Good examples are provided by Ralegh's Notebook hand (nos. 47–8) and by Ben Jonson, whose *Masque of Queenes* elegantly demonstrates that it is possible to write a set variety of this hand perfectly acceptable for use in a presentation copy to a royal personage (46). However, there are quite late examples where the general appearance is more that of *secretary*, as in the case of Heywood's wretched hand, 1624 (no. 55) and later still, the scribe for Herbert's *Temple*, *c*. 1631 (no. 57). But these cases seem to run against the gradual trend, which is for *italic* to take over almost completely, with only the *secretary e*, modified *h* and *r* remaining. By the middle of the 17th century truly mixed hands are dying out, the Vaughan letter, 1673 (no. 61) and the Thomas Browne notebook, *c*. 1680 (no. 64) being fairly late examples. The last letter to go was, fittingly, the cursive reversed *e*, whose lineage went back to *anglicana*, and even some 18th-century hands cling on to it, either out of conservatism or because of its cursive ease.[130]

ii. *Round hand*. Meanwhile, *italic* was continuing to advance, there being for general cursive use two main types: a fairly upright and spiky version as seen in such examples as Overbury (no. 50), Herbert (no. 57), Vaughan and Browne, though the last two are strictly speaking *mixed* hands; and a more rounded, larger, sloping and quite liberally looped one which begins to come into vogue around the middle of the 17th century, as seen in the Pepys longhand (no. 63). This type of writing reflects the changes which had been overtaking *italic*.[131]

In most countries of Europe *italic* was losing something of its ornamental qualities but was gaining in cursiveness by the use of a much rounder style with a profusion of linking loops. Such a change can be easily gauged by sampling the diplomatic correspondence of the early 17th century. The most influential of the writing-masters in propagating the new script is usually considered to be Lucas Materot of Avignon, who published examples of the style of script known as

27. English round hand, *a*. 1659; *b*. 1673

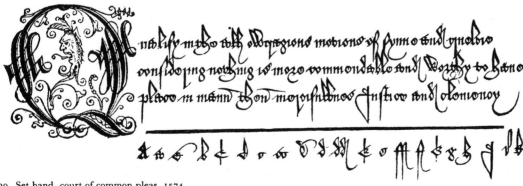

28. Set chancery hand, 1574

bastard italian in 1608. Materot had a marked influence on English writing-masters, who adapted the bastard hand both to commercial and general use, so that as refined and perfected in the hands of such writing-masters as Peter Gery (fl. 1660) and John Ayres (fl. 1680–1705) among others it became known as the English *round hand* and swept the Continent in the 18th century (figure 27).[132]

The period covered by this book closes a little before the perfected English round hand comes into general circulation. But Marvell (no. 60) provides a bold and remarkably early example of its final stages of development, while Dryden (66, 67) comes close to the refinements of the Ayres illustration. Fittingly, his letter of 1699, in marking the end of this text, can be said to point to the beginning of the modern era of English handwriting.

f. **Notes on departmental hands.**[133] Although this book is concerned mainly with literary hands, mention at least should be made of the distinctive government department hands of the period, because some of them had currency beyond their official designation, and in a few cases influenced literary styles, as in the George Cavendish example (no. 22), which shows marks of *chancery* and other legal scripts.

Before the 15th century, documentary hands were on the whole fairly similar to the more formal varieties of cursive book hand, especially in the *anglicana* and early *secretary* periods. The main exception was the *pipe roll* hand in the Exchequer, which originated in the 12th century and had a revered position because it recorded transactions with the sovereign's debtors. It had changed its appearance very little over the centuries and is easily recognized because its minims have the appearance of large colons, since they have head and foot serifs but little or no body.[134]

There were four other important departmental hands, all of which developed in the course of the 15th century. These were *chancery*, used in the court of chancery and for engrossing departmental records; *court of common pleas*, used for that court, the King's bench and in general for legal documents; and two hands of the Exchequer: the *King's remembrancer*, which was close to the *chancery* hand in style, and the *Lord Treasurer's remembrancer*, which had affinities with the *common pleas* hand.[135] The Elizabethan writing-masters took sufficient cognisance of these hands, despite their being limited to a specialist class of clerks, to include specimens of them in their copybooks, the two most commonly illustrated being *chancery* and *common pleas*.

Chancery clearly shows its *anglicana* origins not only in double-lobed *a*, two-compartment *g* and long *r* alternating with the *2* form and sigma *s*, but also in looped *d* and occasional circular reversed *e*. It is quite widely spaced and especially in its less formal grades tends to lose its linking strokes, giving it the impression of a long sequence of parallel lines (figure 28).[136]

The *court of common pleas* hand is extremely narrow, with very tall angular ascenders. Even more than *chancery* it betrays its *anglicana* origins not only in double-lobed *a*, two-compartment *g*, long *r* and a form of sigma *s*, but also in the looped *d* and circular reversed *e* (figure 29).

The departmental hands retained their forms and their mystique for a considerable time, though they were temporarily expelled in the Commonwealth period. They remained a peculiar relic from the medieval period, until an Act of Parliament axed all but the *chancery* hand, which struggled on in a much debased form into the 19th century, when it, too, was dismissed, in 1836, after a reign of 400 years.

29. Set hand, court of common pleas, 1574

5. Abbreviation

The main function of abbreviation is to save time and space, though for the average medieval scribe and, to a lesser extent, his Renaissance counterpart, time was often less important than making the maximum use of the relatively expensive writing surface. Abbreviation has also been used for helping to preserve the secrecy of sacred or highly personal writing or simply for keeping lines of writing of equal length, rather like 'justifying' in printing. It can range from the contraction of a single letter to a complete system, the ancient art of tachygraphy, more commonly known as shorthand, which was practised by Samuel Pepys (no. 63).

For abbreviation to be effective for general circulation, it has to conform to widely recognized and easily assimilated rules, and to be clearly understood in context. Handwriting has not been consistently successful in this, with systems differing not only from place to place but from writer to writer. The abbreviations of the late medieval and Renaissance periods, however, were fairly uniform and confined within reasonable limits, presenting few problems other than whether or not a symbol which usually signifies omission is, in context, simply a meaningless flourish.

Medieval abbreviation derives from Roman times, when three basic systems were in use: the *notæ juris* (*juristic* signs), employed in legal documents, one feature of which was shortening words even to the point of initials, as in *S.P.Q.R.*; Tironian symbols, a shorthand method used by Tiro, Cicero's secretary, from which such signs as *7* for *and* (*et*) were taken; and *nomina sacra*, whereby sacred names, out of deference to the Deity, were reduced often to first and last letters (as in *DS* for *Deus*), a practice common among Early Christians and derived from the Hebrew.[137]

The use of abbreviation for Latin developed considerably, so that by the 12th century it had reached elaborate and complex proportions, requiring of the reader considerable skill in cryptography and linguistics and a flair for inspired guesswork.[138] Thereafter, the range of abbreviated Latin words was reduced and returned gradually to orderly and manageable proportions, though stock formulae were, understandably, still considerably curtailed.[139]

Vernacular languages imitated the Latin system of abbreviation, adopting both its rules and the signs which were readily transferable. For example, English had no need for the *juristic* symbol resembling *H* which signified *enim*, but readily borrowed Tironian *9* representing *com* or *con* at the beginning of a word. In addition, the vernacular devised signs of its own, but its abbreviations never attained the range and frequency they had in Latin. The general pattern in English literary manuscripts was one of gradual reduction, so that by the Renaissance, abbreviations were of modest proportions and, in any case, more abundant in drafts than in formal copies, where the practice was hardly more extensive than in printed books.

Abbreviations are conveniently dealt with under four traditional though sometimes overlapping categories: *contraction*, *curtailment* (or *suspension*), *brevigraphs* (*special signs*) and *superior* (or *superscript*) *letters*. It is also useful to include as a minor but distinct category, *elision*, even though this is more literary and linguistic than palaeographical.[140]

i. *Contraction* was the commonest method of abbreviation, and consisted of the omission of one or more letters from the middle of a word. In general, the number of letters omitted depended on the frequency of the word and how obvious it was in context. In Latin, common polysyllabic words,

especially in formulae, were often reduced to a skeletal form along the lines of *nomina sacra*, so that *Domine sancte Pater* might well become *Dne scte Pr*. In English, such drastic reduction was restricted mainly to modes of address (e.g. *Mr* and *Mrs* for *Master* and *Mistress*), common Christian names (e.g. *Wm* for *William*) and personal adjectives (*y^r* for *your*).

Even if the case of omission was obvious, a sign indicating contraction was almost invariably inserted. A common indication when only the first and last letters remained was a period placed at the end, for example, *Lp.* for *Lordship* and *Sr.* for *Sir*, these illustrations being especially current in the Renaissance. Another method was to place an apostrophe above the place where the letters had been omitted. This occurred frequently in Latin (e.g. *m'iam* for *misericordiam*) and Anglo-Norman (no. 1, *n're* for *nostre*), but in English it usually represented *e*, and combinations of *r* with *e* and *i* (see *curtailment* and *brevigraphs*).

The commonest mark of contraction was the bar, formally known as a *tittle* (*titula*) or *tilde*, which was placed along the top of virtually the whole word in large omissions, and usually above the preceding letter in single letter contractions. Like the apostrophe it was widely used as a general mark in Latin, but in English was a little more restricted. Though it is found for general contraction (no. 4, *lettres*), it is usually reserved for legal terms (no. 26, *presentes*), names (no. 3, *Ihesu*; no. 5, *Willielmi*; nos. 25 and 26, *Spenser*), and, most commonly, for specific single letters: *m*, *n*, and *i* in the *ion* suffix, as well as for final *e* (see *curtailment*).

The bar had various forms, but was generally a simple straight line, or a wavy one like the Spanish *tilde*. An older form, though still in use in the late 15th century, was crescent-shaped, often with a dot below it (cf. no. 10), rather like a music pause (employed as such in no. 11). In addition there were various ornamental forms, especially when the scribe moulded them to his style of writing, and in cursive hands there was a practice of making either the bar or the apostrophe part of the upward curve on the final stroke of a letter, usually at the end of a word (last example, figure 30).

Yet another form of contraction, involving superior letters, is discussed in section iv.

30. Forms of bar (tittle), 15th–17th century

ii. *Curtailment* or *suspension* shortened the end of the word by one or more letters. In its extreme form, as in *notae juris*, only the initial letter remained, called a *sigla*, obvious examples being *B.C.* and *A.D.* A common method of indicating curtailment, especially in the Renaissance, was to place a period or a colon at the end. In the case of the *sigla*, the period was more usual, and, in keeping with earlier practice, one was often placed in front as well. Both marks of curtailment are most frequently found in Renaissance modes of address, which were shortened in varying degrees. Thus *Lordship* might appear as *Lordsh:*, *Lord.*, *Lo:* or simply *L.*, with the plural represented by doubling the *sigla*: *Ll.*, a convention which applied in several other curtailed plurals. *Majesty* also varied in form, for example, *Ma:*, *Mai:*, and *Maiest:*, with many other versions employed with superior letters.

In the medieval period, the bar and the apostrophe were more common marks of curtailment, especially in conjunction with names (no. 1, *Ric'* for *Richard*, an Anglo-Norman example) and for the omission of a single final letter, mainly *e*, but sometimes *m* or *n* (usually signified by the bar). Thus final *g'*, *n'* and *r'* normally stood for *ge*, *ne*, *re*; crossed double *l* for *lle*; and a bar above a final vowel, nasal or *y* generally indicated omitted *m* or *n*. However, the bar and the apostrophe, whether separate or linked to a letter, were sometimes merely ornamental or appeared from force of habit. Since spelling was not normalized either in the medieval or Renaissance period, it is particularly difficult to decide whether or not a final *e* or *n* is intended. The problem of final *e* is an acute one in the late 14th and early 15th century, barred double *l* being a classic case (cf. nos. 11–13). A similar situation exists when there is a curtailment mark above two final minims, which might signify *u* plus omitted *m* or *n*, *n* plus omitted *e*, or simply *n* or *u* with an ornamental second limb (cf. nos. 13 and 24). The solution may be assisted by scansion in a poetry text in which final *e* is pronounced, but usually requires a comprehensive knowledge of the scribal habits, coupled with evidence provided by philology, grammar and orthography. A further complication is that the apostrophe sign also signified combinations of *r* with *e* and *i*, while the bar might well be a general mark of curtailment.

Various other signs attached to the final letter indicated omitted *e*, though they too could be otiose, for example *d* with a long tail from its stem, or *g* with a similar tail from the headstroke. Sometimes a minute curl would be the only indication, particularly when attached to *h* in the definite article, a practice encountered in the late 15th and early 16th century (e.g. no. 19), though this is perhaps more a case of a partly formed letter than a sign of curtailment.[141]

iii. *Brevigraphs* or *special signs*, though not, strictly speaking, shorthand symbols, were somewhat similar to them in use. They generally represented at least two letters or one syllable, and might resemble one of the omitted letters or be apparently arbitrary in shape. Some were immutable in significance, others changed their meaning according to the letter to which they were attached, their relative position in the word, and whether they were on, above or below the line of writing.

For ease of reference, the most common vernacular brevigraphs, together with the Latin ones in the text, are listed in the alphabetical sequence of the first of the letters they represent.[142]

Letters	Symbols	Comments and references
a		Supralinear 14th century *a*, often reduced to a serrated line (really a superior letter). Still used in 16th century (nos. 12, 22). See *ra*.
and		Versions of Tironian nota for *et*. Used in gothic script throughout the period.
and		Common form in *Elizabethan secretary* (no. 22) and occasionally in *italic* (no. 59).
and		Ampersand. Main *italic* form; less common in gothic script.
c		Supralinear for *c* or *ac* (no. 26). Derived from 14th-century form.
ci, ti		More usual simply for *i* in *cion* and *tion* (no. 51).
com, con		In linear, initial position (no. 2). Tironian.
de		Uncommon after 15th century. Can be otiose.
e		In use by late 16th century to denote silent *e* in *ed*, *en* and *est* in poetry; sometimes placed after succeeding consonant (no. 31). See also *curtailment*, *elision*, and *apostrophe* section of *Punctuation*.
etc.		First form is *secretary*, the second *italic*.
er		Supralinear. Very common in all gothic scripts.
es, is, ys		Final linear, or supralinear position. First form more common than second (nos. 4, 13, 19, 20, 22, 26, 32, 40–2). Almost invariably *es* for English post-15th-century MSS, though very occasionally signifies simply *s*. In medieval and Scottish MSS *is* and *ys* are frequently intended.
ge		Uncommon after 15th century. Can be otiose.
i		In combinations *cion*, *tion*, and variants of them (see *contraction*).
ir, ier, ire		As for *er*. Uncommon (no. 26).
lle		See *curtailment*.

Letters	Symbols	Comments and references
m, n	— ‿ ’	See *contraction*.
ne	ꝋ ꞃ	Can be otiose. See *curtailment*.
par, per	ꝑ ꝓ	Basic forms constant for all scripts of the period: *p* with a straight or convex bar through the stem.
pre	ꝥ ꝗ	Same sign as for *er* (nos. 26, 42).
pri	ꝓ	Not very common in English (no. 1).
pro	ꝓ ꝙ	Basic difference from *par/per* is that the curve through the stem is concave not convex (nos. 5, 29, 36, 44).
quam	ẚ̃	Used only in Latin (no. 18).
que	ꝙ ꝗ	Appears in English as well as Latin because *c* and *ck* were often spelt *que* (nos. 6, 14, 18, 23, 56).
quod (quoth)	ꝙ	Used both for Latin and the vernacular, though the word had a different meaning in English.
ra	ꝶ ～	Supralinear. Both forms are current in late medieval period, but rare in the Renaissance (nos. 3, 12). Sometimes used for other combinations with *a*, e.g. *ac, ia* (nos. 26, 42).
re	ꝟ	Common in 15th century (nos. 9, 10).
rum	ꝝ	Used only in Latin.
ser, sir	ꝑ ß	Quite common in period.
sieur	ꝭ	Anglo-Norman, basically the same sign as for *ser* (no. 1).
ter	ꝓ	Basically same brevigraph as for *er*.
ur	ᵃ ꝛ	First sign more common than the second in the vernacular (nos. 5, 6, 10, 22).
us	ꝯ ꝰ	Same sign as for *com/con*, but in final, linear or supralinear position (nos. 4, 44)

iv. *Superior* or *superscript letters* were really a form of contraction, whereby the raised position of one or more letters indicated that letters immediately preceding them had been omitted. Though the presence of superior letters was generally considered sufficient to denote contraction, a bar or an apostrophe was also occasionally added, or, more usually, a period placed at the end either on the line or beside the last superior letter. This method of abbreviation, though popular in the 12th and 13th centuries, seems to have fallen off a little and then to have come back into fashion in the 16th century, when it was extremely common for modes of address, numerals, relative and possessive pronouns and adjectives, and some prepositions. It should be noted that although they usually appeared at the end, superior letters could occur in the middle of a word (e.g. $w^{th}out$ for *without*); and in a few instances, the omission extended beyond the superior letter, as in w^t for *with*. Sometimes the raised letter was there from habit rather than for indicating omission, the most common example being p^e or y^e for *the*. Letters with which this is a frequent occurrence are *a, e* and *r*. The following tables give a sampling of the superior letters in general use both with (*a*) words and (*b*) numbers.

(*a*)

Anno Domini	$A^o\ D^{ni}$	*Regis*	R^e
Bishop	B^p	*regni*	r^{ni}
Christo	X^o	*Signor*	Sig^{or}
Esquire	Esqre	*Sir*	S^r
Highness	$Highn^s$	*servant*	$serv^t, ser^t$ or s^t
Iacobus	Iac^a	*that*	p^t or y^t
Knight	K^t	*the*	p^e or y^e
libri (pounds)	li	*their (theyr)*	$they^r$ or p^r
Lordship	$Lordsh^p$ or L^p	*thou (thow)*	$thou^u, tho^w$ or p^u
Maiestie	$Maitie^p$ or $Matie$	*which (wich)*	w^{ch}
Master	M^r	*with*	wth or w^t
-ment	$-m^t$	*without*	$w^{th}out$
Mistress	M^{rs}	*you (yow)*	yo^u, yo^w, y^u or y^w
our	ou^r or o^r	*your*	yor or y^r
Regina	R^a		

(*b*)

primo	I^o	*decimo*	x^o
secundus	2^{ndus} or 2^9	*eleventh*	IIth or xi^{th}
tertio	3^{io} or iii^o	*twenty*	xx^{tie}
four (fowre)	$iiij^{or}$	*vicesimo*	xx^{mo}

It must be remembered that the use of superior letters was only an alternative method of abbreviation, and a given word might be abbreviated in several different ways, as instanced

24

by *majesty*, which was shortened by contraction or curtailment as well as by superior letters.

v. *Elision*, generally indicated by an apostrophe, differed from traditional forms of abbreviation because it was not primarily concerned with saving time or space but with the silencing of letters for metrical necessity, euphony or colloquial convenience. Further, the abbreviation could take place at the beginning as well as in the middle or at the end of a word. In initial position, elision involved the loss of a single syllable (*aphaeresis*), or vowel (*aphesis*), e.g. *'twixt* for *betwixt*, *'mongst* for *amongst*. Normally the omission was intended to link the word effectively to the preceding or succeeding word, as in *I'll* and *'Twas*. Medial elision (*syncopation*) was extremely common in poetry, especially where *e* and *v* were concerned, as in *e'en* and *off'ring*. Even more frequent was elision at the end of a word (*apocope*), usually enabling it to run on to the succeeding word when this began with a vowel or aspirate, the commonest examples occurring with the definite article: *t'other*, *thaction*, *thandes*, frequently without any break or apostrophe.

Sometimes the elision was so extensive that it swallowed up an entire word, a process called *absorption*. Most of the examples are of short words after a similar sound in the preceding word. Thus *at the* and *this is* might become simple *at* and *this*; while *but it*, *but to*, *but the* could all be reduced to *but*.[143]

There is a marked diminution in abbreviations for literary use from the early 17th century. One of the early casualties was the bar or tittle, which for all its previous popularity seems to die out completely by the end of the century. The other brevigraphs dropped out in the same period, so that from the 18th century there is little more than a few superior letters, the curtailment of titles still in use today and the ampersand. In this respect, handwriting seems very much to have been keeping pace with the printed book.

6. Punctuation
Of the diverse elements that comprise the study of palaeography, punctuation is one of the most rudimentary, yet at times one of the most confusing. It took an extremely long time to evolve. In its earliest form it was little more than a raised point to separate words, and even by the 13th century the point and the inverted semicolon were the only marks of punctuation in England. A number of other signs subsequently emerged, until by the late 16th century there were all the marks now in use and a few others which disappeared in the 17th century.[144] But even then, punctuation was somewhat haphazardly applied in manuscripts and the significance of a given mark varied almost as frequently as spelling did, with a few of the most popular signs acting as general factota. Printing assisted the process of standardization, but its own system did not entirely conform to modern usage, and, in any case, manuscripts generally employed much lighter and less consistent punctuation than printed books. It is not until the 18th century that punctuation fully assumed the strict grammatical function that it generally has today, by which time capitalization and spelling had also been normalized.

Punctuation was not however entirely chaotic in the period covered by this book. The major pauses were generally observed, and some attempt was made to present the material according to manageable units of sense, inadequate though these were. Harington and Jonson give some indication of the consistent and effective use of punctuation (nos. 31 and 46), and John Donne exhibits great sensitivity and modernity in his employment of it in the letter to Sir Robert Cotton (no. 44).

The method of punctuation also becomes more explicable in terms of rhetoric rather than of grammar, though in any case the two often coincide, so that the natural speech pause will often occur at the end of a syntactical unit of sense. Many medieval rhetoricians and grammarians commented on the oratorical function of the major pause marks, among them Alcuin of York and John of Salisbury. The same is true for the Renaissance, when Mulcaster, Puttenham, Jonson and Simon Daines, among others, dealt with the elocutional function of the period, comma, colon, and later the semicolon; while Thomas Heywood (*An apology for actors*, 1612) noted that university performances taught actors how to observe marks of punctuation and 'breathing spaces'.[145] However, the rhetorical theory of punctuation, which is still the cause of much debate, cannot be pushed too far, for, as often happens, the statements of theorists are not always found to be carried fully into practice. Further, the notion of punctuation marks in Renaissance drama as quasi-stage directions indicating how actors were to deliver their lines, is not convincingly supported by the extant holograph play manuscripts, among them the examples in this book (nos. 36, 40, 54–6). Most generalities concerning manuscript punctuation have still to be treated with extreme caution, especially because practice often differed from writer to writer, as indeed, to a lesser extent, it still does today, at least with regard to the pauses within the sentence.

It should also be noted that while in literary manuscripts, under the influence of printing, punctuation increased in range and frequency and eventually in general schematization, the trend was quite the reverse in legal documents. Punctuation is almost completely absent from them by the early 15th century, and the pattern of minimal punctuation has persisted in English legal use.

Quite apart from the question of function, the further problems that sometimes confront the palaeographer are whether the marks are contemporary or added later, as often happened when a text was prepared for publication (no. 24). Those marks added or altered more recently are often in a darker ink, but this is not invariably true, and although the formation of a mark can vary from hand to hand, the differences are not so obvious as for letter formation. Finally there is the question of whether the mark is a sign of punctuation or merely a tiny unintentional fleck of ink, a problem aggravated when dealing with inferior photocopies.

The twenty or so marks of punctuation in the period will be dealt with individually, roughly in their chronological order of appearance and relative importance.

i. The *period* (*periodus*), also known as the *prick*, *point* (*punctum*), *full point*, or more recently, the *full stop*, is the earliest English mark of punctuation, and derives via the Roman from the Greek system, which employed a point in a high, medium or low position according to the degree of pause. From being somewhat arbitrarily used to divide words, when it was normally raised, it came to be a general pause mark, sometimes differing in degree according to whether it was raised or on the line. By the 15th century it was a major pause used on the line with rough equivalence to a full stop, but also did service as a type of comma until the early 17th century (e.g. no. 55). Until about the end of the 15th century it was occasionally employed in raised position as an intermediate or caesural pause (cf. nos. 6 and 13).

Among the other duties assigned to the period or point were, as seen in *Abbreviation*, to enclose the *sigla* and to signify curtailment and contraction generally; to enclose numerals (often in raised position, as in no. 2) or at least terminate them; and to dot certain letters. Until the early 16th century, *u* and *y* were often dotted to distinguish them from *n* and *thorn* respectively; and just as the point ceased to be used for these two letters it took over the role of the diacritic in distinguishing *i* from other minims. (The last example in this book of dotted *y* is in no. 19, and the first for dotted *i* is in no. 17, a good ten years after it came into common use.)

A double period was also used as a separate punctuation mark known as a *gemipunctus* (*double-pricked*) before titles of office and dignity, a practice seemingly derived from the *sigla* punctuation, though it should be added that it is not very common in this period, and is especially rare in vernacular literary manuscripts. Other functions for the point included acting as a mark of expunction (see the section on manuscript corrections) or simply as a pen-rest.[146]

Conveniently treated under the heading of *period*, though strictly speaking it was a separate mark of punctuation, is the *triangle of dots* or *triple period* (∴) sometimes called the *periodus*, thus confusing it with the period. It was to be used 'at the end of a chapter or a whole speech, when nothing further remains to be said'.[147] Though more common on the Continent, and mainly confined to the later medieval period, it was nevertheless used by Skelton (cf. commentary to nos. 14–16) and appeared with exactly the same function in the shorthand of Samuel Pepys (no. 63). An inverted form of it is used by Middleton to introduce the reading of a letter in *A game at chesse* (no. 54).

ii. The '*inverted semicolon*' (*punctus elevatus*, literally, 'raised point') seems gradually to have taken over the function of the raised point in indicating a lighter pause than a full stop, and ranged in emphasis from the comma to the semicolon in present usage. It became a mark of punctuation towards the end of the 12th century, and it lasted until just before the middle of the 15th century (the last recorded instance in this book, no. 7, being dated 1423–30).[148] While in its earlier form, it looked very much like a bold comma written above a point, as its name implies, in its more cursive forms it resembled a horizontal *S* over a point, and by the 15th century was like an elongated upright *S* (nos. 3 and 7). Its functions were gradually usurped by the *virgule* and the comma, but its original shape was to provide the basis for the question mark and the semicolon, for which the marks were in reversed position.

iii. The *virgule* (*virgula*, 'a little rod'), an oblique stroke (/) of varying length, thickness and ornamentation, made its appearance in English manuscripts towards the end of the 13th century and was used as a general factotum by the 15th century, often doing service for the period and the inverted semicolon, though its most frequent function was roughly equivalent to the comma. As the comma came into use, so the *virgule* tended to become the mark for ending the paragraph or other major unit of sense, often accompanied by a period before or after, or with one on either side (no. 51). It was popular for marking the end of a stanza or indicating caesural pause (being doubled in the Langland example, no. 5), and also acted as a substitute for *videlicet*, especially in accounts. Degree of emphasis was given the *virgule* by doubling it or even tripling it, the best example in this book

26

being provided by Cavendish (no. 22), 1558. The *virgule* continued its versatile role until the Jacobean period, but had passed almost completely out of use by the middle of the 17th century. The last examples in this book are in the hand of the somewhat conservative Thomas Heywood (no. 55).

iv. The *comma*, known as *suspensivus* in the medieval period, derives its present name, acquired in the late 16th century, from the Greek, *komma*, a short clause. Though employed on the Continent in the medieval period, it did not make its appearance in England until the early 16th century, owing its introduction in great part to the example set by printing, which first used it around 1521. The earliest instance in this book, in Roger Ascham (no. 23), dates from 1542. It soon came into general use, and while it undertook various duties, it was considered by the theorists to signify the shortest time pause in the sentence. It fully assumed its modern role in the early 17th century. The comma is thought to have evolved from a short form of the *virgule*, which it superseded, and occasionally there is difficulty in distinguishing between these two marks of punctuation, as in no. 30.[149]

v. The *colon* (Greek, *kolon*), which seems to have derived from the raised point, came into fairly common use in the 14th century, and in its early career did service both as a full stop (no. 15) and an intermediate pause (no. 6), being an alternative to the inverted semicolon. In the Renaissance it was employed mainly with curtailment (no. 30), or after numerals (no. 47) as an alternative to the point. In dramatic documents it sometimes introduced stage business, and among its general duties was, in conjunction with the *virgule*, to terminate a paragraph or represent *videlicet*. It did not assume its full modern role until the end of the period, though the employment of it by Dekker and Donne within the sentence seems to provide a rough approximation (nos. 40 and 44).

vi. The *semicolon*, known in Elizabethan times as the *comma-colon* or the *subdistinction*, is remarkably late in English manuscripts. It is said to have been introduced into England in 1569 and was not generally used until about 1580. The earliest instance in this book, the Shakespeare addition (no. 36), is later still, *c.* 1593. Though functioning mainly as an intermediate pause between the comma and the period, it also called attention to a marked transition from one idea to another. By the early 17th century it came to be used in the modern way, one of the first exponents being John Donne (no. 44).[150]

vii. The *question mark* (*interrogativus*) was never particularly common until the 17th century. There was little call for it in documents, and in literary texts the general sense was held to be sufficient to indicate a question, or another mark of punctuation served. Among the early forms were a semicircle above a raised point, a sign resembling the inverted semicolon, sometimes with a comma instead of a point, and later an elongated slanting or supine *S* over a linear point. The form as we know it today appeared in general use in English manuscripts in the later 16th century (the first instance here being the Dekker example, no. 40, *c.* 1593) and even so, the upper part was sometimes reversed, as in no. 53, or shaped like a comma (no. 54), thereby resembling the old semicolon form of Greek interrogation mark.

viii. The *hyphen* is an early mark of punctuation, having been in circulation since about the 13th century. Its main function, even until the end of the 17th century, was to indicate words broken by the end of the line, though it had by that time come to be used for compound words also, as instanced in Ben Jonson's *Masque of Queenes*, 1609 (no. 46) and Dryden (no. 66). The usual medieval form was a thin oblique stroke resembling the *virgule* (which is thought to have derived from it) as exemplified by no. 3. By the later 15th century a double-oblique hyphen was more common (no. 13) and remained the usual form well into the 17th century (nos. 15–16, 23 and 46, 54, where it is horizontal). The hyphen was not any more consistently applied than other marks of punctuation, and until the Ben Jonson practice became standardized, words hyphenated today would either be run together or completely separated (as in the reflexives, *him self, her self*).

ix. *Brackets* were not particularly common in the period. The medieval form consisted of two back to back round brackets linked at the base by a line drawn under the enclosed material:)____(, indicating matter not part of the main narrative (as in no. 7), but also acting as quotation marks. In the Renaissance, brackets were either square (*crotchets*) or, more usually, round (*parentheses*), and faced one another as today. Though sparingly used, they had varied functions: for parenthesis, as in Jonson (no. 46) and Fletcher (no. 52); conversely, for emphasizing significant phrases or exclamations, as in Herrick (no. 53); for indicating the speaker, for example, (*said she*); or, as in Southwell (no. 29), to denote an alternative version in a draft.

x. The *apostrophe* (*apostrophus*) seems basically a simplified version of the old brevigraph for *er* and *e* (see section on *Abbreviation*). It appeared as an indication of the possessive about the middle of the 16th century, though the prevalence of *es* or its brevigraph equivalent made it a rarity until the 17th century. It was also used in elision, and to indicate silent syllables, especially those containing *e* and *v* (see *Elision*). There was no consistency in the position of the apostrophe, which might be found a letter or two earlier or later than the actual point of omission (see nos. 53 and 54).

xi. The *exclamation mark* (or 'admiration' mark as Jonson called it) was long in use in France but was extremely rare in England before the early 17th century, perhaps lending credence to the popular notion of the English as being relatively phlegmatic. In French manuscripts it takes the form of *C*, sometimes surmounted by a comma or a bar, but later assumes its present shape under the influence of printing. The only examples in this book are in the plays of Middleton and Massinger (nos. 54, 56).

xii. *Quotation marks* (formerly *quotation quadrats*) are hardly ever used in the period, since the matter quoted was often underlined or prefaced by an appropriate phrase indicating reported speech; while for direct speech various other punctuation marks might be used, for example a dash or a *virgule* placed at the beginning of each line. However, inverted commas are often found used at the beginning of important passages and noteworthy *sententiae*. There is no example of quotation marks in this book, which may provide some indication of their rarity even in 17th-century manuscripts, though diamond brackets resembling the French quotation marks are used for the 'bob' in Gawain (no. 4).

xiii. The *dash*, looking very much like the contraction bar in its various forms, was, like the exclamation mark, more common on the Continent, especially in France. Even in the 17th century it was not much employed in English manuscripts, and the sole instance in this book may be purely decorative (no. 40). When it did occur, it usually had the force of parenthesis, or indicated a break in narrative or thought, and might also introduce stage directions in dramatic documents.

xiv. *Paragraph marks* are conveniently divided into the *paragraphus* and the *capitulum*. The *paragraphus* had several forms in this period. It could resemble a long doubled *s*, a fat *sigma*, or a large capital *gamma*, from which appearance it came to be known as a *gallows bracket* (nos. 2 and 3, where it looks rather more like a wedge). Another distinct form, thought to represent long *i*[151] came to look like *q* with a thickened bowl. The *capitulum* was denoted by its initial letter, usually in barred capital form, but often a cursive *c* resembling *a* with a headstroke. The exact distinction in the function of these different signs was somewhat blurred, especially in the medieval period. The *paragraphus* might well introduce a new paragraph, but sometimes functioned like a *virgule* (nos. 2 and 3). The *capitulum* usually signified a new heading, book or chapter, though it also acted as a medial pause (no. 3) or formed part of a caesura (no. 5). The function of these marks was more strictly limited in the Renaissance to paragraph and chapter headings, with the *capitulum* often subservient to the *paragraphus*.[152]

xv. The *caret* (literally, 'is lacking') is a very old mark of punctuation to indicate interlineation. It occurs in the 12th century as two oblique strokes, but gradually forms itself into a pointed arch by the 13th century, in which form it has continued with minor variations to the present day (compare, for example, no. 1 with nos. 46 and 64) though it was sometimes inverted. Normally, the caret was inserted a little below the line at the point where the interlineation was intended, but was sometimes misplaced and occasionally forgotten altogether.

xvi. *Braces* of various kinds appeared in the period to link items. They had much the same central culminating point as they have today when used in accounts (nos. 41–3), or they could be square, as when separating stage directions from the text, or connecting rhymes (no. 12).

xvii. *Rules* and *underlining* occurred for quotations, to separate sections of a given work (no. 7), to mark off speeches (nos. 12, 54, 55) and to indicate proper names or personification, thereby serving the function of *italics* (no. 46). They were occasionally used in the medieval period as a method of expunction (see *Manuscript corrections*).

xviii. *Diacritic* and *accents*. The diacritic was an oblique hairline resembling a short *virgule* which was placed over *i* to distinguish it from other minims. It was replaced by the point in the early 16th century, though More was still using it in 1534 (no. 18). To distinguish *u* from *n*, a small inverted semicircle was sometimes employed instead of the point, and is still occasionally found in late 16th-century manuscripts. Accents were usually confined to Latin and the romance languages, but even in these the practice was inconsistent. Most frequently found in Latin are a circumflex over *a* to indicate the ablative (no. 58) and a cedilla under *e* to indicate *æ* (no. 33).

xix. *Reference marks* of diverse kinds were used, many of them based on geometrical symbols or on Greek letters. The *x* figured prominently as a form of asterisk.

xx. *Line-fillers*, as their name implies, were used to ensure that each line was completed for perfect alignment down the page, and also to fill in spaces to prevent illegal additions and forgeries, as in Bunyan's deed of gift (no. 65). Though not, strictly speaking, marks of punctuation, they are sometimes mistaken for them because their components often comprise such marks as periods, question marks, commas, colons (no. 40) and inverted semicolons (no. 3). In a few cases it is impossible to decide whether a line-filler or a mark of punctuation is intended (see the *dash*).

7. Numerals[153]

Roman numerals were dominant in England until the 16th century. Though the form they took was much the same as at present, there were certain variants and extensions. The last in a group of ones was usually written *j* (the *i-longa*), as in *ij* for two and *iij* for three. Four might be written *iv* or *iiij*, and nine *ix* or *viiij*.[154] Hundreds could be indicated by the requisite complement of *C*s or by the number of hundreds with superior *c*. Thus three hundred would be either *CCC* or *iijᶜ*. Five hundred was *D* or *Ɔ* and one thousand *M* or *Mˡ*. Multiples of a thousand were generally written as in the alternative method for hundreds, so that three thousand would be *iijᵐ*. Multiples of twenty were also indicated by the same method in England, so that sixty would be *iijˣˣ*.

Since Roman numerals were unsuitable for arithmetic (even lacking a zero) accounting was usually done by means of a chequered cloth (hence the name Exchequer) divided into columns representing different denominations, reading from right to left, farthings, pence, pounds, scores of pounds, hundreds of pounds and so on. Counters were placed in these columns, their value being determined by their position in relation to the horizontal line drawn across the columns. On or below the line they had a unit value; well above and to the right a value of five; well above and to the left the value of ten for shillings, pounds and thousands of pounds. Farthings (always below the line) only had unit value, and so had the penny except that a counter placed in the very centre and well above the line represented sixpence. An example of the system at work is as follows:

(£1000)	(£100)	(£20)	(£)	(s)	(d)	(¼d)
:.:	..:	...	::.	..	.:.	
£18,000	£800	£60	£13	2s.	10d	½d

$$= £18,873. \ 2s. \ 10\tfrac{1}{2}d$$

or in Roman numerals xviiiᵐ viiiᶜ lxxiii *li.* ii*s.* x*j̈d.*

This method was used by auditors; the merchants had a somewhat different system with the counters in rows rather than columns, the lowest row being for the smallest denomination, with counters above the line for tens (6d in the case of pence) and to the far left for fives (except for pence). Both methods survived well into the 16th century, and an account of them was published by Robert Recorde in 1543.

The system known as Arabic numerals originated in India, was developed by the Arabs around the 8th century, and introduced by them into Europe through Spain by the end of the 10th century. The zero made its appearance around 1150. In 1202 a treatise by Leonardo of Pisa demonstrated how the new numerals could be used for addition, subtraction, multiplication and division, and thereafter they took a firm hold in Europe. By the end of the 13th century they were quite common in England, though they were viewed with suspicion for accounting purposes until the 16th century. It has already been noted in this introduction that Arabic numerals began to supersede Roman numerals in manuscript books for quires and pagination in the 15th century, and shortly after, they became at least as common as Roman for general use, sometimes being actually mixed with them, especially in dates, for example: *i58 i.*

Although in Ugo da Carpi's *Thesauro de scrittori* (1525) the Arabic numerals appeared in practically the same form as today, they had undergone considerable modifications over the preceding two centuries, and even in the 16th century they were not written exactly as set out in the textbook.

The basic ten units are illustrated below (figure 31) in the forms they had between the 14th and 16th centuries. Zero usually took the prevailing form of letter *o*. It could thus be made in two sections, completely rounded, looped, or barred by one or two vertical strokes. *1* was either a simple stroke or had head and foot serifs, causing it to resemble *2*, particularly in the 16th century. *2* was often like a modern *7* in the 14th century, but it also had a recognizably modern shape as well. In the 16th century it was often so malformed when written fast that it resembled *1* if its head and tail were only partly formed, or *3* when it had a pronounced descending tail. *3* could be fairly rounded as today but generally looked like a cursive *z*. *4* was the last letter to attain its modern form, looking first like a looped *e*, or a pair of pincers. Its present form does not become common until the mid-16th century, and even then it leans at various angles. *5* looked like a *G* or an angular *h* until the 16th century, when it gradually changed to its modern form by way of *S*, acquiring an increasingly squarer top. *6* was squat and rounded in the 14th century, developed into a sigma in the 15th, and became slimmer in the 16th, sometimes with a looped stem causing it to look like *b*. Until the early 16th century, *7* was like the top of an isosceles triangle. Its left arm gradually shortened while the right moved to a more vertical position. Its stem was also crossed occasionally in the 16th century as in continental usage. *8* has basically remained the same throughout its history, even if it is close to the supine position in very cursive hands. *9* also retained its basic shape but tended to alter from rounded to pointed head according to the style of script, and the tail could be straight or curled back making it resemble a tadpole, though a curve to the left is more common.

31. Arabic numerals, 14th–16th century

8. Manuscript corrections

In the scriptorium the normal practice was for the scribe to confine himself to correcting the errors in his own copying during the act of writing. The duty of checking and amending the copies by comparison with the exemplar was carried out by the corrector. Professional scribes working on their own would make their own corrections, as would, obviously, an author. By the 16th century the role of official manuscript corrector had virtually disappeared to be replaced by proof-reading which was carried out, albeit sometimes sporadically, in the printing house.[155]

The correction of errors in manuscripts involved *deletion*, *alteration* and *insertion*. There were several methods of deletion, usually depending on the level of formality of the manuscript, the ink, the surface and the writing space available:

i. *Erasure*,[156] by scraping the ink from the surface with a sharp knife or similar implement and then smoothing the area with a boner, usually of ivory, to ensure that the ink did not spread or sink into it too much if anything was to be written over the space. This method of deletion probably was the most frequently employed in formal literary manuscripts of the medieval period written on parchment or vellum, and was especially useful with carbonaceous ink, which could be scraped off quite easily when perfectly dry. It was not suitable for paper, which was likely to tear. Plate no. 2, 1.1 gives an example of an erasure left blank, which, like most erasures, increases in legibility quite considerably under ultra-violet light.

ii. *Cancellation*, by striking through the passage with ink with one or more straight lines, with spirals, or a criss-cross pattern like a trellis (*cancelli*, 'trellis', hence *cancellation*). This is the commonest method of deletion in Renaissance manuscripts, and usually takes the form of one or two strokes through the centre of the words or letters roughly parallel to the base-line, and it is the predominant form in the illustrations in this book, beginning with the Chaucer manuscript (no. 2). A vigorous example of spirals is provided by the Evelyn example (no. 62), while Dryden uses a form of picket fence (no. 66). In some manuscripts, the single-stroke cancellation is so light as to be almost overlooked since it seems to merge with the other pen-strokes, especially when viewed in facsimile.

iii. *Expunction*, by placing a dot under each letter to be left out (or expunged). This was a particularly neat method, though suitable for only short deletions. Indeed it was occasionally used for a single minim to reduce *m* to *n/u*, *n/u* to *i*.[157] Expunction was fairly common in the medieval period but rare by the 16th century.

iv. *Underscoring*, by underlining the word to be deleted. An alternative method to expunction, it was never common in the medieval period and passed out of use by the Renaissance where underlining tended, by contrast, to emphasize the word or passage above it.

v. *Obliteration*, by covering with ink either by blotting, smudging or completely obscuring the word with cancellation, as in the Evelyn illustration (no. 62). An inelegant method, it is rarely to be found in formal manuscripts, and is most common in rough drafts.

vi. *Vacation*, enclosing the passage between the syllables *va* and *cat* (*it is void*).[158] In large deletions, cancellation would be used and *vacat* written in the margin. This method is common in legal manuscripts but unlikely to be found in literary ones. In the Renaissance the marginal notation *del* or *d* was sometimes used in conjunction with the cancellation of an entry.[159]

vii. *Dissolution*, by sponging the ink of the deleted passage until it completely dissolved. Such a method was appropriate only on parchment, with carbonaceous ink, which was soluble, and when the writing surface was large and the letters and words well spaced. Further it could be done effectively only while writing, otherwise the writing to the right and below it was at risk, and the passage for deletion less accessible.

Alterations were used to change letters and word order. Letters were altered by *superimposing* or *superscribing* the correct letter on the deleted one, especially when the two letters shared common features, good examples being provided by the *Massacre at Paris* leaf (no. 35) and the Fletcher letter (no. 52). Occasionally, the superscription extended to a whole word, thereby losing legibility, since it tended to merge with the deletion. For changing the word order, signs, numbers or letters were used. Two thin oblique strokes placed before and after a pair of words indicated that they were to be transposed.[160] The revised sequence of two or more words could be shown by placing below each of them letters of the alphabet or, more commonly in the Renaissance period, Arabic numerals, as in the case of the Milton example (no. 59, l. 9).

Insertions could be effected on the line in the case of small omissions, but were usually made above the line (*interlineation*), either directly over or to the right of where they were intended to go, the precise point of insertion being indicated in most cases by a caret.

9. Scribal errors and textual emendation

Even when a manuscript had undergone correction before passing into use, it was still likely to contain errors, and these were usually augmented in the process of transmission. Establishing what precisely constitutes an error is sometimes difficult for vernacular works in the late medieval and Renaissance periods, because there were no consistently adhered to norms of spelling and punctuation, and syntax and grammar were often acceptably lax. Even when dealing with a holograph by an author whose stylistic habits are known to be fairly predictable, it cannot be unfailingly inferred, for example, that he had intended a different tense, a singular rather than a plural, a more usual spelling, or the inclusion of a particular mark of punctuation. For the editor wishing to produce a text as faithful to the original as possible, the problem of emendation concerns not what the author ought to have written but what he intended to write, which is unfortunately a more hypothetical proposition.

However, it is a reasonable assumption for works of at least moderate literary pretentions that the original made good and complete sense, or was at least intended to, and the editor has a right to consider emending those words and passages which within the context of their period require some alteration in order to make their meaning clear, having first ensured that the fault lies in them and not in his transcription. It is also to be remembered that especially in the case of copies at least two stages removed from the original, a reading that makes good sense may still be wrong, deriving from the guesswork of a scribe trying to unravel an illegible or corrupt passage. This form of error is often difficult to detect when no independent copy of the text exists for comparison, though it may be suspect on stylistic grounds.

Textual emendation is one of the many areas in which palaeography can be useful to literature, often explaining how and why mistakes came to be made, providing at least margins of strong probability for an appropriate amendment and helping to establish the stemma. This usefulness extends to the printed word also, since many of the errors derive not from the mechanics intrinsic to the printing house, but from the copy itself, or from the misreading or mishandling of it by the compositors. Thus it is advisable to seek a palaeographical solution for a textual error wherever manuscripts are directly or indirectly concerned before turning to what are somewhat generously termed 'rational principles'.[161]

Errors vary considerably in nature and range according to the class of manuscript, its exemplar, if any, and the circumstances under which it was written. A presentation copy is obviously likely to have fewer mistakes than a third-hand copy scribbled down in a commonplace book. An author's draft might well be badly written but was not liable to the errors which beset the most conscientious and calligraphically-minded scribe as his eye had to shift continuously between exemplar and copy.

Until recently, most errors in medieval manuscripts were considered to be 'auditory', the theory being that in most scriptoria scribes wrote from dictation. Now that this view has been largely discounted, consideration of auditory errors has been perhaps unduly neglected, especially since there are many instances of authors besides Milton dictating their works; a fair amount of correspondence was written this way; and 'memorial reconstruction' was quite a common occurrence in Elizabethan drama. Further, it has been suggested that since, in the medieval period at least, reading entailed reading aloud, even works copied from exemplars thereby involved auditory errors, a phenomenon still apparent among those who are primarily aural rather than visual readers.[162]

Generally speaking it will be conceded, however, that most scribal errors derive from the imperfect use of sight, aided by lapses of memory and understanding, and abetted by fatigue. They can be conveniently grouped under the headings of *omission, additions, transposition,* and *alterations.*

Omission is one of the commonest forms of error. While it may happen unaccountably at any time, it is usually caused by the scribe resuming his copying at the same word or phrase which occurs a little further on from where he left off, an error known as *homoeoteleuton.* Where this similarity is at the end of the lines of writing it can result in the dropping of one or more lines. Such an omission may also take place when the scribe confuses his points of reference whatever they happen to be. Another common form of omission is writing only once what actually appears twice in the exemplar (*haplography*), frequent examples being *it, that* and similar short words, but it can also occur with syllables (e.g. *pewter* for *pewterer*) or with phrases and longer passages which though not identical are very similar. *Haplography* may be caused simply by optical illusion or by a conscious or unconscious rejection of apparent redundancy.

Additions frequently involve the mechanical repetition of a syllable, word or phrase through lapse of memory or trick of sight (e.g. *þat þat, Gawain,* no. 4), an error of *dittography.* Another form of addition is the inclusion in a word or line of an extraneous element from another part of the page of the exemplar which has been caught up by the wandering eye and accommodated by a process of free association (*contamination*).[163] There are also occasions when a scribe makes insertions because the text appears to be defective. In some cases the text actually is defective though the remedy is incorrect; in others the scribe has misread his exemplar and is simply increasing his error.

Transposition is the transcribing of letters, words or phrases in a different and usually reversed order from that in the exemplar. In the case of reversed pairs of letters the process is known as *metathesis.* While most errors of transposition are due to a lapse of the eye or the memory, some result mainly from a mental re-ordering to provide what superficially appears to be the more obvious meaning. A possible example of this process is in no. 59, where Milton had written *then the entring early* in error for *then the early entring.*

Alterations can be unwitting, based on lack of comprehension of the text or inability to decipher correctly, or they may be wilful, made in the interests of altering or improving the meaning or changing the political, moral or religious connotations. In so far as they are deviations from the exemplar they all count as textual errors. The commonest form is plain mistranscription, which can occur no matter how clear the exemplar, though it is more common in cases where the text being copied is in a rapid and malformed cursive hand. The scribe might also be unfamiliar with the language or dialect of the exemplar, its orthography, system of abbreviation, punctuation or other signs.

The confusing of letter forms is the most frequent cause of misreading. Although scripts generally made provision for ensuring that individual graphs were distinctive, there was always the liability of mistaking one letter or letter group for another, especially if the scribe had strong preconceptions about the word he expected to find. In virtually any period the minims are liable to be confused, thus involving not only *i/j, m, n* and *u* at the very least, but many other linear letters also according to the script, and components of supralinear and infralinear letters (e.g. the second limb of *h*). Even the presence of diacritics and links did not always prove helpful, since the dot intended for an *i* might be several letters away, and links were often made according to the whim of the writer rather than for the distinction of the letter. Thus the linking of two minims of *u,* for example, might be diagonal or at the head. In minim clusters there was also likely to be miscounting, leading to too many strokes, as in no. 36, or too few, as in no. 55. In fairly rapid *Elizabethan secretary,* where linear letters tended to be short and less defined, and rounded graphs often open-headed, there was likely to be a large number of permutations for misreading. Thus in the first folio text of *Antony and Cleopatra,* v, ii. 87, the word *Autumn* was understandably misread as *Antonie* for *Antony,* the first *u* being mistaken for *n,* the second *u* for open *o,* the *m* for *n* plus undotted *i,* and the final *n* for unlooped reversed *e.* The misreading was encouraged by the frequency of the name in the play and its apparent appropriateness in context, and is partly concealed by the spelling being normalized to *Antony.*

Even in book hands with some pretension to *textura,* instances of *confusibilia* abound, *Gawain* (no. 4) providing a very large number of examples, many of which are listed in the commentary. To quote an example from a manuscript contemporary with *Gawain,* the misreading *iolli knyghtus* (*jolly knights*) for *tow knyghtus* (*two knights*) is readily explicable in terms of a short *t* with a high, thin headstroke being mistaken for *i* with a diacritic, and *w* for double *ll* whether with arched, straight, or curved heads, followed by *i* with a head and foot serif. In a later period, even a quite formal hand could produce a misreading like *Bearing* for *Braeing* (*Braying*)[164] by the simple and easily made double confusion of Greek *e* and left-shouldered *r* in an *Elizabethan set secretary* or *mixed* hand. *Italic* was also liable to confuse some of its graphs, an actual instance being the misreading *Trace* for *Face*,[165] since italic *F* and *T* were often distinguished only by the cross-stroke which in this case was mistaken for a simplified form of *r*. This last example is especially interesting because it occurs in a basically *secretary* hand but indicates that its source must have been in either an *italic* or *mixed* hand.

Quite often the misreadings were the result of either ignoring or misunderstanding the abbreviations of the exemplar, especially its brevigraphs. Thus the ignoring of the oblique stroke through the stem of *s* caused the reading *spent* for *serpent*, the failure to note the bar for omitted *m/n* plus the misreading of *e* as *o* resulted in *doeth* for *demeth*, while the misunderstanding of the contraction for *us* converted *Actus 4us* (*Actus Quartus*) into *Actus 49*.[166]

In discerning causes of misreadings it is important to remember that there were many variant spellings for a given word, and in the act of copying and compositing it was always possible for the spelling to be altered in transmission.[167] Thus, in considering the palaeographical possibilities of *A fellow all miss daub'd in a fair wise*, an ingenious emendation of *A Fellow almost dambd in a faire wife* (*Othello*, 1. i. 21, Quarto 1622), a knowledge not only of variant spellings, but also word division, capitalization and punctuation immediately reduces some of the obvious differences. The capitalization, the apostrophe and the final *e* of *faire* can be discounted as being immaterial to this particular comparison. Further, since word divisions are often unclear in handwriting of the period, especially in such compounds as *almost*, which are sometimes written as one and sometimes separately, a further difference is removed, and it is simply a question of setting *all miss* against *all most* (or *allmost*) or *al miss* against *al most* (or *almost*). The difference between the two readings has been already lessened by the quarto spelling *dambd* rather than *damn'd*, the first folio reading. It would be further simplified if the suggested reading were *dawbd*. Having cancelled out what are in fact superficial variations, the only material differences are *iss* for *ost*, *w* (or *u*) for *m*, and *s* for *f*. All these types of confusibilia are extremely common in *secretary* hand: a thick or double-stroked *i* resembled a narrow *o*; ligatures with *s* often looked alike, and in this case a single downstroke from the top of long *s* might serve for *ss* or *st*; the difference between *w* and *m* was negligible when the initial stroke of *w* was short; while the confusion of long *s* and *f* was common in any period or script. Thus the proposed emendation seems palaeographically justifiable even though it might be rejected on other grounds.

Virtually all the types of palaeographical error mentioned provide the means of textual emendation because they are fairly easily traceable, whether they be examples of homoeoteleuton, dittography, transposition or, to a lesser extent, contamination and misreading. However, the permutations for solving misreadings are frequently considerable and in some cases equally plausible, as in the *loue/Ioue/Ione* puzzle occasionally encountered in lyrics and plays.

There is no fool-proof way of predetermining confusibilia, since misreadings depend very much on context and the circumstances under which they occurred, but the following table is provided as a rough guide to many of the commonly confused letters in the period, excluding those which might be mistaken for graphs in modern handwriting (e.g. Elizabethan secretary *c* resembling a modern cursive roman *r*).

Letter	Confused with
A	a, d, de, 15th
a	ct, et, 15th; ii, n, u, 16th; o
B	D, 15th
b	v, 15th; v, 16th
C	D, E, 15th; G, 16th; O, 16th
c	t, 14th; i, 16th; r, v, 16th
D	B, 15th; O, 15–16th
d	e, 15–16th
E	C; k; O
f	long s; long s, 16th
G	B, 14–15th; C, 16th
g	q; y; x, 15th
ȝ	r, z, 14–15th
H	B, 15th; L, 16th
h	s, 16th; th, 16th
I/J	T, 16th
i	minim confusion; o, r, v, 16th
K, k	R
L	H, 16th
l	long s, 14th; e, t, 16th
li	h, 14–15th
lk	w, 14–15th
m, n	minim confusion
O	D, E, G
o	a; i, r, 16th
p	thorn, 15th; x, 16th
q	g, *com, us*
R	K
r	i, z, *and*; t, e, 16th; i, o, v
s	f, l; f, 16th
sa	se, si, so, st, 16th
ss	st, 16th
T	I/J, 16th; o, O, 16th

31

t	c c, 14–15th; t c, 16th; l b, l, 16th
þ	p p, 15th; y y, 15–16th
u	minim confusion;
V	X X
v	b b
w	lh lk, li, 15th; w two or three minims, 16th
x	g g, y, 15th; p p, 16th
y	y thorn, 15th; g g, 16th; q q, 16th
z	z i, r, 3, *and*; 3 yogh, 15th, *que*, 16th

10. Comparison of hands, dating, detection of forgery

These three subjects have been taken together because they are quite closely related and often support one another, but it will be possible only to suggest a few general principles concerning them within the scope of this book.

It should be stated at the outset that none of these subjects is an exact science and, with the exception of really poor forgeries, it is rarely possible to be absolutely certain about any one of them on purely palaeographical grounds. Further, whatever expertise can be brought to bear can only be gleaned over a considerable number of years of concentrated first-hand experience with the manuscripts of a given period. Nevertheless it is possible to arrive at degrees of reasonable certainty on palaeographical grounds given the right conditions and sufficient material to work on.

Comparing handwriting specimens is a useful palaeographical exercise to assist in deciding such matters as provenance, date and authenticity. It is most commonly employed to ascertain whether or not a given manuscript is in the hand of an identifiable scribe or at least from a known scriptorium; and in the period covered by this book it is especially valuable in the quest for holographs. When comparison is used for identification purposes there are important prerequisites to ensure that the conclusions drawn rest on a fairly solid foundation. Ideally, there should be adequate examples of each of the items to be compared, preferably written at roughly the same time, in the same script, for a similar purpose, and at the same level of formality. It is extremely unfortunate that for identifying the most important hand in English literature, none of these conditions is fulfilled. Though three pages containing 147 lines of a play revision are certainly adequate as samples for identification, the basis for the comparison is not, since it comprises six versions of Shakespeare's signature and only two additional short words 'By me', all written roughly twenty years later. The letter samplings and word combinations are not only extremely limited, they are also atypical, as most signatures are, and they do not even resemble one another all that closely.

The Shakespeare specimens do however meet another desideratum, namely that the basis for the comparison should be drawn from undoubted holograph material. This condition is not met in the case of the Chaucer holograph candidates (nos. 1 and 2), but they are mutually supporting, in that no. 2 is obviously an author's manuscript containing his *currente calamo* corrections, while the other at least indisputably relates to Chaucer, being a warrant executed in his name.

The process of comparison is made easier the less formal and the more cursive the examples are, since they are likely to contain more personal idiosyncrasies. It is usually more difficult, for example, to obtain conclusive evidence concerning two specimens of *textura quadrata formata* than it is for two pieces of *rapid Elizabethan secretary*. One should, however, guard against assuming that two rapid cursive hands are the same because they have similar features which might well be common in any rapid cursive of the period. This leads to the next requisite: that there be adequate examples for comparison drawn from manuscripts by other scribes at roughly the same level of script to ensure that supposed idiosyncrasies are not simply general mannerisms of the time. Conversely, when there are diverse elements between the items of comparison, reference to other manuscripts may determine whether these are significant.

The larger the dossier on an author, the greater the chances of establishing the holograph status of a manuscript and, if need be, its date. It is useful to know, for example, that the handwriting of Sidney and Dryden go through distinct and datable phases, that Evelyn used various hands in accordance with his particular purpose, that Ascham wrote *italic* for his Latin works but usually *secretary* for his English correspondence, that Ralegh rarely wrote *secretary* and seems to have abandoned it altogether from the last decade of the 16th century, and that Milton used only *italic e* after his return from Italy.

Even when ideal circumstances exist for a handwriting comparison, it is still as well to ascertain what can be gleaned from other aspects of the item under consideration concerning its provenance, date, watermark,[168] the nature and style of the contents, and various other pieces of information which are appropriate to a given manuscript. In a letter, for example, it is important to examine the address, endorsements, method of folding and sealing, and the seal itself or mark of seal, all of which may provide swifter and more cogent clues than the handwriting.

The actual comparison should include both the general and the particular details. The 'look' of a hand is often telling: the size, word spacing, angle of slope, length of ascenders and descenders, degree of cursiveness, the linking and the loops. Some features stand out immediately, for example in *secretary* hand, the shape, direction and angle of curve of infralinear strokes of *g, h* and *y* or the looping on the stems of *d*. The usual caution has to be exercised, in that a particular calligraphic feature might have been fashionable, just as differences in style could have been dictated by the relative amount of space on the paper and degree of formality. Nevertheless an accumulation of similarities serves to establish the individuality of a hand.

The next phase is the comparison of word-formations, especially of frequently occurring words like the definite article and relatives, since these tend to be the most distinctive and provide generous samplings of possible variations. Particular attention should be paid not only to the general shape but to the actual way in which the strokes are made, if necessary tracing them out from start to finish. The same process should then be applied to individual graphs and common ligatures. No letter should be neglected, but some graphs are more helpful than others, for example, *h* and *s* in the Renaissance, and *g, r* and *w* in the late medieval period. Usually, the more strokes a letter has, the greater the chance of idiosyncrasy, and in this respect capitals are often helpful.

The use of abbreviation, particularly superior letters and brevigraphs, can also be very revealing. The way a tittle or an apostrophe sign is made sometimes varies considerably, and the same applies to otiose flourishes. Punctuation, while usually not quite so rewarding, should be scrutinized with regard to its degree of frequency, the way it is formed, its position relative to the line, and idiosyncrasies of usage.

Before drawing conclusions, which are usually to be stated as probabilities rather than certainties, it is as well to make a final check by comparing the specimen in question with similar manuscripts in other hands to see to what extent the case for individuality holds good. In this respect it is to be noted that the spurred *a* proof for Shakespeare's holograph becomes increasingly weaker as more examples of that particular form come to light, and proof which rests on similarly inadequate foundations is always likely to crumble eventually unless it is backed by an inspired guess, or, more hopefully, strong stylistic support, which is the most eloquent advocate in the Shakespeare case.

Dating manuscripts is always a difficult problem when it has to be based entirely on handwriting. It is hard enough when the scribe is known and his lifespan established. But where no evidence is available to provide a *terminus quo* or *terminus quem*, it is rash to expect to date a manuscript more closely than within about fifty years[169] in the medieval period and about thirty or forty in the Renaissance, when changes are more easily chronicled. In the case of the most formal text hands, as in gothic *textura formata*, the margins of error can be greater because the script is more conservative. It is true that on the accumulated evidence of examples, major changes in script and the evolution of letters can sometimes be placed within a quarter of a century, but this is to deal in general trends rather than in specific instances. Rates of change vary in accordance with the distance and degree of isolation from the centre of influence where the change occurs, how useful or necessary the change is considered to be, the agreed practice of scriveners, the teaching habits in the schools and, above all, the inclination of the individual. A man may well write the same way in his sixties as he did in his twenties whatever changes have occurred in the interim, and in correspondence in particular it seems that old ways died hard. A clear example of how deceptive handwriting can be in dating is provided in a letter by a John Smyth (!) to Henry Gold, dated 1525 which contains mainly *anglicana* features of a hundred years or so earlier.[170]

Given these reservations, the best way of proceeding is to follow the pattern for comparison of hands, moving from the general to the particular. First, it is important to establish the particular style of script and its level of formality. Next, an examination of specific letter forms for those graphs which are known to have evolved or changed in the course of the development of the script will reveal whether the example is early or late. Abbreviations and punctuation also play their part in dating, punctuation being especially important in the Renaissance. The description of the different scripts of the period and the sections on abbreviation and punctuation in this book provide some guide to dating, but it is advisable to check evidence against specialist works in the field, and, above all, against manuscripts of which both the date and provenance are known beyond a shadow of doubt.[171] To make the comparison more exact, it is advisable to compare against manuscripts of the same class and level of formality also.

Usually, supplementary evidence can be obtained from other features of the manuscript: the linguistic characteristics, many of which are at least as closely datable as handwriting, the format, including the use of rules and pricking, the signatures on the quires, the watermark, if any, and possibly the binding.[172] In the absence of an actual date appended by the scribe himself, it is the weight of accumulated evidence rather than one single feature which has to be the decisive factor for proof.

The faking of English literary manuscripts began long after the forging of legal documents, and it was only by the last century that the financial advantages of doing so were realized. There were many expert forgers of non-legal documents long before, but they usually confined themselves to the field of espionage, to provide bogus information or incriminating evidence, the most talented exponent being the *agent provocateur*, Thomas Phelippes, a creature of Sir Francis Walsingham.

Normally, literary forgery for the period covered by this book concerns only the foremost authors of the Renaissance, and with the exception of the ludicrous Ireland attempts (no. 38), tends to be confined to fairly short texts and extracts, not only because of the difficulty of sustaining a forgery, but also on account of the high literary standard and linguistic expertise required, especially to produce a purportedly new or lost work. Further, the likelihood of large-scale works dating from before 1700 appearing suddenly out of the blue is so remote as to deter forgers from making the effort. Thus the question of forgery usually relates to a text on the odd quire or leaf, or additions in commonplace books or accounts, and since most collections are fairly carefully itemized nowadays, any suspect item of this nature in major collections will usually date from the 19th century at the latest.

The poorest forgeries will be executed on artificially aged paper or parchment and with ink made from aniline dyes. A cursory glance will suffice for detection, without laboratory tests, and the use of a metal nib will also leave marks on the paper uncharacteristic of a quill. If the forgery is more clever, but modern materials have been used, micro-chemical analysis will reveal that the paper is made, for example, of wood cellulose rather than of cotton fibre as might be expected; an imitation watermark will usually disappear in an appropriate chemical solution; modern inks will react in special ways with chemical reagents. Various other features will emerge under the use of X-ray or ultra-violet tests.[173]

Quite often, however, the forger will have obtained paper which is contemporary with the author, often in the form of blank leaves or odd scraps, on which laboratory tests would be pointless, and examination of watermarks and chain-lines probably of little avail. If an ink formula similar to the old iron-gall or carbon base has been used, analysis of composition of ink will reveal little when the forgery is quite an old one. Even so, it is sometimes possible to see tell-tale signs on the writing surface. These include traces left of earlier writing either on the page itself or from the page formerly facing it, which are totally out of phase with the writing of the forgery; creases or folds which were made before the writing, so that the ink of the pen strokes seems completely unaffected by them; and wormholes which studiously avoid coming into contact with the ink.

When dealing with isolated items which do not form part of a manuscript book, there is always the pertinent question of pedigree, and it is noticeable that many of the suspect documents have their origins shrouded in mystery after they have been traced back through sales to the late 19th century, though this is sometimes true of authentic manuscripts too. But any manuscript purporting to be a few hundred years old which has no traceable lineage or even immediate history must, of course, be immediately suspect.

The handwriting itself should normally provide invaluable evidence, especially since in many cases there are authentic examples against which to compare. The *Massacre at Paris* leaf, no. 35, still under suspicion of forgery, made its appearance when no known specimen of Marlowe's writing was extant; the discovery of a signature has almost destroyed its claim to holograph status, if not its genuineness. The process of comparison can be carried out in the manner already indicated earlier in this section. There are other important signs to watch for, however, including a lack of integration of style, inconsistency of slope, variable word spacing, awkward retracings, lack of cursive flow, and even a slight tremulousness, known as the forger's 'shake' or 'palsy'. The *Massacre at Paris* does in fact provide an important test case, and the literature concerning it is deserving of scrutiny on the question of method. There are also various models of 'demolition', and one by E. Maunde Thompson on two supposed signatures of Shakespeare has stood the test of time remarkably well.[174]

A further crucial test of authenticity is provided by the contents themselves and their stylistic attributes, but this lies outside the scope of palaeography.

11. Methods of transcribing and editing

There is still no ideal substitute for the original manuscript even though it is now possible to obtain amazingly good facsimiles which match the colour of ink, the texture of the writing surface and simulate the chain-lines and watermarks. A good second-best for palaeographical purposes is an actual-size photographic facsimile with transcription, notes and commentary, thereby combining a fair degree of verisimilitude with an interpretative expansion of it.

It is hard to stipulate what constitutes the ideal edition, because what is appropriate for one purpose may be inadequate or superfluous for another. While theoretically it is best to include every possible detail in a palaeographical description (as is often felt to be necessary in bibliography), practical considerations require some form of compromise. Nevertheless, for an edition to be of enduring value it should contain basic palaeographical data and be of use to the majority of those likely to consult it, including, for example, not only literary critics but also philologists and historians.

There are basically three components in an edition of a manuscript: the description, the transcript, and the textual commentary, which can be subdivided into palaeographical notes and subject-matter. The description should, where possible, include the following information, though not necessarily in the order given here:

1. Present location and call mark.
2. Date, with evidence.
3. Provenance and history, with marks of ownership.
4. Materials: writing surface, ink, binding.
5. General condition.
6. Collation:
   a. Number of leaves in arabic numerals; fly leaves, etc. in roman.
   b. Foliation and pagination.
   c. Quiring, quire and leaf signatures, catchwords.
7. Dimension of page and of written space, height x width in millimetres.
8. Pricking, whether outer margin or inner as well.
9. Ruling, implements used, type of frame (whether open at top).
10. Type of script and level of formality, number of hands, identity.
11. Special features of script, punctuation and abbreviation.
12. Decoration.
13. Contents.
14. The state of the text.
15. Other MS copies, facsimiles, printed texts, editions.
16. Editorial method.

Models for presenting most of this information are to be found in J. M. Manly and E. Rickert, *The text of the Canterbury Tales*, 1940, i, if the description is to be lengthy, and N. R. Ker, *Medieval manuscripts in British libraries*, i, 1969, if a more compact method is required. It should also be remembered that the Ker work takes cognisance of recent developments in palaeography and is therefore preferable for technicalities.

The method of transcription tends to vary in accordance with its purpose. Some record societies propose that a full transcription of the original exactly as it appears should be employed under all circumstances (known as a *diplomatic* transcription). Others suggest that a diplomatic version is advisable as a working copy, but should be converted to a more normalized and modernized form on publication. Certainly, when there is no possibility of obtaining a good photographic reproduction as a check, a full working copy is best; but under normal circumstances, an intermediate stage between the manuscript and the modified transcription is unwise because it increases the possibility of error in the final text.

A diplomatic transcription, though containing many advantages, is somewhat misleading because it rarely reproduces all the features of the original. It is also inadequate in interpretation, since it avoids, for example, expanding the abbreviations. Further, it is laborious to prepare, not being entirely suitable for typescript, is costly to print, and tiresome to read. On the other hand to go to the extreme of normalizing spelling and punctuation, ignoring deletions and completely smoothing out the idiosyncrasies of the manuscript results in a highly uninformative version of very limited use. Here the interpretative faculty is carried too far, with the unwarranted assumption that the editor has a full understanding of the intended meaning of the original and that its system of orthography and pointing are irrelevant. Quite apart from this, it is much more difficult to see where and how errors in transcription might have arisen, and the reader attempting textual emendation is completely deprived of palaeographical help.

A useful compromise between the two extremes is what might be called a *semi-diplomatic* transcription, which provides nearly all that a diplomatic transcription would, but in a more continuous process. It gives scope for editorial interpretation while clearly indicating where this has been carried out. The system is suitable for general working purposes, can easily be used on the typewriter but for a few easily inked-in signs, and is hardly more difficult to print than a simple modernized text. The guidelines for the system, which has been used for the text of this book, are as follows:

Semi-diplomatic transcription

1. Normally the whole text should be transcribed. Where this is impossible or deemed unnecessary, the nature and extent of the omission should be carefully noted.

2. The transcription should be prefaced by the location of

the manuscript, its name, call mark, and the relevant folio, page or membrane number. The foliation (both *recto* and *verso*) and pagination should also be given during the course of the transcription, being placed in the margin in italics and within square brackets.

3. The spelling, capitalization and word division of the original should be retained, including the preservation of *u* for *v*, *i* for *j*. Thorn, wyn, yogh, whether minuscule or capital should be retained, and the digraphs *æ* and *œ*. Ligatures need not be observed, but the general practice in using them can be usefully noted. In dealing with capitals, it is preferable to transcribe *I/J* uniformly as *I*, and to retain *ff* for *F*. When there is doubt whether certain letters are intended as minuscule or capital, it is better to make a consistent decision in the text and to note the difficulty. Numerals should be given in their manuscript form, whether roman, arabic or mixed.

4. The punctuation and paragraphing of the original should be retained. Unusual marks of punctuation can be normalized as follows: the *virgule* or double *virgule* as / and //; *capitulum* (different versions of *C* or *c*) as ❡; the *paragraphus* (resembling long *ss*, *þ* or *q*) and gallows bracket as ¶; the *punctus elevatus* (inverted semicolon) in whatever form as ⁏; carets as ∧. Diacritics for *i* should be normalized as dots. Punctuation marks to distinguish *u* and *y* should not be transcribed but mentioned in a general note.

5. Lineation need not be preserved except in poetry, verse drama, certain forms of accounts and where the original lends itself to this treatment without serious wastage of space.

6. All abbreviations should be expanded, regardless of the language of the text, with the supplied letters italicized, the marks of abbreviation dispensed with and superior letters lowered to the line (e.g. w^t· becomes *with*). Marks of abbreviation which are uncertain in meaning can be retained, being represented by an apostrophe if at the end of the word, but superfluous brevigraphs and otiose flourishes should be ignored and mentioned in a note. Abbreviations still in common use today are better retained (e.g. *Mr.*) as also those in signatures.

7. Deletions should be placed in square brackets.

8. Accidental obliterations should be denoted by diamond brackets, ⟨ ⟩, with dots for the number of letters calculated to be missing or obscured. In case of large obliterations, an estimation of the number of words missing should be given in a note. Conjectural restoration can be supplied within the brackets.

9. Interlineations should be included in their proper sequence in the body of the text but enclosed in 'half-square' brackets ⌈ ⌉. The caret mark if used should be retained in the transcription and placed immediately in front of the first bracket.

10. A brief passage in different script in the body of the text (e.g. an *italic* quotation in a *secretary* hand) can be placed in italics. For longer passages the change is best indicated in a note.

11. Any special features requiring comment, e.g. a new hand, a change of ink, superimposed or altered letters, erasures, etc., should be mentioned in the notes.

12. Insertions and alterations in a hand of a much later date than the main text are to be noted rather than included in the transcript.

For a system closer to a diplomatic transcription the ends of lines in continuous prose could be indicated by a long vertical stroke; and superior letters enclosed in the half-square brackets used for interlineation, or simply left in raised position.

In the section of textual commentary assigned to palaeographical notes, the main ingredients, preferably as brief as possible, are normally textual emendations, variant readings and the other items already noted in the set of guidelines for transcription, e.g. erasures, superimposed letters, changes of hand or of ink, later interpolations, otiose brevigraphs. For easy reference these notes should be placed at the foot of the page of text, but if they are numerous and not easily separable from other sections of the textual commentary, they are best placed at the end of a section, chapter or at the very back of the book according to the nature of the volume.

12. Editorial principles in the text

i. *The plates.* The basic endeavour has been to provide facsimiles from the holographs of major authors in the period or, where these do not survive, from their important works in closely contemporary copies (e.g. nos. 4, 5, 6, 13), while affording a varied selection of scripts and hands, a balanced representation of literary genres and a continuous and fairly well distributed chronological sequence. Sixty of the illustrations are actual size. The remaining seven had to be reduced, but usually only slightly, and in no case has legibility suffered.

The process of selection for lesser authors was somewhat difficult, especially since reputations fluctuate. Literary distinction was sometimes supplanted by palaeographical significance (e.g. Ascham), the need to reinforce a given period (e.g. Paston and Leland), or to provide variety in genres (Camden and Overbury) and in manuscripts (*Westron wynde*); though, in all fairness, the examples cited stand on their own merits and display important types of script.

Major authors were usually assigned a page of plates (e.g. Spenser, Shakespeare, Milton and Dryden). Lydgate also attained full page status, since in a century not over-endowed with literary talent he achieved great popularity, and the two specimens from his *Life of Our Lady* provide markedly contrasting examples of script. Where practicable, two or more illustrations are given of one author as examples of the different scripts he used (More, Ascham), to show how he wrote in different phases of his life (Ralegh, Evelyn, Dryden), or to provide a basis of comparison of known and doubtful holographs (e.g. Skelton, Marlowe, Shakespeare).

In general, lesser authors were placed two to a page, but were paired as appropriately as possible, usually according to genre (e.g. Overbury and Hall), and since Surrey might have been somewhat isolated he was paired with Wyatt, who would otherwise have merited a full page. Occasionally the pairing caused a slight break in chronological sequence, but not in general continuity.

All the common literary scripts of the period are represented, including several versions of *textura*, three grades of *anglicana*, 15th-century *secretary*, hybrid hands, and some uncommon ones, such as the *fere-textura* in no. 8. Understandably, *Elizabethan secretary*, *italic* and *mixed* hands predominate, since the greatest writers in the richest period of English literature wrote in one or other of these scripts. This predominance is not a disadvantage, however, because considerable variety is provided by the individual writers, and the *italic* and *mixed* hands in particular have been somewhat neglected in the past.

Among the genres poetry leads the field, though there are

ample illustrations from prose works and drama. Correspondence is prominent because it is often the only source for holographs (as with Surrey, Kyd, Marvell and Vaughan), it affords generous and dated samples in a fairly compact space, and usually includes a signature. Other types of manuscript represented include diaries (one in shorthand), journals, notebooks, a piece of music, receipts, a warrant, a deed of gift and two forgeries.

Dated material has been used wherever possible in order to denote the phases of development of the different scripts and to provide a more solid basis for comparison of hands. Unfortunately, precise dates are lacking for some of the earlier examples, being particularly uncertain for the Lydgate manuscripts. As a general policy for deciding the chronological sequence, the date of the manuscript has been taken in preference to the birth or death date of the authors, which would have caused in many instances a strange and distorted order of material.

Partly by necessity and mainly by design, nearly all the examples are in English, with five in Latin and one in Anglo-Norman providing a little variety not only linguistically but also in such palaeographic features as script, format and marks of abbreviation. For ease of reference, the illustrations are placed lengthwise for all but the pair of diarists, Evelyn and Pepys, and every fifth line is numbered.

ii. *Text and commentary*. Each text is headed by the author's name and dates, the title of the work, date of composition, class and grade of script, indication of holograph status, and the date of the manuscript if it differs from that of composition. Then follows the full manuscript reference, portion of page reproduced (*in toto* unless otherwise stated) and the scale of reduction, if any, expressed as a fraction. It should be added that the script is named and graded in Latin for texts up to and including Skelton, in deference to the palaeographers who have established a mainly Latin terminology for classifying medieval scripts, but thereafter English is used and could serve equally well for the early period too.

The transcription, given in full for each text, is based on the semi-diplomatic system described in the set of guidelines in the preceding section, to which the reader is referred, though it can be simply restated here that it entails using the original spelling and punctuation, expanding abbreviations in italics, enclosing deletions in square brackets, interlineations in half-square brackets, and accidental obliterations in diamond brackets.

The commentary usually begins with general palaeographical information about the manuscript and its author, and includes details concerning other holograph material and some of the more easily accessible facsimiles and editions. The main part of the commentary is taken up with a description of the salient characteristics of the hand and its individual letters, ending with sections on punctuation and abbreviation.

Notes to Introduction

(1. The survival of medieval and Renaissance literary manuscripts)

1. Cf. John Bale's preface to *The Laboryouse journey*, 1549, quoted in C. E. Wright, 'The dispersal of the libraries in the 16th century', *ELBSH*, 153–4.

2. Betsy is the subject of an article in W. W. Greg, *Collected papers*, ed. J. C. Maxwell, 1966.

3. The nun was Diemude of Wessobrunn, who obtained a farm on Peissenburg in 1057 (cited G. H. Putnam, *Books and their makers in the Middle Ages*, i, 1896, 298, who provides numerous examples of the price of MSS, 225–313). For England *vide* H. E. Bell, 'The price of books in Medieval England, *c.* 1300–1480', *Lib.*, 4th ser., xvii, 1936, 312–32.

4. *vide* R. M. Wilson, *The lost literature of Mediaeval England*, 1952, 168–70.

5. Quoted in H. McCusker, 'Books and mss. formerly in the possession of John Bale', *Lib.*, 4th ser., xvi, 1935, 145–6. (See also note 1.)

6. Useful notes on an author's foul-papers before the introduction of printing are given in H. S. Bennett, 'The production and dissemination of vernacular mss. in the 15th century', *Lib.*, 5th ser., i, 1947, 167–78.

7. About eighty catalogues have survived. See, further, E. A. Savage, *Old English libraries*, 1911; R. M. Wilson, 'The contents of the mediaeval library', *ELBSH*.

8. *vide*, e.g., R. M. Wilson, *The lost literature of Mediaeval England*, 152–5 and *passim*.

9. *Lib.*, 4th ser., v, 1925, 294.

10. Cf. Wilson, *op. cit.*, 241–4.

11. A list of all the manuscripts of English plays with their location is given in A. Harbage, *Annals of English drama*, rev. S. Schoenbaum, 1964 in an appendix; also Supplement, 1966.

12. *vide* H. S. Bennett, *op. cit.*, esp. 170–2; *MEV*, xi.

13. *vide* McCusker, *op. cit.*

14. The image is suggested by Aubrey's description of leaves of manuscripts floating like petals through the streets and thoroughfares. See, further, Wright, *ELBSH*, 151–2. On the subject of the dispersal see also R. Irwin, *The origins of the English library*, 1958, 97–113.

15. J. C. T. Oates, 'The libraries of Cambridge, 1500–1700', *ELBSH*, 1958, 213.

16. *vide* W. W. Greg, 'Books and bookmen in the correspondence of Archbishop Parker', *Lib.*, 4th ser., xvi, 1935, esp. 247–8; Wright, *op. cit.*

17. See, further, F. Madan, *Books in manuscript*, 1927, 97–100; W. D. Macray, *Annals of the Bodleian library*, 2nd ed. 1896; E. Craster, *History of the Bodleian library, 1845–1945*, 1952.

18. See, further, C. E. Wright, 'The Elizabethan Society of Antiquaries and the formation of the Cottonian library', *ELBSH*.

19. *vide* Madan, *op. cit.*, 94–6; G. R. de Beer, *Sir Hans Sloane and the British Museum*, 1953.

20. Madan, *op. cit.*, 101–2, Appendix B; see also note below.

21. On the subject of private collectors *vide* S. de Ricci, *English collectors of books and mss. and their marks of ownership*, 1930. See also comprehensive bibliography in *CBEL*, i, 995–1006.

22. *vide* G. F. Warner, *Catalogue of the manuscripts and muniments of Alleyn's College of God's gift at Dulwich*, 1881.

23. See, further, on American libraries mentioned here: L. B. Wright, *The Folger Library*, 1968; J. E. Pomfret, *The Henry E. Huntington Library and Art Gallery*, 1969; S. Parks, *The Osborn Collection, 1934–74* (exhibition catalogue), 1974.

24. Comprehensive list of catalogues in *CBEL*, i, 987–96.

(2. Writing materials)

25. Term used by Hilliard, Cotgrave and Howell. See, further, W. Lee Ustick, 'Parchment and vellum', *Lib.*, 4th ser., xvi, 1936, 439–43.

26. D. V. Thompson, *The materials of medieval painting*, 1936, 27–8.

27. G. Pollard, 'Notes on the size of the sheet', *Lib.*, 4th ser., xxii, 1941, 112.

28. *vide* Ustick, *op. cit.*, 440, who also quotes a useful passage from a Tudor schoolroom dialogue which indicates that the distinctions mentioned here were also made for general purposes in England in the 16th century.

29. H. Saxl, 'The histology of parchment', *Technical studies in the field of fine arts*, viii, 1939, 1–9; G. Ivy, 'The bibliography of the printed book', *ELBSH*, 34; to be compared with N. Denholm-Young, *Handwriting in England and Wales*, 1954, 58–9. N. Ker, *Medieval manuscripts in British Libraries*, i, 1969, viii, found distinguishing sheep-skin from calf-skin almost impossible, and does not attempt it.

30. For examples of manuscripts mixing vellum and paper, *vide* Pollard, *op. cit.*, 117; Ivy, *op. cit.*, 36, 60–61.

31. So much might be gathered from *EVH*, in which all the illustrations which are not on paper are cited as on vellum.

32. D. V. Thompson, 'Mediaeval parchment-making', *Lib.*, 4th ser., xvi, 1935, 113, n. 1.

33. Thompson, *op. cit.*, 114, quotes from a German manuscript of the 13th century which describes the Bologna method of preparing parchment from goat-skin (Harleian 3915, f. 148).

34. B. L., Cotton Julius D. viii, quoted Thompson, *op. cit.*, 117. For other medieval accounts, taken from Trinity College, Cambridge, manuscript sources *vide* Ivy, *op. cit.*, 35.

35. See, further, D. V. Thompson, *The materials of medieval painting*, 1936, 24 ff.

36. Denholm-Young, *op. cit.*, 59, who dates this practice as late as from the 16th century in England.

37. Cf. L. C. Hector, *The handwriting of English documents*, 1966, 16.

38. Ivy, *op. cit.*, 43. See, however, Pollard, *op. cit.*, 108–9.

39. See, further, R. H. Clapperton, *Paper: an historical account*, 1934, and 'The history of paper-making in England', *Paper-Maker*, 22, 1953; D. Hunter, *Papermaking*, 1947; A. H. Shorter, *Paper mills and paper makers in England 1495–1800*, 1957; A. H. Stevenson, 'Tudor Roses from John Tate', *Studies in bibliography*, 20, 1967. Fuller bibliography in *CBEL*, i, 927–30.

40. For the supply of paper from abroad *vide* M. Plant, *The English book trade*, 2nd ed., 1965, 198–9.

41. It is among the Closed Rolls and relates to Gascon affairs. Cited Denholm-Young, *op. cit.*, 61.

42. Cited Ivy, *op. cit.*, 36, who states that the Red-Book is the first extant record on paper in England.

43. Ivy, *op. cit.*, 36.

44. Facsimiles in *EVH*, 16 and in New Pal. Soc., ser. ii, plate 109. In both examples even the grain and the chain-lines are visible.

45. Ivy, *op. cit.*, 36, based on the collations of Manly and Rickert, *The text of the Canterbury Tales*, 1940.

46. The Skelton works were presented to Henry VIII (see pl. 14–16 and p. 65). By contrast, Johnson's *Masque of Queenes*, presented to Prince Henry, in 1609, a hundred years later, is on very fine quality paper.

47. Hector, *op. cit.*, 16.

48. Significations of excommunication dated 1601, for example, are all on parchment (Ellesmere MSS, 2159 ff., pr. A. G. Petti, *Recusant documents from the Ellesmere MSS*, 1968, 102–44).

49. An indispensable guide to the study of watermarks is C. M. Briquet, *Les filigranes*, 4 vols. 1907, repr. 1923 and 1968.

50. Ivy, *op. cit.*, 36, notes that the paper of the hustings court records of 1309 (B.L., Add. 31223) is 'uneven and fibrous'.

51. Pollard, *op. cit.*, 115, refers to Paris students being expected to buy their vellum in small quantities, and to Oxford students buying a couple of skins at a time for a penny or twopence. Paper, being infinitely cheaper, would of course have been bought in larger quantities by the later medieval period.

52. For example, Bolognese parchment was usually quired in tens (Pollard, *op. cit.*, 108, 116); manuscripts of the university of Naples were usually in twelves, as were those of Oxford and Paris (J. Destrez, *La pecia dans les manuscrits universitaires du XIIIe et du XIVe siècle*, 1935, 47).

53. Ivy, *op. cit.*, 40, found from a survey of medieval English manuscripts in Trinity College, Cambridge, that over 60 per cent were quired in eights, the rest being mainly in twelves with a few tens.

54. *vide* E. K. Rand, *A survey of the mss. of Tours*, 1929, i, 11–18.

55. Pollard, *op. cit.*, 109.

56. 'Multifolded' is used by Ivy, *op. cit.*, 38, and 'undivided' is coined by Pollard, *op. cit.*, 107.

57. The difference between the manuscripts of the two universities was noted by Destrez, *op. cit.*, 46, and explained by Pollard, *op. cit.*, 113 ff.

58. Pollard, *op. cit.*, 110.

59. Madan, *op. cit.*, 14–15.

60. Pollard, *op. cit.*, 116–17.

61. *vide* L. W. Jones, 'Pricking manuscripts: the instruments and their significance', *Spec.*, xxi, 1946, 389–403; Ker, *op. cit.*, ix, esp. with ref. to frames, pricking after folding, and use of dry point.

62. J. de Yciar, *Arte subtilissima*, 1550, trans. E. Schuckburgh, 1960, 37–8, 60. Yciar also refers to the set square and dividers and ruling with lead. R. W. Hunt has noted the use of dry point in early humanistic manuscripts of Italy (quoted in Ker, *op. cit.*, ix, note).

63. Ivy, *op. cit.*, 44–5.

64. Ker, *op. cit.*, ix–x; Denholm-Young, *op. cit.*, 59–60.

65. *vide* Destrez, work cited note 52.

66. It is very doubtful that many manuscripts were compiled from dictation. Cf. Denholm-Young, *op. cit.*, 57. It is likely, however, that in small-scale works in the later period, an author might dictate to his secretary much as he often did for letters, though usually even here the secretary worked from the author's rough draft for important and lengthy correspondence.

67. Denholm-Young, *ibid.* It should be remembered that much of the foliation and pagination found in manuscripts were added much later, the 19th-century librarians being especially fond of foliating in bold black ink, though their 20th-century counterparts have restricted themselves to light pencilling.

68. See, further, on bookbinding: G. D. Hobson, *English bookbinding before 1500*, 1929; H. M. Nixon, 'English bookbindings', *BC*, i, 1952– (in progress); H. G. Pollard, *Lib.*, 5th ser., xi, 1956; xvii, 1962; xxv, 1970; and for a brief, simple history, J. P. Harthan, *Bookbindings*, 1961.

69. Yciar, *op. cit.*, 30.

70. Steel pens came into use in the 1820s and were in vogue by the 1830s (cf. Hector, *op. cit.*, 19). A preliminary stage was an attempt to combine a quill nib and reservoir with a silver body containing a flow control.

71. John de Beauchesne and John Baildon, *A booke containing divers sortes of hands*, 1570, and Francis Clement, *The petie schole*, 1587, refer to raven's feathers as a satisfactory alternative. Tagliente, *La vera arte*, 1524, pr. in O. Ogg, *Three classics of Italian calligraphy*, 1953, 104, comments that many good writers liked the swan's quill because it was large and firm and especially useful for the cursive chancery hand. Cf. Yciar, *op. cit.*, 30, 38.

72. *F. & W.*, 42–3.

73. Choosing the left wing was apparently a matter of much controversy, cf. Yciar, *op. cit.*, 38–9.

74. Nearly all the Renaissance writing-masters gave instructions for cutting the pen, including Arrighi, Tagliente and Palatino (*vide* O. Ogg, *Three classics of Italian calligraphy*, 1953, 39 ff., 103 ff., 242 ff.). One of the most detailed descriptions (with diagrams) is by Wolffgang Fugger (*Handwriting manual*, 1553, trans. F. Plaat, 1960) and among the most lucid is that by Yciar, *op. cit.*, 39–41, on which the present account relies.

75. Yciar, *op. cit.*, 41 ff. A set of four identical illustrations of the right and wrong way of holding the pen appear in de Beauchesne and Baildon, *op. cit.* and *A newe booke of copies*, 1574, ed. B. Wolpe, 1962.

76. A good though late set of four illustrations of the relative positions of the pen is given in J. Langton, *A new copy book of the small Italian hand*, 1727.

77. Hector, *op. cit.*, 20.

78. The designations are taken from the verse recipes for ink printed in de Beauchesne and Baildon, *op. cit.*, and reprinted in *A newe booke of copies*.

79. Madan, *op. cit.*, mentions that this ink is to be found on the Herculanean rolls and at Pompeii. J. Grant, *Books and documents*, 1937, 41, gives the year 1020 as the beginning of the gradual transition from carbon to iron-gall inks.

80. Recipe taken from a composite of de Beauchesne and Baildon (repeated in *A newe booke of copies*) and Francis Clement's *The petie schole*. See, further, *F. & W.*, 43–5. The recipes in de Beauchesne are written in doggerel by 'E.B.', whose identity is unknown.

81. H.L., MS 31191, f. 34.

82. Cf. *F. & W.*, 43; Yciar, *op. cit.*, 33–4, suggesting rainwater.

83. E.B.'s recipe referred to in note 80.

84. Hector, *op. cit.*, 20. Denholm-Young, *op. cit.*, 62 refers to a copper additive being used from the later 14th century, giving a greenish black colour to the surface.

85. H.L., MS 31191 (the same source as in note 81); Yciar, *op. cit.*, 35, has a similar recipe for the russet, which he calls red.

86. Quoted Hector, *op. cit.*, 19. On lack of evidence in the medieval period *vide* Ivy, *op. cit.*, 45.

87. Cf. Parkes, xxvi, which has proved useful for this paragraph; Denholm-Young, *op. cit.*, 7.

88. Parkes, *loc. cit.*, distinguishes between *script*, 'the model which the scribe has in his mind's eye' and *hand*, 'what he actually puts down on the page'. But this distinction, though useful, is rarely observed by palaeographers, perhaps because the shortage of synonyms requires that the terms be interchangeable.

89. S. A. Tannenbaum, *The handwriting of the Renaissance*, 1930, 6, employs these categories.

90. Cf. Denholm-Young, *op. cit.*, 6.

91. Description taken from Tannenbaum, *op. cit.*, 23. The spur is mainly a manifestation of late *Elizabethan secretary*, and is confined to *a* and *c*.

92. Term used by N. Ker, *English manuscripts in the century after the Norman Conquest*, 1960, 38.

93. The distinction between the two terms is taken from Tannenbaum, *op. cit.*, 17.

94. I am very grateful to Professor T. J. Brown for allowing me to glean ideas for this section on scripts from his valuable tabulation of Gothic scripts of northern Europe. An important work on the terminology of scripts is the Bischoff, Lieftinck and Battelli, *Nomenclature des écritures livresques du IX au XVI siècle*, 1954.

95. E.g. *ECH* and *Later court hands in England*, 1927, esp. 14.

96. Cf. Lieftinck, 1964, i, text, xv; preferred also by Brown (*vide* note 94).

97. S. Morison, *Lib.*, 4th ser., xxiv, 1943, pl. opp. 24, uses *fere* as a prefix with humanistic hands.

98. Lieftinck, 1964, i, plates, 320–30, uses *hors système*. (See also note 100.)

99. *Formata* has long been accepted by palaeographers (cf., e.g., Morison, *op. cit.*, pl. opp. 24).

100. Lieftinck, 1954, uses *currens*; Morison, *op. cit.*, *corrente*; see also Denholm-Young, *op. cit.*, 31. The term *free hand* comes from Jenkinson (cf. *Lib.*, 4th ser., iii, 1923, 8–9). Jenkinson also uses it as a substitute for all *documentary* scripts not in *set* hand (*id.* 5–9); cf. Hector, *op. cit.*, 59.

101. *A coppie book*, 2nd ed. 1637. Billingsley uses three grades for *secretary*: 'the Sett, Facill and Fast hands'. The suggestion of *rapid* is an adaptation of Billingsley's third category. T. J. Brown uses *media* as a middle category.

102. The idea of intermediate grades derives from T. J. Brown.

(4. The succession of literary scripts)

103. For surveys of the period *vide* E. M. Thompson, *Introduction to Greek and Latin palaeography*, 1912; B. L. Ullman, *Ancient handwriting and its influence*, 1969; Denholm-Young, *Handwriting in England and Wales*, 1954; L. C. Hector, *The handwriting of English documents*, 1966; E. A. Lowe, *Handwriting: our medieval legacy*, 1969 and *English uncial*, 1960; T. A. M. Bishop, *English caroline minuscule*, 1971; N. R. Ker, *English mss. in the century after the Norman Conquest*, 1960.

104. The alphabet illustrations provided here are intended only as a rough guide. Letters isolated from context can rarely give other than indications of the character of a script, especially a cursive one; neither is it possible to demonstrate adequately the different variations which graphs are subject to, even in a very formal script.

105. The derivation of *Carolingian minuscule* has been the subject of much debate which is conveniently summarized in Denholm-Young, *op. cit.*, 21 ff.

106. An indispensable work for literary hands in this period is M. B. Parkes, *English cursive book hands 1250–1500*, 1969, which has created order out of what was a somewhat chaotic and ill-defined area, and the sections dealing with *anglicana*, *secretary* and *hybrid* scripts are very heavily indebted to it.

107. This section on the main text hands is based on S. J. P. van Dijk, 'An advertisement sheet of an early 14th century writing master at Oxford', *Scriptorium*, x, 1956, esp. 55 ff. For further categories *vide* S. H. Steinberg, 'Medieval writing-masters', *Lib.*, 4th ser., xxii, 1941, 1–24.

108. See, further, Parkes, xiv–xvi, pl. 1–6; N. Ker, *Medieval manuscripts in British libraries*, i, 1969, xi ff.

109. See, further, Parkes, xix–xxii, pl. 9–13; N. Ker, *op. cit.*, xii.

110. See, further, Parkes, xvii ff., pl. 7–8, 14–15.

111. For refs. to further examples *vide* commentary to nos. 14–16.

112. *vide*, e.g., Parkes, pl. 20 (ii), where it is used for the translation, with the original Latin in *hybrid italic*, and the commentary in *set secretary*. Examples of *hybrid secretary* for display in accounts and registers are to be found in G. Dawson and L. Kennedy-Skipton, *Elizabethan handwriting*, *1500–1650*, 1968, pl. 16, and H. E. P. Grieve, *Examples of English handwriting*, *1150–1750*, 1954, pl. 15.

113. The problem of distinguishing 15th-century *secretary* from 16th-century has been dealt with in this book by the use of the three qualifying terms for the 16th century, and *secretaria* for the 15th (see Editorial method).

114. Cf. *secretary* examples no. 11, Parkes, pl. 12 (ii); 13 (ii), 21; *anglicana*, nos. 9, 11; Grieve, *op. cit.*, pl. 3. A close antecedent to *early Tudor secretary* is seen in Dawson and Kennedy-Skipton, *op. cit.*, 1B.

115. Cf. Grieve, *op. cit.*, pl. 4, churchwardens' accounts, 1528. Examples of the hands of Henry VIII and Katherine of Aragon are contained in B.L., Cotton, Vespasian, F. xiii, f. 138 and F. iii, f. 33 respectively. Scottish examples are a little more compressed and angular (*vide* G. G. Simpson, *Scottish handwriting*, *1150–1650*, 1973, pl. 12 ff).

116. For another illustration *vide* Dawson and Kennedy-Skipton, *op. cit.*, pl. 5, dated 1549. Like the Surrey example in this book (no. 20), it is a rather sprawling hand.

117. Cf. note 101. Examples of the different grades are given in the text of this volume, e.g. *set*, no. 32; *facile*, no. 35; *rapid* or *fast*, no. 55.

118. Figure 21 is taken from *A newe booke of copies*, 1574. Examples of the small set hand appear in de Beauchesne (labelled *glosing*) and in Hondius, *Theatrum artis scribendi*, 1594 (termed *anglicana*).

119. Adapted from *A newe booke of copies*, 1574. A rather full illustration has been used because the capitals are relevant to 15th-century gothic hands also.

120. See, further, S. Morison, 'Early humanistic script and the first roman type', *Lib.*, 4th ser., xxiv, 1943, 1–29; J. Wardrop, 'Civis Romanus sum', *Signature*, 1952, 3–39; B. L. Ullman, *The origin and development of humanistic script*, 1960; A. de la Mare, *The handwriting of the Italian humanists*, i, fasc. i, 1973.

121. Figure 24 is taken from Arrighi's *Modo di temperare le penne*, 1523, and is, strictly speaking, *letera da brevi*.

122. Examples of *cancellaresca bastarda* are given in Palatino (repr. in O. Ogg, *Three classics of Italian calligraphy*, 1953, 171) and in Lucas, *Arte de escrevir*, 1577 (repr. *F.&W.*, 81–4). See also Wardrop, *op. cit.*, pl. 5.

123. Examples in Palatino (repr. Ogg, *op. cit.*, 158 ff.).

124. See, however, G. Battelli, 'Nomenclature des écritures humanistiques' in B. Bischoff, G. I. Lieftinck and G. Battelli, *Nomenclature des écritures livresques*, 1954, 35 ff.

125. *F.&W.*, 29–30, which reflects the traditional view. Additional points are made by Denholm-Young, *Handwriting in England and Wales*, 1954, though he seems unduly to discount the influence of *cancellaresca* and other forms of *italic* in England in the 16th century.

126. Examples of Udall, Edward VI and Arbella Stuart in *F.&W.*, pl. 23, 25, 56.

127. An early example of Queen Elizabeth's *hybrid italic* is her prayer book, 1545, in the B.L., Royal 7D X. See also *F.&W.*, pl. 28 for another example, dated 1552.

128. All the Elizabethan writing-masters include examples of *testeggiata* and it is the predominant *italic* style in de Beauchesne (1570), from which figure 25 is taken.

129. Examples from *A newe booke of copies*, 1574. S. Morison in his masterly section on the development of handwriting in A. Heal, *The English writing-masters and their copy-books*, 1931, refers to *piacevole* as 'particularly lascivious' (xxxi).

130. The characteristics of individual mixed hands are dealt with at length in the text, which makes fuller treatment here unnecessary.

131. English palaeography of the later 17th century is a very grey area though illuminated by the useful work of Heal and Morison mentioned in note 129.

132. See, further, Morison, *op. cit.*, esp. xxix ff. The illustrations are taken from Gery, *Gerii viri in arte scriptoria*, 1659, and Ayres, *The accomplish'd clerk*, 1673? (adapted).

133. See, further, on Departmental hands: H. Jenkinson, *The later court hands in England*, 1927; Hector, 64—8 and plates.

134. Cf. Hector, pl. XXIa.

135. For illustrations of these four hands *vide* Hector, pl. XIV ff.

136. Figures 28 and 29 derived from *A newe booke of copies*, 1574.

(5. Abbreviation)

137. See, further, L. Traube, *Nomina sacra*, 1907; W. M. Lindsay, *Notae latinae*, 1915; D. Bains, *Supplement to Notae Latinae*, 1936; A. Mentz, *Die tironischen Noten*, 1944.

138. Some idea of the extent of Latin abbreviations can be gained from the excellent *Lexicon abbreviaturarum*, 1889, repr. 1961, by A. Cappelli.

139. See, further, concerning medieval Latin abbreviations: Cappelli, *op. cit.*; L. A. Chassant, *Dictionnaire des abréviations latines et françaises*, 1846, repr. 1965; C. T. Martin, *The record interpreter*, 1910; L. Schiaparelli, *Avviamento allo studio delle abbreviature latine nel medioevo*, 1926; M. H. Laurent, *De abbreviationibus et signis gothicae*, 1937; and A. Pelzer, *Abréviations latines médiévales*, 1964. Hector is also useful for abbreviations in Latin documents in England (29 ff.).

140. The four categories derive from Chassant, *op. cit.* The *elision* category is adopted from Tannenbaum, *The handwriting of the Renaissance*, 1931, together with the use of the term *curtailment* as being now more easily recognizable than *suspension*.

141. Useful examples of the ways in which final *e* was indicated are given in *ECH*, 67 ff.

142. Earlier examples of brevigraphs are given in *ECH*, 59 ff.

143. The section on *elision* and *absorption* is based on Tannenbaum, *op. cit.*, 121–4, including some of the examples. These two categories pose problems if abbreviations are to be expanded in a transcription. It would seem best not to expand either, or at least not in poetry where scansion is involved. See, further, on these two categories: A. Western, 'Aphesis, syncope and apocope in Middle and early Modern English', *A grammatical miscellany offered to Otto Jespersen*, 1930; and A. C. Partridge, *Orthography in Shakespeare and Elizabethan Drama*, 1964, 94 ff., and *passim*.

(6. Punctuation)

144. Denholm-Young, 77, notes that the Wolsey Gospel Book, Magdalen College, Oxford, *c.* 1520, contains the full range of modern punctuation marks except for the exclamation mark.

145. One of the modern pioneers of the 'elocutionary and rhetorical' theory of 16th-century punctuation was Percy Simpson, e.g. *Shakespearean punctuation*, 1911, 'The bibliographical study of Shakespeare', Oxford Bibliographical Society, *Proceedings*, i, 1923, *Proof-reading in the 16th, 17th and 18th centuries*, 1935. Simpson's investigations were continued by C. C. Fries, 'Shakespearean punctuation', University of Michigan Publications, i, *Studies in Shakespeare, Milton and Donne*, 1925, 67–86, who reacts somewhat negatively, and W. Ong, 'Backgrounds to Elizabethan punctuation', *PMLA*, 59, 1944, 349–60, who supports Simpson's findings. Among the useful works on Renaissance punctuation are S. A. Tannenbaum, *The handwriting of the Renaissance*, 1931, 139–52; A. C. Partridge, *Orthography in Shakespeare and Elizabethan drama*, 1964, esp. 124 ff. and append. VIII; and M. Treip, *Milton's punctuation and changing English usage, 1582–1676*, 1970, which distinguishes theatrical, verse and prose punctuation, and traces the changing styles in punctuation in the early and middle periods of the 17th centuries.

146. An example of a pen-rest is given in G. G. Simpson, *Scottish handwriting, 1150–1650*, 1973, no. 7.

147. Hector, 47, translated from the appendix to the 1709 edition of Mabillon's *De re diplomatica*, which quotes a description of punctuation in an undated medieval manuscript from Vallombrosa.

148. It has twice been stated recently that the inverted semicolon passed out of use by the end of the 14th century, but it is clear that the *terminus quem* has to be extended by almost fifty years. Cf. example in *ECH*, 76, dated 1439.

149. See, further, Hector, 47; Partridge, *op. cit.*, 190; Treip, *op. cit.*, 26 ff.; Ong, *op. cit.*, 357–8.

150. See, further, Tannenbaum, 142; Treip 28 ff.; Partridge, 190–2.

151. Cf. *ECH*, 77. Presumably the *i* stood for *item*, though the whole question of paragraph marks seems confused.

152. Tannenbaum, 145.

(7. Numerals)

153. This section on numerals is indebted to Hector, 41–5, Tannenbaum, 153–9, *ECH*, 73–5, and to the pioneer work of G. F. Hill, *Development of Arabic numerals in Europe*, 1915.

154. The use of diacritic and points to mark out the Roman units corresponded with the practice for letter *i/j*.

(8. Manuscript corrections)

155. That proof-reading was far more frequent and thorough than has hitherto been assumed is ably demonstrated by P. Simpson, *Proof-reading in the 16th, 17th and 18th centuries*, 1935, though his case for the 16th century is possibly overstated.

156. The order of deletions here is based on that in *ECH*, 78, though some of the terms have been altered and a seventh category added.

157. Hector, pl. IIIb, contains an example of *u* altered to *i* by expunction.

158. Cf. Hector, 50, pl. IXb; *ECH*, 78.

159. Tannenbaum, *The handwriting of the Renaissance*, 1931, 147.

160. Hector, *op. cit.*, 50, pl. IVa and Va.

(9. Scribal errors and textual emendation)

161. Ways in which palaeography can assist in textual emendation are ably demonstrated by E. Vinaver, 'Principles of textual emendation', in *Studies in French language and literature presented to M. K. Pope*, 1939, 351–69.

162. Cf. Denholm-Young, 58. It will be noticed from Simpson, *op. cit.*, 130, that the corrector in the printing house sometimes had the text read aloud to him.

163. Examples of contamination are provided in Vinaver, *op. cit.*, 358–60.

164. Donne, *Satire II*, 71.

165. No. 20, l. 9, of a group of twenty-nine sonnets by Sir Toby Mathew (*vide* A. G. Petti, *Recusant History*, ix, 1967).

166. Example from Heywood, *The wise woman of Hogsdon*, quarto, 1604.

167. One of the most useful sources for variant spellings is still the *Oxford English Dictionary*. For a brief account of Renaissance orthography *vide* A. C. Baugh, *A history of the English language*, 1951, 255 ff. See also A. C. Partridge, *Orthography in Shakespeare and Elizabethan drama*, 1964.

(10. Comparison of hands, dating, forgery)

168. For pre-1600 watermarks *vide* C. M. Briquet, *Les filigranes*, 4 vols., repr. 1968; and for post-1600, W. A. Churchill, *Watermarks in paper in Holland, England, France in the 17th and 18th centuries*, 1935; E. Heawood, *Watermarks mainly of the 17th and 18th centuries*, 1950; E. J. Labarre, *The study of watermarks in Great Britain*, 1952. See also A. H. Stevenson, 'Paper as bibliographical evidence', *Lib.*, 5th ser., xvii, 1962; and *Studies in Bibliography*, 6, 1954. A comprehensive bibliography is provided in *CBEL*, i, 927–30.

169. The fifty-year rule seems to derive from Francis Wormald.

170. Hector, pl. XVI.

171. See bibliography for a list of palaeographical handbooks. It cannot be said that aids to dating are sufficiently comprehensive or illuminating.

172. For further details *vide* section on the manuscript book in *Writing materials*. References on watermarks are given in note 168. For early bookbinding *vide* J. B. Oldham, *Blind panels of English binders*, 1958.

173. One of the most authoritative works on forgery in general is W. R. Harrison, *Suspect documents: their scientific examination*, 2nd imp. and suppl., 1968. Still quite useful, though somewhat outdated, is C. A. Mitchell, *Documents and their scientific examination*, 1935.

174. 'Two pretended autographs of Shakespeare', *Lib.*, 3rd ser., viii, 1917, 193–217. For literary forgeries see T. J. Brown, 'The detection of faked literary mss', *BC*, 2, 1953, 6–23, and for documents, L. C. Hector, *Palaeography and forgery*, St Anthony's Hall Publ., no. 15, 1959.

List of Plates

Alphabetical List of Identified Hands in the Plates

In the name of god pitos & merciable saide the largere þt þilk makeþ this
instrument the largere ben thi chef devisiouns the largere þt ben tho devisiouns
in hem may ben mo smale fracciouns / & euere the mo of smale fracciouns
the ner the trouthe of thy equaciouns / tak therfore a plate of metal or elles
a bord þat be smothe shaue by leuel & euene polised / of which whan it is
[5] rounded the hole diametre shal contene 72 large enches or elles 6 fote of
mesure / the whiche rounde bord for it shal nat warpe ne krooke the egge of
the cyrcumference shal be bounde with a plate of yren in maner of a karte whel
this bord yif the lyketh may be vernissed or elles glewed with perchemyn for
honestye / tak thanne a cercle of metal þat be 2 enches of brede & þat the hole
[10] diametre set in this cercle shal contene the forseide 68 enches or 6 fote 2 & 8 enches & subtili lat this cercle
be nayled vp on the cyrcumference of this bord or ellis mak this cercle of
glewed perchemyn / this cercle wole I clepe the lymbe of myn equatorie
þt was compouned the yer of crist 1392 complet the laste meridie of decembre
this lymbe shaltow deuyde in 4 quarters by 2 diametral lynes in maner of
[15] the lymbe of a comune astrelabye & lok thy croys be rekke proued by
geometrical conclusiouns tak thanne a large compas þat be stif & set the fix
point on the middel of the bord which middel shal be nayled a plate of
metal round / the hole diametre of this plate shal contene 16 enches large
for in this plate shollen ben perced alle the centris of this equatorie / & ek in
[20] pces of tyme may this plate be turned a bowte after þat auges of planetes
ben moeued in the 9 spere / thus may this instrument laste perpetuel / tak thanne
as I haue seid by forn the fix fot of thy compas & set it in the middel of
this plate & with the moeuable point of thi compas descryue a cercle in the

1 Memorandum of Chaucer's appointment of a deputy
controller for the wool quay, Port of London, May 1378.
Anglicana facilis, Anglo-Norman, holograph?
P.R.O., E 207/6/2 (56).

Geffrey chauce⟨r⟩ conterollour de le Wolkeye en le Port de loundris *par* lauis
∧ [& assent] du cou*n*seil *n*os*t*re *sieur* le Roy a constitut Ric*hard* baret de estre sou*n*
lieutenau*n*t en l*o*ffice[1] auant dite de le xvj Iour de maii lan du Roy Ric*hard* le
P*ri*mer Iuq*ue* a sa reuenue a loundris

1. *l* superscribed on *c*.

2 *The Equatorie of the Planetis*: first page of text proper,
1392. *Anglicana facilis*, holograph?
C.U.L., Peterhouse MS 75. i, f. 71v., excluding last eight
lines. Reduced by $\frac{1}{4}$.

In the name of god pitos & *me*rciable seide [keyk][1] the largere þat thow makest this
instrume*n*t / the largere ben thi chef deuisiou*n*s / the largere þat ben tho
deuisiou*n*s / in hem may ben mo smale fracciou*n*s / & euere the mo of smale
fracciou*n*s the ner the trowthe of thy *con*clusiou*n*s / tak ther fore a plate of metal or
elles a bord þat be smothe shaue / by leuel / & euene polised ¶ of which whan it is
Rownd ∧ [by compas] / the hole diametre shal *con*tene .72. large enches or elles .6.
fote of mesure / the whiche Rownde bord for it shal nat werpe ne krooke / the
egge of ∧ [the] circu*m*ference shal be bownde wi*th* a plate of yren in maner of a
karte whel. / ¶ this bord yif the likith may be vernissed or elles glewed wi*th*
*per*chemyn for honestyte ¶ tak thanne a cercle of metal þat be .2 enche of
brede / & þat the hole dyamete ∧ [wi*th* in this cercle shal] *con*tene [the forseide]
.68. enches / or .5 fote [& .8. enches] / & subtili lat this cercle be nayled vp on the
circu*m*ference of this bord or ellis mak this cercle of glewed *per*chemyn. / this
cercle wole I clepe the lymbe of myn equatorie þat was *com*powned the yer of
crist .1392. *com*plet the laste *me*ridie of dece*m*bre ¶ this lymbe shaltow deuyde in 4
quarters by .2. diametral lynes in man*er* of the lymbe of a comune astrelabye &
lok thy croys be trewe proued by geometrical *con*clusiou*n* / tak thanne a large
*com*pas þat be trewe & set the ffyx point ou*er* the middel of the bord ∧ [on] which
middel shal be nayled a plate of metal Rownd ¶ the hole diametre of this plate
shal *con*tene .16. enches large for in this plate shollen ben perced alle the centris
of this equatorie / & ek in p*ro*ces of tyme may this plate be turned a bowte after
þat auges of planetes ben moeued in the .9. spere thus may thin instrume*n*t laste
*per*petuel. ¶ tak thanne as I haue seid by forn the fix fot of thy *com*pas & set it in the
middel of this plate & wi*th* the moeuable point of thi *com*pas descriue a cercle in the

1. *keyk* erased but visible under ultra-violet light. Price (see below) reads *leyk*.

Notes

No undisputed specimen of Chaucer's handwriting has come to light, but two
mutually supporting claimants are sufficiently
strong to justify reproduction here. The first is a
memorandum which T. M. Manly (*MP*, xxv,
1927, 123) thought could have been written by
Chaucer or at least passed through his hands.
The writing is less formal than a clerk's or a
secretary's, and if, as seems likely, the document
is holograph, then it also contains a form of
signature. The case for the other claimant, *The
Equatorie of the Planetis* has been circumspectly
put by D. J. Price in his edition of the work
(1955, 149–66). Unfortunately, he limited his
palaeographical investigation mainly to a
comparison of *chauce*⟨r⟩ in the memorandum
with the apparent reading of the name on f. 5*v*.
of the *Equatorie*, and the case for authorship has
been somewhat cavalierly dismissed by F. N.
Robinson (*Works of Geoffrey Chaucer*, 2nd ed.,
1957, viii–ix).
Characteristics. Both examples, though
quite pleasing to the eye, are a little irregular
in letter formation, somewhat splayed, and with

a mixed impression of roundness, partly given by
the loops and bowls, and of angularity,
suggested by the thin diagonal links, which form
a sharp angle with the minims. Word-spacing is
fairly generous. The writing of no. 2 is larger
than that of no. 1 in the original, a little more
formal and less cursive, as might be expected
from a treatise as compared with a jotted and
blotted memorandum, but like no. 1 it contains
currente calamo corrections suggestive of an
author's holograph. Among the letter forms to
be noted are the wide varieties of both long *s*
and sigma *s*, the former used initially, medially
and when doubled, and the sigma finally,
though a large sigma is sometimes used initially
in no. 2, possibly as a capital (e.g. ll. 3, 5). Two
common forms of *r* appear, forked *r* as the norm,
and the tagged *2* form after *o* (with a rather
longer tag in no. 2 than in no. 1). A
calligraphic *m* is used in no. 2, with the end of
the initial minim curled inwards with a little
hook, and the final minim ending in an
infralinear clockwise curve similar to the limb
of *h* (e.g. ll. 1, 4, 8). Final *e* sometimes has a
tagged lobe (e.g. no. 1, ll. 3, 4; no. 2, ll. 1, 2, 5),
or a rather clumsy ascending curve from the
tail (no. 1, ll. 1, 3; no. 2, ll. 1, 10).
Punctuation. Common to both are the caret,
dotted *y* to distinguish it from *thorn*, and the
diacritic to identify *i* (e.g. *lauis*, no. 1, l. 2).
Appearing only in no. 2 are the virgule as general
factotum, the paragraphus (ll. 5, 9, 10, etc.),
the period, sometimes in conjunction with the
virgule, and raised points to enclose numerals
(transcribed as ordinary points).
Abbreviation. Both contain a curved bar
for omission of *m* and *n* (no. 1, l. 2; no. 2, l. 2),
crossed *þ* for *par* and *per* (no. 1, l. 2; no. 2, ll. 10,
13, 23) and the Tironian nota **ꞇ** for *and*,
sometimes with a bar above it in no. 2 (ll. 3,
16). Found in no. 1 are crossed long *s* for *sieur*;
q3 for *que*; ' linked to final letter for
curtailment and contraction (e.g. l. 2, *Ric*',
and *nre*', a common Norman French
abbreviation for *nostre*); and another form of '
occurs over *P* (l. 3) for *ri*. Additionally in no. 2
are the straight bar for *m* or *n*; *g* for *com*, *con*
(ll. 4, 11, 14, 17, 23) the heavy *s* form of '
for *er* (ll. 1, 14, 15, 18), and *þ* with looped
cross-stroke for *pro* (l. 21).
Comparison of hands. Apart from the
differences listed above, of which only the
relative size and the initial *m* are of possible
significance, the two hands look almost identical,
even though dated fourteen years apart and
employed for different purposes. It should also
be noted that with the exception of the looped
P (ll. 1, 3) and *q* (l. 4), those letters and
brevigraphs of no. 1 which do not appear in
no. 2 have their counterparts in other places in
the *Equatorie* (e.g. capital *I/J*, f. 78, 3rd line
from bottom; ' linked to final letter, f. 62v.,
l. 2). The many close similarities between the
hands cannot be entirely explained as features
common to *anglicana* and the case for both being
Chaucer's holograph is a strong one.

Now preye I to hem alle that herkne this litel tretys or rede
that if they be any thyng in it that liketh hem that they of
they thanken oure lord Ihu crist. of whom proceedeth al
wit and al goodnesse. And if ther be any thyng that displese hem. I

preye hem also that they arette it to the defaute of myn vnkonnynge
and nat to my wyl. that wolde ful fayn haue seyd bettre if I hadde
had konnynge. ffor oure book seith al that is writen is writen for
oure doctrine. and that is myn entente. Wherfore I biseke yow
mekely for the mercy of god that ye preye for me that crist haue mercy
on me and forzeue me my giltes. and namely of my translations
and enditynges of worldly vanitees the whiche I reuoke in my re
tractions As is the book of Troilus The book also of ffame The
book of the xxv ladies The book of the Duchesse The book of
seint Valentynes day of the parlement of byrdes The tales of
Caunterbury thilke that sownen in to synne The book of the leon
and many another book if they were in my remembrance And
many a song and many a leccherous lay. that crist for his gre
te mercy forzeue me the synne But of the translacion of Boece
de consolacion and othere bookes of legendes of seintes and
Omelies and moralitee and deuocion that thanke I oure
lord Ihu crist and his blisful mooder and alle the seintes of he
uene bisekynge hem that they from hennes forth vn to my lyues
ende sende me grace to biwayle my giltes and to studie to the
saluacion of my soule and graunte me grace of verray penite
ce confession and satisfaction to doon in this present lyf thurgh
the benigne grace of hym that is kyng of kynges and preest
ouer alle preestes that boghte vs with the precious blood of his her
te so that I may been oon of hem at the day of doome that shulle
be saued Qui cum patre &c

Heere is ended the book of the tales of Caunterbury
compiled by Geffrey Chaucer of whos soule Ihu crist
haue mercy Amen

3 Ellesmere MS of *Canterbury Tales* (*c.* 1387–): the
Retraction. *Anglicana formata, c.* 1400–10.
H.L., EL 26, C.9, lower portion of f. 236v. Reduced by $\frac{1}{10}$.

Now preye I to hem alle that herkne this litel tretys or rede that if ther be any
thyng / in it that liketh hem / that ther of they thanken oure lord Ih*e*su crist /. of
whom procedeth al wit and al goodnesse. And if ther be any thyng that
displese hem. I preye hem also that they arrette it to the defaute of myn
vnkonnynge and nat to my wyl. that wolde ful fayn haue seyd bettre / if I
hadde had konnynge. ffor oure book seith / al that is writen / is writen for oure
doctrine. and that is myn entente ⟨ Wherfore / I biseke yow mekely for the m*er*cy
of god / that ye preye for me / that crist haue m*er*cy on me and foryeue me my
giltes. and namely of my translacions and enditynges of worldly vanitees / the
whiche I reuoke in my retracciou*n* ⟨ As is the book of Troilus ⟨ The book also of
ffame ¶ The book of the .xxv. ladies ⟨ The book of the Duchesse ⟨ The book of
seint valentynes day of the p*ar*lement of briddes ¶. The tales of Caunt*er*bury / thilke
that sownen in to synne ⟨ The book of the leou*n* And many another book / if they
were in my remembrance / and many a song and many a leccherous lay. that
crist for his grete m*er*cy foryeue me the synne ⟨ But of the *translaciou*n of Boece de
consolacio*ne* / and othere bookes of legendes of seintes / and Omelies / and
moralitee / and deuociou*n* / that thanke I oure lord Ih*e*su c*ri*st / and his blisful
mooder / and alle the seintes of heuene / bisekynge hem / þat they from hennes
forth vn to my lyues ende / sende me *grace* / to biwayle my giltes / and to studie to
the saluaciou*n* of my soule / and graunte me *grace* of v*er*ray penite*n*ce /
confessiou*n* and satisfacciou*n* to doon in this p*re*sent lyf / thurgh[1] the benigne
grace / of hym þat is kyng / of kynges / and preest / ouer alle preestes / that
boghte vs w*ith* the p*re*cious blood of his herte / so þat I may been oon of hem at
the day of doome that shulle be saued? Qui cum patre &c

⟨ Heere is ended the book of the tales of Caunterbury compiled by Geffrey
Chaucer of whos soule Ih*e*su crist haue mercy Amen

1 Bar on final *h* otiose.

Notes

Of the 83 or more extant MSS of the
Canterbury Tales, the Ellesmere Chaucer is one
of the most authoritative and earliest, being
dated 1400–10 in J. M. Manly and E. Rickert,
The text of the Canterbury Tales, 1940, i, 148. It is
also one of the best preserved and has the most
elaborate decoration. On the basis of dialect
and orthography it is thought to have been
compiled in the London area. Among previous
owners was apparently Baron Ellesmere
(Thomas Egerton), and it remained in the
possession of his descendants until purchased for
the Huntington Library in 1917. The
Canterbury Tales section of the MS (ff. 1–232v)
was transcribed by F. J. Furnivall for the
Chaucer Soc., 1868, and a colour facsimile of
the whole volume was published by
Manchester U.P. in 1911. For a description
vide H. C. Schulz, *The Ellesmere Manuscript of
Chaucer's Canterbury Tales*, 1965, and Manly and
Rickert (*op. cit.*, 148–59, 565 ff.), who
justifiably suggest that the scribe is the same as
for the Hengwyrt MS of the *Tales* (Nat. Lib. of
Wales, Peniarth 392 D).
Characteristics.   A large, bold and clear
hand, though the thickness of the strokes and
the proportionately narrow space between
words gives it a slight impression of heaviness
and congestion when compared with other
examples of *anglicana formata* in the period, e.g.,
three of the *Piers Plowman* MSS (no. 4; Greg,
FTTC, VII; Skeat, *TOEM*, IX). There is the
typical calligraphic use of high gothic-arched

ascenders for headings, incipits and explicits,
while, in general, ascenders end in a short,
thick, angled arch, and descenders are quite
short, though they taper slightly. The minims
are separate and have small curled or hooked
foot-serifs. A broken-stroked squarish figure *8*
form of *s* is used in final position, sigma
initially, and long *s* medially and in ligatures. A
circular reversed *e* is occasionally used in final
position when preceded by the forked *r* (ll. 6,
7); a broken-stroked *2* form of *r* appears with a
tag after *o* (ll. 1, 3) and without after *þ* (ll. 3,
26, 7); in all other cases the long, forked *r* is
used. *Thorn* occurs only in conjunction with
superior *t* in the abbreviation for *that* (ll. 22, 28).
Rounded capitals have the characteristic gothic
decoration of a single or double vertical bar, and
final letters with cross-strokes often have a
pendant hair-line (ll. 4, *thyng*, 12, *book*), which
could be mistaken for a virgule.
Punctuation.   The range and form of
punctuation marks are as in Hengwyrt: point,
virgule, capitulum and, occasionally, the
paragraphus (noticeably similar to the type in
the *Equatorie*, so that it is possible that
Chaucer's original pointing is being followed in
Ellesmere); *y* is dotted; a small, crescent-shaped
diacritic is used to distinguish *i*; a flourish
resembling a sloping *s* serves as a *punctus elevatus*,
i.e. an inverted semicolon (l. 29); the same
flourish and a type of three-minim figure act as
line-fillers (ll. 3, 8, 19, 31, etc.). A light,

oblique and barely visible hyphen occurs at the
end of ll. 11, 17 and 27.
Abbreviation.   There are the usual
brevigraphs: crossed *þ* for *par* (l. 14); ' with an
elaborate flourish ending in a heavy
downstroke curving back to the right is used for
er (ll. 9, 24) or in a smaller version above *þ* for
re; the bar for *m* or *n* (ll. 12, 15), or linked to the
final letter for *e* (l. 19). The bar is also used in
Ihesu (ll. 3, 21), a Latin abbreviation of the
Greek, the *h* originally representing the Greek
eta, though its significance was apparently lost
by this time. Other brevigraphs and superior
letters include *i* for *ri* (*crist*, l. 21), *a* with a
headstroke for *ra* (*grace*, ll. 24, 26) and a serrated
line for *ra* (*translation*, l. 18).
Illumination.   Initial *N* is in pink veined in
white, with pink, red, white and blue foliation
on a gold ground. The left of the double-barred
border is gold, the right alternates pink and
blue; the interlaced knots are in pink and deep
blue on a gold ground. The trefoils and oak
leaves also alternate mainly between pink and
blue, the tendrils are often tipped with gold
balls, and the four pairs of daisy buds are
pink-tipped with olive green calixes. At the
bottom there appear to be, appropriately,
Canterbury bells, coloured alternately red and
blue. The first capitulum marks on lines 12
and 13 and the one on line 18 are in blue with
red ink flourishes; the rest are in gold with
violet ink flourishes.

þat þay þus lyst ferolayke lee hit me þynk
who wyȝtes vp þis beriage þis bargayn is maked
So sayd þe lorde of þat lede þay laȝed vchone
þay dronken & daylyeden & diten vntyȝtel
5 þise lordeȝ & ladyeȝ quyle þat hem lyked
& syþen wt frenkysh fare & fele fayre loteȝ
þay stoden & stemed & stylly speken
kysten ful comlyly & kaȝten her leue
wt mony lede ful lyȝt & lemande torches   ful sofrt
10 vche burne to his bed wat broȝt at þe laste
to bed ȝet er þay ȝede
recorded couenaunteȝ ofte
þe olde lorde of þat londe
cowþe wel halde layk aloffte

15 Ful erly bifore þe day þe folk vp rysen
gestes þat go wolde hor gromeȝ þay calden
& þay busken vp bilyue blonkkeȝ to sadel
tyffen he takles trussen her males
richen hem þe rychest to ryde alle arayde
20 lepen vp lyȝtly lachen her brydeles
vche wyȝe on his way þer hym wel lyked
þe leue lorde of þe londe watȝ not þe last
arayed for þe rydyng wt renkkeȝ ful mony
ete a sop hastyly when he hade herd masse
25 wt bugle to bent felde he buskeȝ bylyue
by þat þat any daylyȝt lemed vpon erþe
he wt his haþeles on hyȝe horses weren
þenne þise cacheres þat couþe cowpled hor houndeȝ
vnclosed þe kenel dore & calde hem þer oute
30 blwe bygly in bugleȝ þre bare mote
braches bayed þerfore & breme noyse maked
& þay chastysed & charred on chasyng þat went
a hundreth of hunters as I haf herde telle   of þe best
to trystors vewters ȝod
35 couples huntes of kest

4 *Sir Gawain and the Green Knight* (*c.* 3rd quarter of 14th century): ll. 1111–47, including the beginning of Book III. *Fere-textura rotunda facilis?* *c.* 1375–1400. B.L., Cotton Nero A.x, art 3, f. 106.

& þat yow lyst forto layke lef hit me þynk*es*
who bry*n*geӡ v*us* þis beu*er*age þis bargayn is maked
so sayde þe lorde of þat lede þay laӡed vchone
þay dronken & daylyeden & dalten vntyӡtel
5 þise lordeӡ & ladyeӡ quyle þat hem lyked
& syþen *with* frenkysch fare & fele fayre loteӡ
þay stoden & stemed & stylly speken
kysten ful comlyly & kaӡten her leue
with mony leude ful lyӡt & lemande torches ≪fulsofte[1]
10 vche burne to his bed watӡ broӡt at þe laste
to bed ӡet er þay ӡede
recorded coue*n*aunteӡ ofte
þe olde lorde of þat leude
cowþe wel halde layk a lofte
15 Ful erly bifore þe day þe folk vp rysen
gestes þat go wolde hor gromeӡ þay calden
& þay busken vp bilyue blonkkeӡ to sadel
tyffen he takles trussen her males
richen hem þe rychest to ryde alle arayde
20 lepen vp lyӡtly lachen her brydeles
vche wyӡe on his way þer hy*m* wel lyked
þe leue lorde of þe londe watӡ not þe last
a rayed for þe rydy*n*g *with* renkkeӡ ful mony
ete a sop hastyly when he hade herde masse
25 *with* bugle to bent felde he buskeӡ by lyue
by þat þat[2] any day lyӡt lemed vpon erþe
he *with* his haþeles on hyӡe horsses weren
þe*n*ne þise cacheres þat couþe cowpled hor hou*n*deӡ
vnclosed þe kenel dore & calde hem þ*er* oute
30 blwe bygly i*n* bugleӡ þre bare mote[3]
braches bayed þ*er*fore & breme noyse maked
& þay chastysed & charred on chasy*n*g þat went
a hundreth of hunt*er*es as I haf herde telle ≪of þe best
to trystors vewters ӡod
35 couples huntes of kest

1. The 'bob' *fulsofte* is a line too early. 2. *þat*, dittography. 3. The scribe has apparently omitted ӡ.

Notes

Pearl, Cleanness, Patience and *Sir Gawain* form a remarkable group of four poems by the same unknown author which survive only in the one MS volume, probably the earliest in the vernacular to contain illustrations (ff. 37, 38, 125, 125v, 126), if rather crude in execution. The date of composition is usually placed in the third quarter of the 14th century (though E. V. Gordon in his edition of *Pearl* suggests 1360–95) and the manuscript is thought to be somewhat later, being a scribal copy at least one stage removed from the original. However, details of costume in the illustrations and such features as the consistent use of *thorn* for *th*, and more especially of *yogh*, would seem to suggest the manuscript was compiled before the end of the 14th century. The poems are thought to derive from the North-West or the West Midlands, and the names of Hugh Masy and John de Massey have come to the fore as possible authors in recent years. Scholarship is undecided on whether or not the scribe came from the same region as the author, but Gollancz has noted his Anglo-French mannerism in writing *tӡ* for *s*.

Although the MS is in mainly one hand, a corrector has been at work occasionally, and nearly illegible passages have been retraced. Further, it is to be supposed that the initial capitals were added by yet another scribe, possibly the person who made the illustrations. A facsimile of the whole manuscript made by I. Gollancz, E.E.T.S., o.s., 162, 1923, is on the whole clearer than the original, which appears to be fading, with ink gradually falling off the pen strokes. For transcriptions *vide* editions by Gollancz, Day and Serjeantson, E.E.T.S., o.s., 210, 1940, and J. R. R. Tolkien and E. V. Gordon, rev. N. Davis, 1967. For the rather sparse palaeographical material *vide* the introductions to the three works cited above, esp., respectively, 7–11; ix ff.; xi ff.; also, W. W. Greg, *Lib.*, 4th ser., xiii, 1933, 188–91; J. P. Oakden, *Lib.*, 4th ser., xiv, 1934, 353–8; F. P. Magoun, *A*, lxi, 1937, 129–30; D. R. Howard and C. Zacher, *Critical studies of Sir Gawain and the Green Knight*, 1968, ix ff., 3–4. The illustrations are discussed in R. S. and L. H. Loomis, *Arthurian legends in mediaeval art*, 1938, 138 ff., and recent suggestions on authorship are summarised in *YWES*, 1971, 86.

Characteristics. An extremely small, compressed and angular book hand, with an impression of irregularity both in size and formation of letters, and closest in category to *textura rotunda*, being sparing of breaking and serifs. It is probably one of the most distinctive and easily recognizable vernacular book hands of the period, though this is the only example that has come to light. It is also a difficult hand to read, not only because it is small with very short ascenders, but because many of the letters, especially the minim formations, have the barest of distinguishing features. Among the examples of confusibilia are: *n* and *u* (l. 9), *et* and *ec* (l. 12), *l* and long *s* (l. 3), *b* and *v* (l. 17), *2* form of *r* and *ӡ* (l. 9), *ut* and *itt* (l. 29), *ll* and *n* (l. 33), *þ* and *v* (l. 34). In general, the pen strokes are comparatively thick, but fine hairlines form the tails of the *h* and *y*. The biting characteristic of the book hand is present in *de* (ll. 3, 5, 7) and *da* (ll. 4, 15). Ordinary continental *r* is used except that the *2* form appears after *o* (l. 12); a short squarish *5* or *8* form of *s* is used in final position; the bottom lobe of the *a* is open so that it resembles a small roman capital. *Yogh* serves many phonetic purposes: *gh* (l. 9), *y* (l. 11), *w* (elsewhere in the MS), *s* (ll. 2, 5) and *s* also in the combination *tӡ* (l. 10). The initial *F* is coloured in blue and red and decorated in long flourishes as if implying a structural division (as also at ll. 491 and 1998).

Punctuation. There is no punctuation apart from a bar of braces to separate the 'bob', l. 33 and a flower-like flourish for the 'bob', l. 9, both reproduced here as ≪.

Abbreviation. The bar for *n* (l. 12); an *s* form of ' for *er* (l. 2), for *and* (l. 4), superior *t* with *w* for *with* (l. 6), ℭ for *es* (l. 1) and *9*, normally for *us*, though possibly simply for *s* (l. 2, *vus*).

How we ladde oure lyf here and his ...
and how we dide day by day the dome ...
a pouche ful of pardon þer ne prouincials lete
þogh we be founde in þe fraternite of alle fyue o...
and haue indulgences double folde but dowel ve he
I sette noght by pardon a pese ne nat a pye hele
ffor þy I counseile alle cristne to crye god mercy
and marie his modur be oure mene to hym
þat god zif vs grace her ar we hennes wende
þat after oure deye day dowel reherse
at þe day of dome we dide as he taghte amen

Explicit visio Willi·W·de Petro le plowman
Et hic incipit visio eiusdem de Dowel

Thus yrobed in russet I romed aboute
Al a somer sesoun for to sele dowel
and frayned ful ofte of fole þat I mette
Jf eny wight wiste wher dowel was at inne
and what man he myghte be of many men I asked
was neuer wight in þe worlde þat me wisse couthe
where þis longeth I lasse no more
Til it bifell on a friday two freres I mette
maistres of þe mendinauntz men of grete witte
I hailsede hem hendely as I hadde leyed
and prayed hem pur charite er þey passed forþe
Jf þey knewe eny cuntre er costes aboute
where þat dowel dwellede dere fiendes telley me
ffor ze aye men of þis molde þat most wide walken
and knowen cuntrees and courtes a many kyn places
boþe princes paleys and pouer men cotes
and dowel and do euele wher þey duellen boþe
Comely sayde þe frere he soiourney with vs freres

5 *Piers Plowman*, C-text (*c.* 1393–8): end of Passus X and opening of Passus XI. *Anglicana formata, c.* 1400. U.L.L., V. 88, f. 53.

How we ladde oure lif her*e* ⁋ and his ⟨lawes kepte⟩[1]
and how we dide day by day ⁋ þe dome ⟨wol reherce⟩
a powhe ful of p*ar*doun þer // ne prouynciales lett*r*es
þogh we be founde in þe frat*er*nite of alle fyue o⟨rdres⟩
5 and haue indulgences dowblefolde ⁋ but dowel vs he⟨lpe⟩
I sette noght[2] by p*ar*doun a pese ⁋ ne nat a pye hele
ffor þy I counseile alle c*r*istne ⁋ to crie god mersy
and marie his mod*er* ⁋ be oure mene to him
þat god ʒif vs *grace* her ⁋ ar we hennes wende
10 þat aft*er* oure deþe day // dowel reherse
at þe day of dome we dide as he taghte amen
Explicit visio willi*elmi* w.[3] de Petro le[4] Plowma*n*
Et[5] hic incipit visio eiusdem de Dowel
Thus yrobed in russet ⁋ I romed aboute
15 al a somer sesoun / for to seke dowel
and frayned ful ofte of folc // þat I mette
If eny wight[2] wiste ⁋ wher dowel was at Inne
and what man he myghte be // of many men I asked
was neuer wight[2] in þe worlde ⁋ þat me wisse couþe
20 where þis longed ⁋ lasse no more
Til it bifell*e* on a friday ⁋ tuo freres I mette
maist*er*es of þe menour ⁋ men of gret witte
I hailsede hem hendely ⁋ as I hadde lered
and prayed hem þur charite ⁋ er þey passed forþere
25 If þey knewe eny cuntr*e* // oþ*er* coostes aboute
where þat Dowel dwellede dere frendes telleþ me
ffor ʒe are men of þis molde ⁋ þat most wide walken
and knowen cuntrees and courtes ⁋ & many kyn places
Boþe p*r*inces paleys ⁋ and pour*e* men cotes
30 and dowel and do euele wher þey duellen boþe
Soþely saide þe frer*e* ⁋ he soiourneþ *with* vs freres

1. Obliterations supplied from Skeat, p. 176. 2. Bar through *h* seems otiose but may represent final *c.* 3. Possibly dittography. 4. Only MS with *le.* 5. *Et* unnoted by Skeat (E.E.T.S., o.s., 54, 1873, 176–9).

Notes

About 53 MSS of *Piers Plowman* survive, 19 of them being C-text. None of them is holograph, and little is known of the author or authors. The present MS is one of two C-text manuscripts housed in the Senate House Library, University of London (the other being MS V. 17), having previously belonged to the Earl of Ilchester. It is described by N. R. Ker, *Mediaeval manuscripts in British Libraries,* I, 1969, 377–8; E. T. Donaldson, *Piers Plowman, the C-text and its poet,* rev. 1966, app. A; R. W. Chambers, *HLB,* VIII, 1935, 19–20; and by Skeat in his edition of the C-text, E.E.T.S., o.s., 54, 1873, xxxiii–viii, who collates it as manuscript I. Although basically an imperfect C-text contaminated by a bad A-text, it contains some very good readings which, according to Skeat and Chambers, may derive from the poet's first drafts (e.g. Passus X, 128–40). Even in Skeat's time the damaged state of the manuscript was much in evidence, it being described by him as 'spoiled by damp and much injured by rats' with nearly every page lacking corners.

Characteristics. The manuscript is a fine example of *anglicana formata* penmanship. It not only has the characteristic boldness and clarity of the script, but is remarkably regular in the size of letters, well spaced, and has a pleasing appearance of roundness conveyed mainly by the minims, which often have curved links at both ends, and some of the ascenders, though the heads of some of the letters, notably *a* and *e,* are generally pointed. The hand is certainly rounder than Ellesmere's and somewhat smaller. The ascenders of *f* and long *s* are noticeably shorter too, and *a* barely rises above the bodies of the other letters. Instead of the squarish *8*-form final *s* of Ellesmere there is, as in 15th-century *secretary,* the French cursive *B* form (which may perhaps explain the intrusion of *le* in line 12). *Thorn,* used throughout for *th,* is quite squat and resembles a *wyn* (as in the *Gawayn* MS). The usual forked *r* and the *2* form after *o,* tagged or untagged, are present, and there are instances of *ʒ g, y* (ll. 9, 27). Initial *T* is in gold on a blue

ground blocked in light brown and veined in white. The attached daisy buds have olive green calixes and brown tops also veined in white. The explicit and incipit (ll. 12–13) are rubricated.

Punctuation and abbreviation. The point is used twice in l. 12 to denote curtailment, and the double virgule (in one case a single virgule, l. 15) indicates the caesura, being usually surmounted by a red or blue capitulum (the latter showing up darker in the photograph). The capitulum seems to have been added later, and is sometimes accidentally omitted. Occasionally, caesural indication is entirely lacking. Abbreviation includes the bar for general contraction (l. 3, *lettres;* l. 12, *Willielmi*), for final *e* (l. 21, *bifelle*), and *n* (l. 6, *pardoun*); ' for *er* (l. 3) and, linked to final *r,* for *e* (l. 25); crossed *þ* for *par* (l. 6), *þ* with the concave curve for *pro* (l. 3, *prouynciales*); superior *i* for *ri* (ll. 7, 29), *w^t* for *with* (l. 31); the symbol resembling single-lobed *a* for *ur* (l. 22) and the Tironian nota surmounted by a bar for *and* (l. 28).

Wher of may wel be iustified
pat yei may nought be deified
And wip pat taketh alwey theonõ
Which due is to ye creatour

5 And yifey it to ye creature
He dop to greet aforfaiture
But of Chaldee natheles
Vpon yis feith· pough it beles
They holde affermed ye creance

10 So pat of helle ye penance
As folk Which stant out of beleue
Yei schul receyue as ye bileue
Of ye Chaldeus lo in yis wise
Stant ye beleue out of assise

15 But in Egipte worst of alle
ye feyp is fals hou so it falle
ffor yei diuise bestes there
Honoure as pough yei goddes were
And napeles zit forth wip al

20 Yre goddes maost in special
They haue· forth wip a goddesse
In whom is al her likernesse
Yoo goddes be zit clepid thus
Orus· Typhon· and Isirus

25 They were dreyen alle yre
And ye goddesse in hir degre
Hir suster was and pis highte
Whom ysirus forlay be nyghte
And helde hir after as his wyf

30 So it bifel pat vpon stryf
Typhon hap yslawe his broy Clayn
Which hadde a child to sone Orayn
And he his fadir dey toherte
So tok· pat it may nough asterte

And pat ye lond bigan to greyne
Which Whilom hadde be bareyne
ffor ye erye lay aftir ye kinde
His due charche· yis I finde
pat sche of verye ye goddesse
Is cleped· so pat in destresse
The women yer vpon childinge
To hire depe· and here offringe
yei beren· Whan pat yei ben lighte
lo hou Egipte al out of sighte
ffro resou stant in misbileue
ffor lack of lore as I beleue
Among ye Greks out of ye were
As yei that resou putte alwey
Ther was as ye Crounq seith
Of misbileue anoy feith
pat yei her goddes and goddesses
As who seip token al to gesses
Of suche as were ful of vice
To whom yei maden here sacrifice
ye hihe god so as yei seide
To whom yei most worschipe leide
Saturus highte· and king of crete:
He hadde be· but of his sete
He was put don: as he which stood
In frenesie· and was so wood
pat fro his wif Which Rea highte
His owne children he toplighte
And eet hem of his comun wone
But Jupiter Which was his sone
And of ful age his fadir bond
And cutte off wip his owne hond
His genitals· Which also faste
Into ye depe see he caste

52

◉ John Gower (*c.* 1330–*c.* 1408)

6 *Confessio Amantis* (final rev. 1393): Book V, ll. 775–808;
823–55. *Textura semiquadrata formata*, early 15th century.
U.C.L., MS Frag. Anglia I, f. 1, upper portion.

Wher of may wel be iustifyed
Þat þei may nought be deified
And who þat takiþ awey theonour
Which due is to þe creatour
5 And ʒifeþ it to þe creature
He doþ to greet aforfaiture
But of Chaldee natheles
Uppon þis feith · þough it beles
They holde affermed þe creance
10 So þat of helle þe penance
As folk which stant out of beleue
Þei schul receyue as we bileue
Of þe Chaldeus lo in þis wise
Stant þe belieue out of assise
15 But in Egipte worst of alle
Þe feiþ is fals how so it falle
ffor þei diuerse bestes there
Honoure as þough þei goddes were
And naþeles ʒit forth wiþ al
20 Þre goddes moost in special
Thei haue · forth wiþ a goddesse
In whom is al her sikernesse
Þoo goddes be ʒit clepid thus
Orus · Tiphon · and Isirus
25 Thei were breþeren alle þre
And þe goddesse in hir degre
Hir sustir was and Isis highte
Whom ysirus forlay be nyghte
And hield hir after as his wyf
30 So it bifel þat vppon stryf
Tiphon haþ Isre his broþer slayn
Which hadde a child to sone Orayn
And he his fadir deþ to herte
So tok · þat it may nough asterte

And þat þe lond bigan to greyne
Which whilom hadde be bareyne
ffor þe erþe bar aftir þe kinde
His due charche · þis I finde
Þat sche of berþe þe goddesse
Is cleped · so þat in destresse
The wommen þer vppon childinge
To hire clepe · and here offringe
Þei beren · whan þat þei ben lighte
Lo how Egipte al out of sighte
ffro resoun stant in mysbilieue
ffor lack of lore as I beleue
Among þe Greks out of þe weie
As þei that resoun putte aweye
Ther was as þe Cronique seith
Of mysbelieue anoþer feith
Þat þei her goddes and goddesses
As who seiþ token al to gesses
Of suche as were ful of vice
To whom þei maden here sacrifice
Þe hihe god so as þei seide
To whom þei most worschipe leide
Saturnus highte · and king of crete:
He hadde be · but of his sete
He was putt doun ⸵ as he which stood
In frenesie · and was so wood
Þat fro his wif which Rea highte
His owne children he toplighte
And eet hem of his comun wone
But Iupiter which was his sone
And of ful age his fadir bond
And cutte off wiþ his owne hond
His genitals · which also faste
Into þe deepe see he caste

Notes

The *Confessio Amantis*, which like *Piers Plowman* exists in three different versions, was an extremely popular work, and 50 complete or nearly complete MSS of it have survived (33 of A text, 7 of B, 10 of C) as well as 10 MS extracts (*vide MEV*; *MVS*; C. C. Macaulay, E.E.T.S., e.s., 81, 1900, cxxvii–clxx; J. Fisher, *John Gower*, 1964, pp. 116–27, app.). The present example is a fragment of four leaves from Book V, containing ll. 775–966, 1159–1542 and 1735–1926, and may well be part of an apparently lost manuscript of the complete work. Formerly Phillipps MS 22914, it was presented to University College London in 1911, and is discussed in D. K. Coveney, *A descriptive catalogue of manuscripts in the library of University College London*, 1935, 18, with an illustration (plate 3) from f. 4v. Macaulay in his edition of *Confessio Amantis* (*op. cit.*, clxvi)

mentions the fragment but had not seen it.
Characteristics. A careful and evenly written gothic book hand, with lozenges and broken strokes at the heads of many of the letters, but usually with rounded serifs at the base, hence the name *semiquadrata*. There is also forking at the tops of many ascenders. Two types of *a* appear: the usual straight-sided, small capital form, (a, ll. 1, 2) and one with the open or absent upper lobe (b, ll. 6, 8, 9). Biting occurs in *de*, *do* and *ba* (a, ll. 2, 6; b. l. 3). Ligatures include *pp* (a, l. 8) and occasionally *st* (b, l. 6). Short *s*, somewhat resembling a closed *9*, is used invariably in final position. The regular form of book hand *r* is used except after *o* when the *2* form occurs as expected (b, l. 3). *Thorn*, looking much like a straight-tailed *y*, alternates with *th*, and *yogh* appears occasionally

(a, ll. 5, 19, 23). Capitals are decorated with parallel lines, and hairstrokes often act as tags and finials, e.g. final *t*, *f* and *s*. Initial *O* is in gold with purple ink flourishes; initial *A* in deep blue with red ink flourishes. The page has running title, ❡ *Quintus*; marginal heading opposite initial *O*: ❡ *De secta Egiptorum*; opposite initial *A*, right margin: ❡ *De secta Grecorum*.
Punctuation and abbreviation. There are four marks of punctuation: the lozenge-shaped raised point, inverted semicolon, colon (b, l. 23), and the diacritic for *i*. Abbreviation comprises a curved bar resembling a comma on its side for *m* or *n* (b, ll. 7, 11), raised *a* symbol for *ur* (a, l. 3; b, l. 23), a lozenge-shaped raised point, presumably intended as ' for *er* (b, l. 16), and *3* for *ue* (b, l. 15).

Oon tyme was no enyvhethy trwm na they
Ne no manhode sheeld in no wyse
But Oldcastel colde his thankes be they
Hoc hath the cursid feend changid thy gyse
Flee from him and all his workes despyse

5 And yt y doon on to our cristen kyng
Thee hie as faste / as y thow canst dryvse
And humble eck thee to him / for any thyng
ꝗ III   III

) Cest tout

10 Cy ensuyt la male regle de T. Hoccleue.

O precious tresor incomparable
O ground & roote of prosperitee
O excellent richesse commendable
Aboven all yt in eerthe be
15 Who may susteene thyn aduersitee
What wight may thy auante of worldly welthe
But if he fully stande in grace of thee
Eerthely god, piler of lyf, thow helthe
ꝗ III   III

7　Closing lines of *Address to Sir John Oldcastle* (1415) and beginning of *La male regle* (1406). *Secretaria formata/facilis*, with heading in *secretaria hybrida*, holograph, *c*. 1425–30. H.L., HM 111, f. 16v.

Sum tyme was no knyghtly[1] turn nowher*e*
Ne no manhode shewid in no wyse
But Oldcastel wolde his thankes be ther*e*
How hath the cursid feend changid thy gyse
5　fflee from him and all*e* his wirkes despyse
And þ*at* y doon ⸳ vn to our cristen kyng
Thee hie as faste / as þ*at* thow canst dyuyse
And humble eek*e*[2] thee to him / for any thyng

———————

) Cest tout (

10　Cy ensuyt la male regle de T. Hoccleue.

O precious tresor inconparable
O ground & roote of Prosperitee
O excellent richesse commendable
Abouen all*e* / þ*at* in eerthe be
15　Who may susteene thyn adu*er*sitee
What wight[1] may hi*m* auante of worldly welthe
But if he fully stande in grace of thee
Eerthely god / piler of lyf / thow helthe

———————

1. otiose bar through *h*. 2. Normally abbreviation for *es* or *is*.

———————

Notes

Hoccleve, perhaps because he was a trained scribe, is the only early English poet whose works have survived in great abundance in holograph, proof of his hand having been securely established by H. Schulz in *Spec.*, xii, 1937, 72–81. Schulz demonstrates that, despite variations in style of writing, Hoccleve's poems in Durham Univ., Cosin MS V. iii, 9, and Huntington Library, HM 111 and 744 are all holograph, and he provides two plates of examples from four MSS (Croft, no. 3, gives a further example from HM 744). The present MS, previously Phillipps MS 8151 and once part of the library of James I's son, Prince Henry, was transcribed by F. J. Furnivall, E.E.T.S., e.s., 61, 1892 (*vide* esp. 24–5). **Characteristics.** A fairly compact, neat and fluent book-hand form of 15th-century *secretary*, certainly when compared with his more current hand in B.L., Add MS 24062, f. 101v (Schulz, *op. cit.*, pl. Ia) where the letters are spread out, with many more ligatures, cursive reversed *e*, and with the *anglicana* forked *r* and sigma *s*

quite prominent. Here, most of the features of 15th-century *secretary* are present. There are horns and indentation on many of the letters, especially *a*, *e* and initial *d* (possibly a capital *d*, ll. 5, 6, 7); long tapering descenders for *f* and long *s* (both usually in two strokes); *a* has a single compartment; the lower bowl of *anglicana g* has given way to a tail. Forked *r* is now infrequent, being confined mainly to final position (ll. 6, 18) often in conjunction with ' for *re*, and the most common *r* is the *v* type, though the *2* or *z* form is present not only after *o* but after þ and *t* as well (l. 11). Final *s* is the small capital *B* type, often with a little spur at the top (l. 5). Schulz (*op. cit.*, 72 ff.) draws attention to four letters as determinants of Hoccleve's hand: *A*, *g*, *w*, *y*, and certainly these have distinctive features, especially the *A* with its large initial figure *8* loops (ll. 6, 8), the *y* with a tail often ascending well above the line, (l. 6) and the 'circle and 2' form of *w* which dates back to the early 14th century, as in the Harley Lyrics (*EVH*, 9) and as recorded in

ECH (53, no. 9). The *w* is here transcribed as a minuscule except at the beginning of a line when it is capitalized (ll. 15, 16) to conform with practice in the other lines. The heading (l. 10), which contains a form of signature, is in a *hybrid* or *bastard secretary* (a mixture of formal book hand and cursive) with typical forms of *a* and *g*, and Hoccleve generally uses this hand for his titles and incipits, e.g. in HM 111, f. 26; B.L., Add MS 24062, f. 194v (Schulz, *op. cit.*, pl. I, b, c).
Punctuation and abbreviation. Punctuation includes the point (l. 10); the virgule (l. 7); the inverted semicolon, shaped like *S* (l. 6); the diacritic for *i* (l. 5); and a form of brackets (l. 9), normally used to enclose material not part of the main text (*vide* Hector, 48). Common marks of abbreviation are used: crossed *ll* for *lle* (l. 14), the bar for *m* (l. 16), ' for *er* when linked to *u* (l. 15) and for *e* when linked to *r* (l. 1), þ*t* for *that* (l. 6), and the Tironian nota resembling *z* enclosed by an arc for *and* (l. 12).

	And eke my master chaucers þ nou is graue
	The noble rethor poete of Britayne
	That worthi was þe lauret to haue
	Of poetri and þe palme atteyne
5	That made first to distille and reyn
	The goldyn dropis of speche & eloquence
	In to our tunge þronze his excellence
	And fonde þe flouris first of rethorike
	Our rude speche for to elumine
10	That in our tunge was neu oon hi like
	for as þe son dope in heuē schyne
	In mydday spere down to vs by shne
	In whos presence no sterr may appere
	Ryzt so his ditees wtout eny pere
15	Eny makyng wt her lizt disteyne
	In sopfastnes ho so takiþ hede
	Wherfor no wonder þou my hert pleyne
	Vppon his dey & for sorow blede
	for want of hi now in my gret nede
20	That scholde allas couuey & directe
	And wt his supporte amende & correcte

	And eke my mastur Chaucers is grad
	The nobill rethor and poete of Brytayn
	That worthy was the lauuer for to hade
	The poetre and the palme attoyn
5	Wich makid furst for to distill & reyn
	The gold selue droppis of spech & oloquence
	Into our tung þrwth his excellence
	And fond the fflouris furst of rethorik
	Our rude speche ouly for to enlumyne
10	That in our tunge wes nobir noon hym like
	ffor as the sune dorth on heuen shyne
	In mydday spere down to vs be hne
	In whose presence no sterr mey apper
	Ryzt so his detees with out eny fere

56

8 *Life of Our Lady* (*c.* 1409–11?): Bk. II, ll. 1628–48, Chaucer eulogy. *Fere-textura rotunda formata, c.* mid-15th century?
C.U.L., Mm. 6.5, f. 61.

And eke my master chaucers þat now[1] is graue ⟦ 30
  The noble rethor poete of Britayne
  That worthi was þe lauret to haue
  Of poetri and þe palme atteyne
5 That made first to distille and reyn
  The goldyn dropis of speche & eloquence
  In to our tunge[2] prouȝe his excellence

⟦And fonde þe flouris first of rethorike
  Our rude speche for to elumine
10 That in our tunge[2] was neuer oon him like
  ffor as þe son doþe in heuen schyne
  In mydday spere doun to vs by lyne
  In whos presence no sterr may appere
  Riȝt so his ditees without eny pere

15 ⟦Euery makyng with her liȝt disteyne
  In soþfastnes ho so takyþ hede
  Wher for no wonder þon my hert pleyne
  Vppon his deþ & for sorow blede
  ffor want of him now in my gret nede
20 That scholde allas conueyn & directe
  And with his supporte amende & correcte

1. The red marks above *now* possibly indicate deletion: many MSS do not have the word, and the line does not scan with it. 2. Bar above *n* probably otiose.

9 *Life of Our Lady* (*c.* 1409–11?): Bk. II, ll. 1628–41, Chaucer eulogy. *Anglicana formata/media* mixed with *secretaria, c.* mid-15th century.
C.U.L., Kk. 1.3, pt. x, f. 40v, lower portion excluding last four lines.

And eke my mastir Chawcere is grave
  The nobill[1] Rethor and poete of Brytayne
  That worthy was the laurer for to have
  The Poetre and the palme atteyne
5 Wich makid first for to distill[1] & reyne
  The gold dewe droppis of spech & eloquence
  In to our tung þurh his excellence

And fond the fflouris first of Retherik
  Oure rude speche oonly for to enlumyne
10 That in our tunge was nevir noon hym like
  ffor as the sone doith on heben shyne
  In mydday spere down to vs be lyne
  In whose presence no Sterr may appere
  Riȝt so his detees with out eny pere

1. Bar through *ll* probably otiose.

Notes

Though Lydgate holographs are still lacking, there is no shortage of MSS of his copious works. His *Life of Our Lady*, a lengthy poem of 5936 lines in *rime royal*, one of the most widely read works in the 15th century, exists in 42 MSS, collated in the critical edition by J. A. Lauritis, R. A. Klinefelter and V. F. Gallagher, Duquesne Studies, 1961. The two Cambridge University MSS reproduced here have not been adequately collated in this edition and contain important variant readings, not all of which have been recorded. This is especially true of no. 8. (l. 1, *chaucers þat now is graue* for *Chauser is ygraue*; l. 3, *lauret*, probably a misreading of *laurer*; l. 6, *goldyn dropis* for *golde dewe, dropes*; l. 15, *her* for *his*; cf. ed. cited above, 426–7). Whereas the MS of no. 8 contains only the *Life* and is in excellent condition, that of no. 9 is part of a much larger collection and is badly damaged by damp (see further ed., 34–6; *Catalogue of the mss. in the library of C.U.*, 1861, III, 554; IV, 383).
Characteristics of no. 8. An individual and beautifully executed book hand which seems based on *textualis rotunda* from its general

appearance, proportions, rounded serifs, the *g* (l. 1), and biting in *de* (l. 5). It also shows *anglicana formata* influence, seen in the double-lobed *a*, used throughout, but also suggested by the shafts of long *s* and *f*, which go slightly below the line, and the short loops on *h* and *l*. *Bastard* or *hybrid anglicana* forms are present, in particular *d* (though this is also influenced by *rotunda*). The *6* form of final *s* appears to be a compromise between the cursive sigma of *anglicana* and the *B* form of 15th-century *secretary*. If the hand had to be placed in an established category, it would be closest to *hybrid anglicana*, but the designation *fere-textura* or quasi-text hand seems most appropriate (cf. examples in Parkes, 8, ii; *EVH*, 19). *Thorn* alternates with *th*; *yogh* is used for *gh* (l. 7). Initial *A*, one of the many fine illuminations in the MS, is in gold on blue and violet quarters. First letters of lines are decorated with a vertical red stroke.
Punctuation and abbreviation. Proper names are underlined (ll. 1, 2), *y* is dotted, the point is used after the numeral (margin), and a long diagonal diacritic for *i*. Abbreviation

comprises the bar for *m* and *n* (ll. 10, 11); ' formed like *c* for *er* (l. 10); *w*[t] for *with* (l. 21); þ[t] for *that*; and the symbol resembling crossed *i* with a bar above for *and* (l. 6).
Characteristics of no. 9. This has the typical heavy-stroked compact look of *anglicana formata* but a greater degree of cursiveness. All the usual *anglicana* letter forms are present: double lobed *a*, looped *d*, sigma *s* in final position, ordinary *e* and reversed *e* of cursive *anglicana*, long *r* (l. 13) and two compartment *g* (l. 6). There are several letters from 15th-century *secretary*, e.g. the v type of *r* (l. 6) and *r* with the detached headstroke (l. 1, *mastir*); the tailed *g* with a crossbar, especially common in the 2nd quarter of the century (l. 1, *graue*); and the backwards leaning *w*. *Thorn* is occasionally used (l. 7) and ȝ for *gh* (l. 14). There are no marks of **punctuation**, which is generally very sparse in the MS.
Abbreviation. A hook linked to the arm of long *r* indicates *e* (l. 13); the curved bar on final *n* may be otiose but probably signifies omitted *e*.

5

10

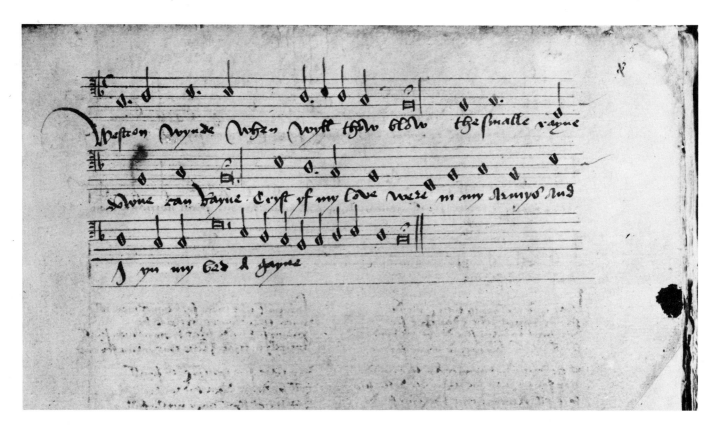

10 Letter to John Norwode, *c.* 1453. Late *anglicana currens*.
Last 3½ lines and signature Paston, the rest in hand of
James Gloys.
B.L., Add MS 27444, f. 20, lower portion. Reduced by 1/10.

I*tem* the seid litill[1] hows drawyth not v thowsand tyle which aft*er* xvjd the
Thowsand shuld drawe vjs[1] viijd Notwithstandyng if s*ir* Thom*a*s thynk that he
shuld be a lowyd m⟨o⟩ he shall be // [but] [and] ye must remembre [in this newe
werk] how that he [for the seid caret [werk] nobill[1]] hath receyvid vjs viijd of you
and [viijs] of Robert Tolle be fore halwemesse as apperth in his accompt[1] / [viijs]
and [what] he hath receyvid of Tolle sith halwemesse [vs iiijd] [Tolle can telle
you I suppose it is xs[1]] and than be this rekenyng he shuld be [xviijs] [xiijs iiijd] a
fore hand / Which Ī wuld ye shuld gader vp in this newe werk aswele as ye
myght[1] for I am be hold to do hym but litill[1] favo*ur* //[2] I*tem* be ware þer leve no
firsis [mo] in þe deke / þat ye rep*ar*re / & þat þe wode be mad of fagot & leyd vp
forthwoth as it is fellid for taki*n*g away // I wold ye we*re* her on satirday at Euy[3]
thow ye red ageyn on moneday

Ion[4] Paston

1. Otiose brevigraph. 2. Paston's hand begins with the double virgule. 3. *n* probably omitted
(*Euyn* for *even*). 4. The flourish may represent *h*.

Notes

The letters of the Paston family of Norfolk form the largest and most varied collection of English private correspondence in the 15th century. They are now mainly housed in the B.L. and Part I of a new and comprehensive edition of them has been published by N. Davis, *Paston letters and papers*, 1971 (*vide* transcr. 74–5), together with 11 plates illustrating hands of the different members of the family. John Paston senior, son of William, is among the second generation of letter writers in the series. He was educated at Cambridge and the Inner Temple, married Margaret Mautby *c.* 1440, and his chequered career included three periods of imprisonment. James Gloys, the scribe for most of the letter, was chaplain and secretary to John and Margaret Paston, and many of their letters are in his hand (*vide* Davis, *op. cit.*, liv ff., lxxvi). Other scribes for John and Margaret were James Gresham and John Pampyng (*id.*, lxxvii).

Characteristics. Somewhat hastily written throughout, the Gloys portion is broad, bold and somewhat clumsy, with generous loops and long descenders; the Paston section is in a thin scrawl, perhaps partly explaining why so little of his correspondence is in his hand. Both writers are, however, attempting much the same letter forms. As in many other Paston letters, even those written as late as in the 1480s, the two hands are basically *anglicana* (*currens*) though with some *secretary* forms (cf. Parkes, pl. 24, iii). The most prominent *anglicana* letters are the cursive sigma *s*, always in final position and sometimes initially (l. 1, *seid*); long-stemmed forked *r*, *d* and *h* with looped stem (l. 1, *drawyth*), and the double-lobed *a* looking much like a capital *A*—a particularly common form in this period—(l. 2, *that*). Among other *anglicana* letters may be counted *b* and *l*. The *secretary* letters include the single-lobed *a* and *g* which curls counter-clockwise and ends in a flourish above the line (l. 2, *Notwithstandyng*); but there is also apparently a modified *anglicana* two-compartment *g* (l. 7, *myght*). Reversed or circular *e* and '*ll* and reversed *c*' form of *w* used here are common in 15th-century *secretary*, though both derive from *anglicana* (cf., e.g., *EVH*, pl. 17). Gloys uses a distinctive *5* form or open sigma *s* after *i* (*this*, l. 6). Paston employs *thorn* fairly frequently, in a form closely resembling *y* (l. 8, *þer*).

Punctuation comprises an occasional single virgule, and double virgule for paragraphing (l. 8).

Abbreviation includes crossed *þ* for *par* (l. 9), a hooked ' linked to crossbar of *t* for *er* (l. 1, *after*) or simple curtailment (l. 1, *Item*); and elaborate ' on the end of *r* for *e* (l. 8, *be ware*); a symbol for *ur* (l. 8, *fauour*); a curved bar, sometimes with a point below it, for *m* or *n* (l. 10, *taking*) and the symbol like *z* within an arc for *and* (l. 9).

Westron wynde (*c.* end 15th cent., anon.)

11 *Secretaria facilis*, *c.* end 15th century.
B.L., Royal, append. 58, f. 5.

Westron wynde when wyll*e* thow blow
the smalle rayne downe can Rayne
Cryst yf my love were in my Armys
And I yn my bed A gayne

Notes

One of the most famous and shortest love lyrics in the English language, this poem survives only in the one MS, a tenor part-book. It is often mistranscribed: *yf* being misread as þ*t*, though a *thorn* would be more upright than the *y* of this text, and *f* is easily distinguished from *t* by its long stem and hook at the top. The bar on *will* is sometimes taken as otiose rather than as an abbreviation for *e*. Grammatically, the best reading is *wilt*, and it is possible that the scribe misread *lt* in his copy as crossed *ll*. For a bibliography *vide MVS*, 3899.3.

Characteristics. An angular and somewhat splayed hand typical of the later 15th century, necessarily compact to fit beneath the notes in this mainly monosyllabic setting. Particularly noticeable is the pointed appearance of the minims, *g*, *I* and *w*, and the wide variety of letters, including three types of *r*: book-hand *r* (*Cryst*), *v* form (*rayne*) and modified *z* form (*were*). There are four graphs of *d*: three have a diamond-shaped body, but the shaft is straight and oblique (*wynde*), or ends in a curl (*bed*), or has an *anglicana* loop (*And*); and the fourth has a larger and indented body (*downe*). There are no marks of **punctuation**, nor is any usual in underlay in this period, and a space rather than a hyphen is common for indicating syllabication (e.g. *A gayne*). The bar through *ll* is the only **abbreviation**, and even this may be a misreading, as suggested above. The same hand occurs on the facing page of the MS, f. 4v.

Fulle Hym þat all this world has wroght
Nowe kysse me hartely I þe pray
Isaak I take my leue for ay / þe bus ye mys
my blissyng haue you euerlay
5 And I beseke god all myghty / þe kysse þe his
Thus aren we samyn assent
Eftur thy wordis wyse
Lorde god to þis take tente
Ressayue thy Sacrifice
10 This is to me A perles pyne
To se myn awne dere childe þus bonne
He had wele leuer my lyf to tyne
Than see þis sight þus of my sone
It is goddis wiłł it sall be myne
15 Agaynste his saande sall I neuer stone
To goddis cummaundement I sall enclyne
That in me fawte non be fonne
Therfore my sone so dere
If you wiłł any thyng saye
20 Thy dede it drawes nere
Fare wele for anes and ay

Isaac

Now my dere fadir I wolde you praye
Here me thre wordes graunte me my bone
25 Sen I fro this sall passe for ay
I see myn houre is comen full sone
In worde in werke or any waye
That I haue trespassed or oght mysdone
Forgiffe me fadir or I dye þis daye
30 For his luffe þat made boye sonne and mone
Here sen we two sall twynne
Firste god I aske mercy
And you in more and myne
35 This day or ells I dy

Abraham

Now my grete god Adonay

60

12 'Abraham and Isaac', ll. 229–63. *Secretaria hybrida formata*, *c.* late-15th century.
B.L., Add MS 35290, f. 35v.

The parchemynars and bokebyndars

Tylle hym þat all[1] this world has wroght
Nowe kysse me hartely I þe pray
Isaak I take my leue for ay // Me bus þe mys
5 My blissyng haue þou enterly
And I beseke god all myghty — He giffe þe[2] his
Thus aren we samyn assent[3]
Eftir thy wordis wise
lorde god to þis take tente[4]
10 Ressayue thy Sacrifice
This is to me a perles pyne
To se myn nawe dere childe þus boune
Me had wele leuer my lyf to tyne
Than see þis sight þus of my sone
15 It is goddis will it sall be myne
A gaynste his saande sall I neuer schone
To goddis Cummaundement I sall enclyne
That in me fawte non be foune
Therfore my sone so dere
20 If þou will any thyng saye
Thy dede it drawes nere
ffare wele for anes and ay
————————————————— Isaac
Now my dere fadir I wolde you praye
25 Here me thre wordes graunte me my bone
Sen I fro this sall passe for ay
I See myn houre is comen full sone
In worde in werke or any waye
That I haue trespassed or oght mysdone
30 ffor giffe me fadir or I dye þis daye
ffor his luffe þat made boþe sonne and mone
Here sen we two sall twynne
ffirste god I aske mercy
And you in more and myne
35 This day or euere I dy
————————————————— Abraham
Now my grete god Adonay

1. Every final *ll* has a bar, probably otiose, possibly brevigraph for *e*. 2. Beginning of *h* above þe. 3. Erasure of three words, the last of which is possibly *witnyse*. 4. The 1568 Protestant reviser has enclosed ll. 7–10 for deletion, marking the cut by *hic* in the right margin (cf. Craig, *English religious drama*, 1955, 201).

Notes
The York cycle of plays survives in a single MS which originally belonged to the city corporation of York and was for a time in the care of Holy Trinity Priory, Micklegate. It passed into the hands of the Fairfax family of Yorkshire and belonged to Lord Ashburton prior to being acquired by the British Library. It is mainly in one hand throughout, thought to be about a century later than the final form of composition (Craig, *op. cit.*, 200, dates it 1430–40), and is considered to be a fair copy rather than a prompt copy. Here, as elsewhere, the name of the craft responsible for the play appears as a running title, rhymes are indicated by braces, long red rules mark off speeches, and characters' names, also rubricated, are given in the right margin. Initial letters of each line are stroked in red. For a transcription *vide* L. Toulmin Smith, *The York Plays*, 1885, repr. 1963, with introduction and facsimiles.
Characteristics. Apart from the names of characters which are in *hybrid anglicana* (and possibly by a different scribe), the text is in *secretary* with some basic *textura* features in the formation of the bodies of letters, especially *o, e* and *d* and to a lesser extent in the minims. Descenders are quite long and tapering, and ascenders generally have small rounded arches, except that in the top line, as was customary, they are much taller. A typical *hybrid* letter is *g* with the short tail and headstroke (l. 5). Single-lobed and pointed *secretary a* is generally used, though there is occasionally the capital form or variant of the double lobe (l. 3), transcribed here as a minuscule except at the beginning of a line and in proper names. Final *s* is the *B* form but sometimes the top is open like a *6* (l. 14; cf. pl. 8). Short *r* with a slightly curled base regularly occurs and has a flourish in final position (l. 13) but the *z* form appears not only after *o* but occasionally *a* and *e* also (ll. 3, 5). *Thorn* is almost indistinguishable from *y*.
Punctuation consists of rules, braces, diacritic for *i* and a double virgule form of caret (l. 4).
Abbreviation includes the bar for *m* (l. 17), ' for *er* (l. 35), *a* with a headstroke for *ra* and a serrated line for *a* (l. 36, cf. pl. 3).

So aftir thes questis of Sir Gawayne Sir
Tor and kynge Pellynore than hit be felle that Merly
on felle in dotage on the damesell that kynge Pellynore
brought to courte and she was one of the damesels of the lady of the
lake that hyght Nenyve But Merlion wolde natt lette her have
no reste but all wayes he wolde be wyth her And ever she made
good chere tylle she had lerned of hym all man of thyng
that she desyred and he was assoted uppon hir that he
myght nat be frome hir So on a tyme he tolde to kynge
Arthure that he scholde nat endure longe but for all
his craffte he scholde be putte in to the erthe quyk and so
he tolde the kyng many thyngis that scholde befalle
but all wayes he warned the kyng to kepe well his swer
de and the scawberde scholde be stolyn by a woman frome
hym that he moste trusted Also he tolde kyng Arthure
that he scholde mysse hym And yett had ye lever than all
youre londis have me agayne A sayde the kyng syn ye
knowe of youre evil adventure purvey for hit and putt
hit a way by youre crauffte that mysse adventure Nay seyde
Merlion hit wolt not be he departed frome the kyng And within
a whyle the damesell of the lake departed and Merlyon
went with her evermore where som ever she yeode and oftyn ty
mes Merlion wolde have had hir prevayly a way by his subtyle
crauffte Than she made hym to swere that he scholde never do
none inchauntemente uppon hir if she wolde have his will
And so he swore Than she and Merlyon wente on the see un
to the londe of Benwyke there as kyng Ban was kyng
that had grete warre ayenste kyng Claudas And there
Merlion spake with kyng Ban wyff a fayre lady and a good and hir
name was Elayne And there he sawe yonge Launcelot
And there the queene made grete sorowe for the mortal
werre that kyng Claudas made on hir londis Take

13 *Morte Darthur* (1469/70): beginning of 'The Death of Merlin', Bk. IV. Scribe A, ll. 1–6, *textura quadrata* (l. 1) and *secretaria (hybrida) formata*; Scribe B, ll. 7–32, *secretaria formata/facilis, c.* 1470–80.
Winchester College, Malory MS, f. 45.

So aftir thes questis of Syr Gawayne Syr Tor and kynge Pellynore Than hit be felle that Merlyon felle in dotage on the damesell[1] that kynge Pellynore brought to courte and she was / one of the damesels / of the lady of the laake that hyght Nenyve But Merlion · wolde nat lette her haue no reste but / all wayes / he wolde be wyth . her And eu*er* she made M*er* good chere tylle sche had lerned of hym all man*er* of thyng*e* that sche desyred and he was assoted vppon*e* hir that he myght nat be from*e* hir // So on a tyme he tolde to kynge Arthure that he scholde nat endure longe but for all his craft*es* he scholde be putte In to the erthe quyk and so he tolde the kyng many thyngis that scholde be falle but all wayes he warned the kyng to kepe well his swerde and the scawberde scholde be stolyn by a woman frome hym that he moste trusted // Also he tolde kyng Arthure that he scholde mysse hym. And yett had ye levir than all youre londis haue me a gayne // A sayde the kyng*e* syn ye knowe of youre evil · aduenture purvey for hit and putt hit a way by youre crauft*es* that mysse aduenture Nay seyde M*er* · hit woll not be. he dep*ar*ted from*e* the kyng*e* And w*ith* In a whyle the damesell of the lake dep*ar*ted and Merlyon*e* went w*ith* here euermore where som eu*er* she yeode and oftyn tymes M*er*. wolde haue had hir prevayly a way by his subtyle crauft*es*. Than she made hym to swere that he sholde neu*er* do none inchauntemente vppon hir if he wolde haue his wil· And so he swore · Than she and Merlyon wente ou*er* þe see vn to the londe of Benwyke there as kyng*e* Ban was kyng*e* that had grete warre a yenste kyng*e* Claudas And there M*er*· spake w*ith* kyng*e* Baya*n*s wyff a fayre lady and a good hir name was Elayne And there he sawe yonge launcelot And there the queene made grete sorowe for the mortal · werre that kyng*e* Claudas made on hir lordis // Take

1. Bar through *ll* probably otiose in all cases.

Notes

Although the MS of Malory's *Morte Darthur* (discovered in 1934 by W. F. Oakeshott) is at least two stages removed from the original, it is more authoritative and probably earlier than Caxton's edition of 1485. It is thought to have been copied out in London, where Malory was in prison for a time and where the volume seems to have been repaired around 1500. The watermark on the paper is nearly identical to one on a document dated 1485, and Oakeshott (*The Times*, 25 Aug. 1934) has suggested 1470–80 as the date of the manuscript, a perfectly feasible one palaeographically. The copying is the work of two scribes, termed **A** and **B**, **A** apparently being the supervisor, for on two occasions (here and on f. 35) he began a new book and left **B** to carry on. **A** certainly appears to be the more experienced and superior penman, but is a more careless copyist and limits his corrections to those noticed while writing. Apart from the sharing of ff. 35 and 45, the work was divided as follows: **A**, ff. 9–44v, 191–229, 349–484v; **B**, ff. 45–191, 229v–346. They seem also to have done their own rubrication. Oakeshott (*TLS*, 27 Sept. 1934) saw similarities between hand **A** and Machlinia type used in London in 1486, while A. J. Collins (*ibid.*) found affinities with chancery hand of the period, noting that 'Know all men by these presents' had been written at the top of one of the pages. See, further, articles by Oakeshott cited above and in *Gutenberg-Jahrbuch*, 1935, 113–14, and his chapter in J. A. W. Bennet, *Essays on Malory*, 1963; E. Vinaver, *Works of Thomas Malory*, 1967, the standard edition based on the manuscript and collated with Caxton, (*vide* esp. i, c ff. and facsimiles of ff. 35, 70v. and 409).

Characteristics. The chancery features mentioned by Collins (see above) are not particularly evident from this page, and although they can be seen elsewhere in **A** when his hand is narrower and with more distinctive Chancery parallelism of minims (e.g. f. 35), there seems to be little trace of them in **B**. Both hands show affinities with the rather thick-stroked cursive book hands of Northern Germany and the Low Countries in the period (cf. Parkes, 24, ii; Lieftinck, 1954, figs. 21 and 31). In addition, **B** bears a strong resemblance to the hand in John Capgrave's *Lives of St. Augustine and St. Gilbert*, 1451 (Kirchner, pl. 59, *EVH*, 21), and Vinaver (*op. cit.*, i, cii) has noted a similarity between **A** and the script of the Arthurian section of the English *Brute* in Alnwick Castle.

Hand **A** uses a bold, calligraphic *quadrata* for the opening line, though final *s* is too rounded and elongated for authentic *quadrata*. His remaining five lines, in uniformly heavy strokes and with many looped ascenders are basically a formal *secretary* book hand, though it has some appearance of *hybrid*, especially in the proper names. Typical *secretary* features include the generally pointed appearance of the minims and the heads of many of the letters, the single-lobed *a*, short *r* with a curved base almost touching the head stroke (l. 4, *courte*) the *B* form of final *s* (l. 4, *was*) and unlooped *d* (l. 3, *dotage*), though a looped and indented *d* is also present (l. 4, *damesels*). Indentation also occurs frequently on the *b*, *l* and *w*; final *t* has a calligraphic pendant hairline on its cross-stroke. Among the unusual forms should be noted the 7 shaped infralinear *r* (l. 6, *reste*), presumably a variant of long forked *r*.

Hand **B** is more cursive and has a decided slope to the right, especially noticeable in the loops. It is also a larger hand with much taller ascenders, though it contracts somewhat around l. 16, when the pen strokes also become lighter. Although many of the basic letter forms are the same, **B** uses sigma *s* with a long arched top in final position, and the stem of *d* is perpendicular rather than slanting to the left. *A* has single lobe with a high-arched stem (l. 15, *Also*) by contrast to the two-lobed form in **A** (l. 6, *And*, possibly a large minuscule). Hair-lines also hang from the cross-strokes of other letters as well as *t* (e.g. *g*, l. 15, *f*, l. 29). All proper names throughout are in red.

Punctuation and abbreviation. Both use the point and raised point. In **B** the point also occurs in curtailment (l. 20, *Mer.*, left in abbreviated form because of doubtful spelling). **A** has single virgule, **B** the double virgule. A long diacritic is often used for *i* in **B**, and the double oblique hyphen (ll. 13, 22). *Abbreviations*, appearing only in **B**, include crossed *þ* for *þar* (l. 21), *5* form of ' for *er* (l. 22), *ꝯ* for *es* (l. 24), bar for omitted *n* (l. 29), upward curl on *g* (a form of ') for final *e* (l. 20), *w^t* for *with* (l. 20), *þ^e* for *the* (l. 26), and an upwards curl (a form of attached bar) on final *g*, *m*, *n*, *r* for *e* (l. 7, *thynge*, l. 9, *frome*, l. 8, *uppone*, l. 22, *here*), though in some or all of these cases it could be otiose, the interpretation given here to crossed *ll* in either hand (ll. 3, 6, 7, 10, 13, 16, 20, 21).

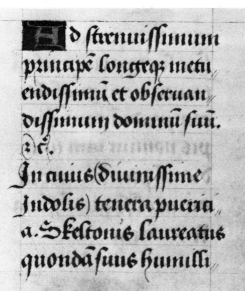

5

5

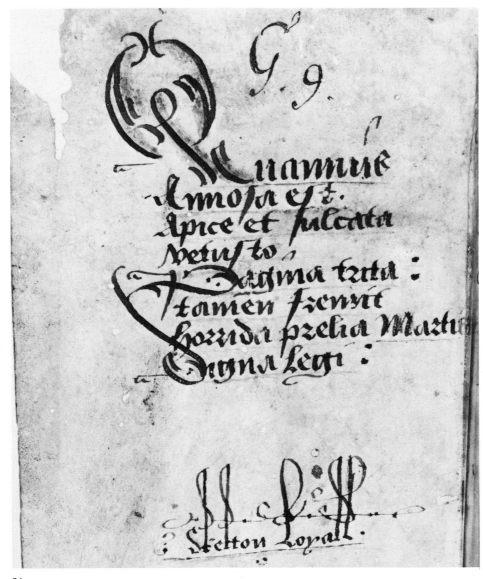

5

⊛ John Skelton (1460?–1529)

14, 15 Beginning and end of *Speculum Principis* (1501).
Secretaria formata hybrida (*lettre bourguinonne*), holograph, 1509.
B.L., Add MS 26787, ff. 2, 29.

Ad strenuissimum principe*m* longeq*ue* metuendissimu*m* et obseruandissimum
dominu*m* suu*m*. &c.
In cuius (diuinissime Indolis) tenera puericia. Skeltonis laureatus quonda*m* suus
humilli

Skeltonis Laureatus Didasculus quondam Regius. &c. tacitus secu*m* in
soliloquio. ceu vir totus obliuioni Datus. aut tanquam mortuus a corde. &c

16 First leaf of dedication to *Chronique de Rains*. *Secretaria
hybrida formata* (*lettre bourguinonne*), holograph, 1511–12.
Corpus Christi College, Cambridge, MS 432, f. 1v.

℃ Quamuis
　　Annosa est.
　　Apice et sulcata
　　vetusto
℃ Pagina trita:
　　tamen fremit
℃ horrida prelia Martis
　　Digna Legi:

　　Skelton Loyall.

Notes

Two holographs of Skelton's works are known for certain to exist. The first (16) is the dedication (f. 1v–3) to the 13th-century MS of *Chronique de Rains* presented by Skelton to Henry VIII in 1511–12, transcribed and dated by H. L. Edwards, *PMLA*, 53, June 1938, 601 ff. The second is *A lawde and prayse made for our Souereigne Lord the Kyng*, P.R.O., E.36/228. ff. 7–8, reproduced in M. Pollet, *John Skelton*, 1962 (transl. J. Warington, 1971, between 62 and 63) and in Croft, 6–8. A probable third is *Speculum Principis* (14–15), formerly in Lincoln Cathedral library, discovered by F. M. Salter, *Spec.*, ix, 1934, 25 ff., who transcribed it and identified it as the copy presented in revised form to Henry VIII in 1509. Salter later suggested that the hand was also Skelton's on the grounds that it is 'precisely in the same style and in what seems to be the same hand as the dedication to the *Chronique de Rains*' (*Diodorus Siculus*, E.E.T.S., 233, 1956, xii–xiii). It is true that the use of very few words per line is common to 14–15 and 16, and that both are in the distinctive script called *lettre bourguinonne*. It could be added that the scroll work in both is similar (initial *S*, no. 14, initial *Q*, no. 16; cf. also *Speculum*, f. 21 and *Chronique*, f. 2v);

that the form of the name *Skelton*, discounting some of the flourishes, is very similar (14, l. 8; 15, l. 1; 16, l. 9; also *Chronique*, f. 2v, l. 6). Further, the use of colons and a triangle of points is also characteristic of both MS (cf. *Speculum*, f. 20v, 22v; *Chronique*, f. 1v, l. 5; f. 2v, ll. 3, 4, 11). On the other hand, the punctuation marks could have been executed by a copyist faithful to Skelton's MS draft, and the *Speculum* hand looks too regular and more skilfully calligraphic than that for the *Chronique*, though both purport to be the fairest hand possible. Nevertheless, there seems to be a very good case for the *Speculum* being an example of Skelton's most formal and compact hand, so that three grades could be extant: a middle-grade *hybrid secretary* with *bourguinonne* influence, a large formal but somewhat clumsy *bourguinonne*, and a smaller, highly artistic and regular *bourguinonne* in which book-hand influence is at its greatest.

Characteristics. Both examples are typical of the *bourguinonne* hand which was mainly in use in the court of Burgundy in the 15th century and derived from the French Chancery (*vide* Lieftinck, 1964, i, text, xvi ff.; plates 268–82, esp. 277–8). The main characteristics of this

script are the minimal use of loops (virtually non-existent in 14–15); a slope to the right in the shafts of *f*, *s*, and sometimes *p*, and in the head of *t*; long finely tapered descenders for *f* and *s*; hairline links, especially between minims; and broken strokes giving the impression of *textura quadrata*. The tops of minims are often spurred, heads are generally arched, and final *s* is an angular *B* form. It should be noted that book hand *r* is predominant in 14–15, with the *z* form appearing only after *o*, whereas in 16 the *z* form is used exclusively. Among other differences between 14–15 and 16 is that whereas *d* in 14–15 has a short back with an upward curl and sometimes a hairline tail (14, l. 6), in 16 it has a long diagonal back.
Punctuation. 14–15 have the period, the diacritic for every *i*, normally hardly more than a point, but occasionally with an upright hook, a short double hyphen, and elsewhere (ff. 20v, 22v) the colon and a pyramid of points. 16 employs the period, colon, diacritic for *i* varying greatly from a long, upright hook to a short, thin diagonal, and elsewhere in the MS (f. 2v) a pyramid of points.
Abbreviation consists mainly of the bar for *m* and *n*, *3* for *ue*, *zc* for *et cetera*.

shall have herd of the good & prosperous ende of
this affaires agaynst Scotland which god willing he
trustith shalbe shortely than forthwt to repaire to wyndesore
and there somewhat be till his grace & his councel and
determyne ferther. Whom both o lord send well & shortely
to gether and long preserve you both in helth & myche honor
At woodstok the ffryday before all hallowen day &c

yor humble orato & most
bounden bedman

Thomas More

ut omnes in me scandalu
pateremini. omnes hoc futurum negastis.
Et qui id negauit maxime, praedixi,
fore ut priusq cantaret gallus,
ipse me ter negaret. Institit affirmare
no futurum esse gz moriturum secum potius
q me negaturum. Siliter et omnes dixistis.
Ego ne tentatione re tam lenem dixeretis
iterum atqz iterum vos vigilare iussi
et orare ne in tentatione intraretis.
et vos tam procul tamen ab estimanda
tentationis violentia semper abfuistis,
ut nec orare aduersus eam
nec vigilare curaueritis. arati
fortassis inde ad contempnedas

17 Conclusion of letter to Cardinal Wolsey, 30 October 1523. *Facile early Tudor secretary*, holograph.
B.L., Cotton, Galba B. viii, f. 95, lower portion, signature raised.

shall haue herd of the good & prosperouse ende of his affeires agaynst scotland which god willyng he trusteth shalbe shortely than forthwith to repaire to wyndesore and ther to demurre vn till his grace & yours deliver And determyn[1] ferther. Whom both our lord send well & shortely to gether And long preserve you both in helth & mych honour At woodstoke the ffryday byfore all hallowen evyn[1]

your humble orator & moost
bounden beedman
Thomas More

1. Otiose flourish but possibly brevigraph for *e*.

18 A page from *De Tristitia Christi*, 1534. *Facile italic* (*antiqua cursiva*) mixed with *secretary*, holograph.
Royal College of Corpus Christi, Valencia, *De Tristitia Christi*, f. 83v.

ut omnes in me scandalum [in me] pateremini. omnes hoc futurum negastis. Ei qui id negauit maxime / predixi / fore ut priusquam quam cantaret gallus / ipse me ter negaret. Institit affirmare non futurum / se que moriturum mecum potius quam me negaturum. Similiter et omnes dixistis. Ego ne tentationem rem tam leuem dureretis / iterum atque iterum vos uigilare iussi et orare ne in tentationem intraretis. et vos tam procul tamen ab estimanda tentationis uiolentia semper abfuistis / ut nec orare aduersus eam / [nec] nec uigilare curaueritis. armati fortassis inde ad contempnendas

---

Notes

More's holographs comprise correspondence, housed mainly in the P.R.O. and the B.L., sundry signatures, a collection of prayers and meditations written in the top and bottom margins of 16 pages in a 1530 edition of the Sarum Book of Hours (Yale U.L.), and the MS of *De Tristitia Christi* (also known as *Expositio Passionis*), written in the Tower, which was discovered by G. Bullough in the library of Corpus Christi College, Valencia, in 1963 (*The Tablet*, 21 Dec. 1963). See further for sources, facsimiles and transcriptions, *Correspondence,* ed. E. F. Rogers, 147 (facs. opp. 282); R. W. Gibson and J. Max Patrick, *St. Thomas More: a preliminary bibliography*, 1961; *Moreana*, 5, 1965; E. E. Reynolds, *The field is won*, 1968, 351–7; *Thomas More's Prayer Book*, ed. L. L. Martz and R. S. Sylvester, 1969; *De Tristitia Christi*, ed. C. Miller, 1976.

Characteristics of no. 17. In keeping with common practice in the period, More seems to use *secretary* for his English writings and correspondence, and *italic* for Latin. His English hand is a characteristic *early Tudor secretary*, with its openness, breadth and firmness of stroke. It is also very clear and fluent, with More's general tendency to slope his lines upwards (cf. no. 18). The transitional phase from 15th-century cursives (both *anglicana* and *secretary*) to Elizabethan *secretary* is quite apparent. Looking back to the 15th century are: *A* buckled in the middle (l. 7, *At*) and a smaller version of *A* for the minuscule (l. 1, *shall*); *c* with a curved stem (l. 2, *which*); unlooped *d* with rounded or broken-stroked bowl (l. 5, *lord; determyn*) or hybrid *d* with looped stem and spurred bowl (l. 4, *deliver*); *g* with headstroke and simple tail (l. 6, *long*); *h* with fat curved body (l. 6, *helth*); *z* form of *r* (l. 5, *ferther*); and *t* with curved shank and bold cross-stroke (l. 3, *than*). The most prominent graph anticipating *Elizabethan secretary* is reversed *e*, whether linked (l. 3, *shortely*) or detached (l. 4, *deliver*), and sometimes with the head separated from the body (l. 9, *bounden beedman*). Others include *f* with the loop intersecting the shaft to form the cross-stroke without a pen lift (l. 5, *ferther*); double-looped *h* with no body (l. 5, *both*); long *s*, like *f*, having a fairly long descender–ascender shaft, with the characteristic round head when separate or in ligatures (l. 1, *prosperouse*) except for the usual right-angled top in *sh* (l. 3, *shalbe shortely*); and sigma *s*, though its ascender is rather high and irregular (l. 2, *his affeires*). Among graphs in a transitional phase are *d* with open body and linking loop (l. 1, *ende*) and

w, still rather broad and a little clumsy (l. 5, *well*).
Punctuation comprises the solitary period, l. 5.
Abbreviation relies on superior letters: *w*[t] (*with*); *yo*[r] (*your*), with occasional doubt whether raised *r* signifies omitted *o* (l. 8, *orato*[r]); and a symbol resembling *c* above *p* for *re* (l. 6, *preserve*). The Tironian sign resembling *z* enclosed by a large *C* is used for *and*.

Characteristics of no. 18. A small humanistic cursive hand (*italic*) of the facile grade, similar to many of the more compact humanistic hands of Italy in the late 15th and early 16th century (cf. M. G. Battelli, *Nomenclature des écritures humanistiques*, 1954, figs. 40, 41; B. L. Ullman, *The origin and development of humanistic script*, 1960, pl. 69). Its comparative uprightness, the detachment of many of its letters (e.g. l. 11, *et vos*, *procul*), the simplicity and the thinness of uprights, suggest at least the indirect influence of the *littera antiqua corsiva* as used by Niccolò Niccoli (1367–1437), particularly in his texts of Ammianus Marcellinus and Lucretius (*vide* S. Morison, *Lib.*, 4th ser., xxiv, 1943, 1–29, esp. pl. 8, 9). Among the characteristic graphs the present hand shares with the early Italian *humanistic cursives* are *g* with a narrow head and fairly long tail usually ending in a round and often closed loop (l. 14, *uigilare*), *h* with a curved tail descending a little below the line, and a small capital *S* used as a minuscule especially in final position, also with its tail slightly below the line (l. 7, *dixistis*). Letters often shared by *humanistic* and *secretary* hands in the period are *c* with a short straight head and curved stem (l. 6, *mecum*), and simple form of long *s* with medium-sized shaft, especially in the combination *st* (l. 5, *institit*). However, the larger form of *c* with straight head and curved stem (l. 4, *cantaret*) seems to derive from early *secretary*, and so probably does the bolder form of long *s* with a split shaft (l. 9, 1st *s* of *iussi*). In particular, there are *secretary* graphs which point to similarities with More's English hand, which at first sight looks so different: *f*, uniformly as described in no. 17 (l. 4, *fore*) and the small form of capital *a* used as a minuscule (l. 14, 1st *a* of *armati*).

Punctuation consists mainly of the period and a short virgule which might represent a comma. A diacritic is occasionally used to mark the *i* (l. 6, *moriturum*; l. 10, *intraretis*) as an alternative to the point.
Abbreviation is quite frequent, as might be expected of a Latin text written on small pages probably in short supply. The most common form is the bar for *m* and *n*, varying considerably in size and degree of curve, and in one case surmounted by *i* as part of the *abbreviation* (l. 7, *Similiter*). Two contractions are used with *q*, which followed by ȝ represents *que* (l. 6), and with a stroke through its tail and a serrated line above stands for *quam* (ll. 4, 7).

Tagus fare well that westward with thy streames
torns up the grayns off gold already tryd
with sonne and syle for I go seke the temmes
gaynward the sonne that showth her welthi pryd
and to the town which brutus sowght by dremes
5 like bendyd mone doth lend her lusty syd.
My kyng my contrey for whome alone I lyve
of myghty love the wynge for this me gyve

T.

---

ensend imediatly uppon the advertisement
to send hym to my lord the dyllysseur
to awayte uppon his lordshyp ther furst
leo[...] off thynge as suport
5 to his maiestis of his hoste that now my
lord to have me hartely comendyd to
hym / thus wyshyng your lordshyp aswell
to do as my self / from shyppis
the vth of october 1545.

10 I pray the money by the
off edward watton payd to barnard gysor
when as I frayt m[...] edward wattoye
by hauntasshly a greut soldyour off myne
y standith in callais who is blynd and waynd
15 I am ashamyd to gyve hym but iff it plese hym to take hym till I
be able to gyve hym a better / I shall desyer hym so to do

your lovyng cossyn
SURREY

Sir Thomas Wyatt (1503?–1542)

19 Poem 105, Egerton MS. *Early Tudor facile secretary* mixed with *italic*, holograph, *c.* 1539.
B.L., Egerton 2711, f. 69, upper portion.

Tagus fare well yat westward with thy strems
torns vp the grayns off gold alredy tryd
with spurr and sayle for I go seke the tems
gaynward the sonne[1] yat shewthe her welthi pryd
5 and to the town [yat] ∧ [wyche] brutus sowght by drems
like bendyd mone doth lend her lusty syd.
My kyng my Contry ∧ [alone] for whome [only alone] I lyve[2]
of myghty love the winges for this me gyve
        Y T[3]

1. Otiose bar. 2. *l* superscribed on *s*, apparently part dittography of *syd* (l. 6.) 3. Monogram.

Notes
The Egerton MS, one of the main sources for Wyatt's poems, contains twelve holographs and several others with autograph corrections (*vide* K. Muir and P. Thomson, *Collected Poems of Sir Thomas Wyatt*, 1969, esp. xi–xii, 1–125, and plates facing 84 and 100; Croft no. 9; R. Harrier, *The canon of Sir Thomas Wyatt's poetry*, 1975). Originally the poet's own MS, most of the section containing his poetry was copied out in or before 1537, but the autograph poems were written during or after Wyatt's period in Spain, probably between 1537 and 1542, the present poem dating from the time of his leaving Spain, June 1539. The volume passed into the hands of the Harington family and contains autographs of Sir John Harington (*vide* no. 30).

Characteristics. Fairly compact, though words and letters are widely and somewhat irregularly spaced. It is also economical and undecorated (apart from the high-hooked ascender on sigma *s*), and final *e* after *h* is usually reduced to a barely distinguishable curl (l. 2). Loops are mainly confined to *f*, *l* and occasionally *b* and double-looped *h*, which alternates with the unlooped shaft and wide-curved body variety. The *s* is used in a variety of ligatures: *sa*, *se*, *sh*, *so*, *sp* and *st*. Though at much the same state of development of *secretary* as More's (no. 18), it includes the two-stroke *e* (l. 1) as well as open reversed *e* (l. 4), and the open *d* (l. 6, *doth*) characteristic of *Elizabethan secretary*. The influence of humanistic hands is present in *C* (l. 7) and in *r* (l. 1, *fare*), sometimes with a foot-serif (l. 7, *for*) though the *z* form is also found. Other letters suggestive of a humanistic hand are *t*, *y* and the straighter unlooped forms of *b* and *d*. Thorn is now replaced by *y* with curled tail (l. 1).

Punctuation includes the period, dotted *y* and caret and, elsewhere, the virgule.

Abbreviations are the common ones of ꝫ for *es* (l. 8), *wt* for *with* and *y*[4] for *yat* (*that*).

Henry Howard, Earl of Surrey (1517?–1547)

20 Letter to Lord Cobham, 20 October 1545. *Mid-Tudor rapid secretary*, holograph.
B.L., Harleian 283, f. 329, lower portion. Reduced by ¼.

entend immediatly vppon your advertysement to send him to my Lord with dyllygence to awayte vppon his lordship ffor suche declaration off thynges as emporte to his maiestis service ∧ [here] besechyng yow my Lord to have me hartly commendid to him / thus wishyng[1] yowr lordship aswell to do as my self ffrom Boloygne[1] the xxth off October 1545
    Your loving[1] cosyn
    H Surrey
wher as I perceyve [master] sir edward wottones son ffantasyth a genet geldyng off myne yat standith in Callais whiche is blynd and ruyned I am ashamyd to gyve him but iff it pleas him to take him till I be able to gyve him a better / I shall desire him so to do I shall[2] also send the money by philleret yat sir edward wotton payed to barnard grete by my appoyntement /

1. Otiose flourish. 2. *I shall* of 2nd P.S. begun immediately above 1st P.S., then cancelled.

Notes
There are no known holographs of Surrey's poems, and relatively few of his letters are in his hand apart from the signature. Another reproduction of Surrey's hand (from Cotton, Titus B. ii) is given in G. F. Nott, *Works of Henry Howard*, i, 1815, facing 167. A new edition of the complete works is long overdue, though Nott was reprinted in 1965.

Characteristics. A sprawling and clumsy hand, with a lack of definition in the minims. Alternating with the double-looped *h* (l. 4) is the wide-bodied *h* (l. 2) which looks back to an earlier *secretary* form, and the long straight-tailed *y* is like Wyatt's, but the general formation of the letters and greater cursiveness are moving close to *Elizabethan secretary*, especially the reversed *e*, open *d* (l. 2, *send*). They are now joined by the right-angled *c* (l. 3, *such*), the *p* with introductory *2* stroke, and the double-stroked *ff* sharing the same looped cross-stroke. Two letters showing humanistic influence, though they become fairly common in *secretary*, are the *v* form of *r* (also derived from 15th-century *secretary*) and roman *s* in final position. Other features to note are *t* with a linking loop at its foot (l. 1) and the consistent use of *v* medially.

Punctuation depends almost entirely on a long virgule. There is also a caret.

Abbreviation. The bar for *m* or *n* is in the form of a very long, arched horizontal loop (ll. 1, 6) which is occasionally otiose (ll. 7, 8). Among superior-letter contractions are *yor* for *your* (l. 1) and *wt* for *with*. ꝫ appears for *es* (l. 4).

In right harty maner J comend me o to yow
And where as Master Leylande at this pre
sente tyme cumith to Byri to see what bookes
be lefte yn the library there or translation thens
ynto any other corner of the late monastery
apon iuste consideracion
J shall desier yow right redily to forder his
cause And to permitte hy to have the use of
such as may forder hym yn setig forth nch
maters as he writith — or the kiges matie te
In o doyng ye haulbjnde me to showr on to yow
df al tymes like gratitude for it J there
present at this tyme w you J wolde gladly my
self fulfil his honeste reqneste. Thus fare ye
wel this ie o Nouebre at Barnewelle

21 Copy of letter of introduction on his behalf. *Facile italic*, holograph, *c.* 1540.
B.L., Add MS 38132, f. 16v, middle portion.

In right harty maner I com*m*end me *o*n to yow And where as Master Leylande at this præsente tyme cum*m*ith to Byri to see what bookes be lefte yn the library there or translatid thens ynto any other corner of the late monastery. I shaul desier yow ∧ [apon iuste co*n*sideration] right redily to forder his cause And to permitte hy*m* to haue the use of such as may forder hym yn setti*n*g forth such matiers as he writith for the Ki*n*ges maieste In so doyng ye shaul by*n*de me to show on to yow at al tymes like gratitude: for if I were present at this tyme *with* yow I wold gladly my self fulfil his honeste requeste. Thus fare ye wel this ix of Noue*m*bre at Barnewelle.

Notes

This letter of introduction for access to the monastic library at Bury St Edmunds is probably connected with Leland's antiquarian visitation of England (1536–42) and must date from after the dissolution of the monasteries in 1536. The MSS of his *Itinerary* (most recent complete ed. by L. Toulmin Smith, 1907, repr. 1964) are in the Bodleian Library. For other facsimiles *vide* Greg, CI, and *F. & W.*, no. 23 (a *bastard italic* text, with marginalia in Leland's *facile italic*). Leland was appreciative of good penmanship and took a practical interest in teaching *italic* handwriting (*F. & W.*, 62).

Characteristics. A large, squarish, partially cursive *italic* hand, which presumably Leland learned in his Cambridge days, Cambridge being a main centre for the humanistic scripts in England, with Cheke and Ascham especially prominent there, though after Leland's time. The letters are well-proportioned, even if idiosyncratic and with hairline links which do not quite fulfil their function, and the total effect would have been very pleasing had Leland not been economizing on space between lines. Among the distinctive letter forms are *e* made in two pen lifts, looking like a *c* intersected by an acute angle forming the lobe; *d* with a cross-stroke linking the bowl to the shaft; and *w* comprising large *v* intersected by a smaller *v*, which usually has a horizontal introductory stroke.

Punctuation comprises the period, colon, caret and dotted *i*.

Abbreviation consists of diagonal bar for *m* and *n*, and *w*ᵗ for *with*.

George Cavendish (1500–1561?)

22 *Life and death of Cardinal Wolsey*: excerpt from Wolsey's dying words. *Early/mid Tudor facile secretary* mixed with *chancery*, holograph, 1558.
B.L., Egerton 2402, f. 90, upper portion.

*per*son / to whome god gave the victory /// Alas m*aster* kyngeston / if thes be not playn *p*resedent*es* and sufficyent *per*swasions to admonysshe a prynce to be circumspect ayenst the semblable[1] myschefe / and if he be neclygent / than wyll[1] god stryke and take frome hyme his power / and dymynysshe[1] his regally / [as] takyng frome hyme his prudent councellou*r*s and valy*a*unt capteyns / and leave vs in *our* owen hand*es with*out hys helpe & ayed / And than wyll[1] ensewe [myschefe vpon /] myschefe vppon myschefe / Inconvenyence vppon Inconvenyence / barynes & skarcyte of all[1] thyng*es* / for lake of good order in the co*m*en welthe / to the vtter distruccion & desolacion of this noble[1] Realme / ffrome w*hi*che myschef*es* god for hys tender m*er*cy defend vs / Mayster kyngeston farewell[1] I canno moore but whyshe all[1] thyng to haue good successe / my[2] tyme drawyth on fast I may not tary *with* you. / And forgett not (I pray you) what I haue seyd & charged you wi*t*hall[1] ffor when I ame deade / ye shall[1] *per*auenture remember my word*es* myche better //

1. Otiose flourish. 2. Beginning of *d*? between *my* and *tyme*.

Notes

Characteristics. A small, angular and basically *secretary* hand, though its marked vertical compression and *anglicana* graphs of double-lobed *a* and long *r* obviously show it has close affinity to *facile chancery*, as might be expected of Wolsey's secretary. It should be noted that *anglicana a* and long *r* were preserved in most court and legal hands of the period, but the open lower lobe of *a* is most common in *chancery* and *pipe office* hands (Cavendish's father, incidentally, having been a clerk of the pipe). Alternating with long *r* is the *z* form common in *early Tudor secretary*. Also typical are the double-looped *h* with top and bottom loops crossing the shaft (l. 1, *thes*) and the fat-bodied *h* (l. 8, *this*), and *g* with a pointed head and a crossbar link (l. 1, *god*). Final *e*, as in Wyatt's hand (no. 20), is sometimes a mere curl (l. 1, *the*). The MS is described and dated in R. Sylvester's edition of the biography, E.E.T.S., 243, 1959, with an illustration from f. 88v.

Punctuation. The virgule is the most prominent mark of punctuation, used as general factotum, the degree of pause apparently being indicated by doubling or tripling it (ll. 1, 12).

Abbreviation includes *p* crossed by a *2* form of bar for *per* (l. 1); ɛ for *es* (l. 5); ' for *er* (l. 9) or *re* when above *p* (l. 2); *w*ᵗ for *with*; *w*ᶜʰ for *which*; the somewhat archaic superior *a* symbol for *ur* (l. 4), and serrated line with flourish for *a* (l. 5). ɛ serves for *and*; and a number of ascenders are crossed with an otiose bar (note 1). Details of punctuation and abbreviation in the MS are given in Sylvester, *op. cit.*, xxxix–xli.

uiter strictim̄q; tantum tacta esse
uideantur, cum cuncta ea alias
in cæteris Eplis, præcipue in utraq;
ad Timotheum fusius ac copiosi
us sint pertractata

    Postremo Eruditissime Præsul
si quid in hac versione (quæ pri
ma n̄ræ tenuitatis periclitatio
est) animaduertatur, quod, uel
negligentia oscitanter perpendi
mus, uel imperitia potius non ple
ne assequuti simus, a Domina
tione tua moniti, erratum liben
ter agnoscemus.
D. IESVS Christus Domina

tionem tuam perpetuo seruet in
columem. Cantab. E Col
legio D. Ioan. Euangeliste.

Dominationis tuæ
obseruantissimus

Rogerus Aschamus.

---

if it woto pleaße you, of good will to make the tolt6 for me, and when you haue
iß done, by y⁰ wißdom to drawe for me to, I am aßured my woke ßhall be good,
the woßire onely I committ to goddes p̄oudence and y⁰ intelwiße. I ßend you,
S⁰, by m̄ Raynley a mappe, the beſt y̶ euer I founde, in all my bußineßē here
abode, eſpetiallie for Germanie, Italie, and Hungarie. it vetaynets tofi Europe
and ſo muche of Aßia and africke, as is eythez knowen by men, or ßpoken of
in wurnyng. Iohn onelie in the eaſt parte is ſtraoghte not far enowgh to
the indies and perßians. And as it is generall, for the hole, ſo it is
in moſt places, ſo particulare for euy citie and touwn, as the like y̶ I haue
not ſeen. The worthie ambaßador of venice i Sig̶⁰ Marco Antonio Damula
in this court did geue me two of them, the on I ſend to you, thother to m̄
Chooke, wuhiche youw token̄ of good will, I truſt ye will boke take in good parte
ſent this the lowd preſerue you to my good lady Cicill. from Spira
the vßon of nouemb̄ 1552

y⁰ I m̄ Shyp̄o moſt bownden
ß to ße R. aſcham

23 Dedicatory epistle to his Latin translation of *Oecumenius*.
Set italic book hand (*cancellaresca formata*), holograph, 1542.
Bodleian, Rawl. D. 1317, ff. 4v–5.

uiter strictim*que* tantum tacta esse uideantur, cum cuncta ea alias in cæteris
Ep*isto*lis, præcipuè in vtra*que* ad Timotheum fusius ac copiosius sint pertractata.

   Postremo Eruditissime Præsul si quid in hac versione (quæ prima n*ost*ræ
tenuitatis periclitatio est) animaduertatur, quod, uel negligentia oscitanter
perpendimus, uel imperitia potius non plene assequati sumus, à Dominatione tua
moniti, erratum libenter agnoscemus. *D*ominus IESVS Christus Dominationem
tuam perpetuo seruet incolumem. Cantabriæ E Collegio *Domino* Ioan*ne*
Euangeliste.

Dominationis tuæ obseruantissimus
Rogerus Aschamus.

24 Letter to Sir William Cecil (later Lord Burghley),
28 November 1552. *Facile Elizabethan secretary* mixed with
italic, holograph.
B.L., Lansdowne 3, f. 5v, middle portion.

if it wold please yow, of good will to make the[1] lotes for me, and whan yow
haue so done, by yo*ur* wisdom to draw for me to, I am assured my lucke shall be
good the which holy I com*mi*tte to goddes *p*rovidence / and yo*ur* ientlenesse I send
yow S*ir* by mr Yaxeley a mappe, the best y*at* ever I fownd, in all my businesses
here a brode, speciallie for Germanie, Italie, and Hungarie. it conteyneth hole
Europe and so moch of Asia and africke, as is eyther known[2] by men, or spoken
of in lernyng, save onelie in the East parte it streacheth not far enowgh to the
Medes and Persians. And as it is generall, for the hole, so is it in most placese, so
particulare for any*e* Citie and town, as the like yet I haue not seen. The worthie
Ambassador of venice *il Signor Marco Antonio Damula* in this Corte did give me
two of them, thone I send to yow, thother to mr Cheke, whiche poore tokens of
good will, I trust ye will both take in good parte And thus the lord preserve yow
w*ith* my good lady Cecill. from Spira the xxviij of nouemb*er* 1552

Yo*ur* W*or*ships most bownden
so to be R. Ascha̅m

1. The crosses, underlining and small commas in dark ink are the work of a later hand, probably
an editor. 2. Otiose bar above final nasal, omitted in transcription except in signature.

Notes

Ascham, a pupil of Sir John Cheke, the influential proponent of *italic* handwriting in England in the early 16th century, himself became extremely influential because he was tutor to Elizabeth before she was queen, and also gave writing lessons to Edward VI (boasting that he had taught him to write better than any child in England). He was also Latin secretary to Queen Mary and to Elizabeth for a brief time on her accession. As public orator for Cambridge, Ascham wrote a large number of official letters on behalf of the university (see further *F. & W.*, 30–3; A. Fairbank and B. Dickins, *The italic hand in Tudor Cambridge*, 8 ff.). Ascham seems to have observed consistently the convention of employing *italic* for Latin and *secretary* for the vernacular in correspondence, even with his signature. Further, he wrote an amazingly varied number of forms of each type. In general, there are three main degrees of formality in his *italic* (cf. Fairbank and Dickins, *op. cit.*, plates 4, 5, 7) and the same number in *secretary* (cf. Greg, LXIII), but in no case is grace sacrificed completely for speed. Notes on the sources of Ascham holographs are contained in

L. V. Ryan, *Roger Ascham*, 1963, e.g. 300 ff., 326 ff.

Characteristics of no. 23. The hand, basically derived from *cancellaresca* and *letera da brevi*, is Ascham's most formal and beautiful *italic* and is strongly influenced by John Cheke, as is noted by A. Fairbank and R. W. Hunt (*Humanistic script of the fifteenth and sixteenth centuries*, 1960, 7 and pl. 18), who draw attention to the distinctive use by both writers of digraph *æ* (a, l. 3), omega (not represented here), and looped *ss* (b, l. 5). The same form of looping is used for *ct* and for *st*, which are sometimes ligatured even when there are intervening letters. Ascham also seems to derive from Cheke the same generous and elegant curves of ascenders and descenders, especially on the double-length long *s*. Distinctive letters include *e* shaped like a *c* with a hook near the top (a form of eta?), a version of long *s* in final position as an alternative to short *s* (a, l. 3, *cæteris*), and an occasional *h* with an open curved bowl (a, l. 4).

Punctuation comprises the point, dotted *i*, the single and double hyphen at the end of the line,

and (for the first time in these illustrations), the comma.

Abbreviation. An elaborately looped bar acts as a general mark of contraction; *q* with a small *2* or small *3* symbol stands for *que*.

Characteristics of no. 24. A compact fully fledged *Elizabethan secretary* with a few *italic* forms, sometimes used for capitals of proper names: *C* (ll. 12, 13), *E*, *G* (l. 5) and *S* (l. 4), and one complete proper name (l. 10). The *h* has now lost most of its large rounded body and has a long linking tail, and all the *secretary* letters are as might be found in a late Elizabethan *secretary* hand, including the two forms of *d* and *e*, though the two types of *r* (modified *z* and *v*) are usually found only in the more current hands.

Punctuation includes the period and, as in 23, the comma. Superior letters form the bulk of the **abbreviation**: y^t = *yat* (*that*); yor = *your*; S^r = *Sir*; m^r = *master*; Sig^{or} = *Signor*; p^o = *pro* (l. 3, instead of the more usual *p* with concave cross-stroke through tail); and *y'* for *ye* (l. 9). The bar is used for omitted *m* and *n*, but is frequently superfluous.

gentlemen in due performance of the marryge in there owe
them, restored the pray and isterlye, there Thomas
Browne, in one or ij other lyvestmes, woomld solick
Bredeme very bee, nys it said to bee dead synn and
5 took my guifts from them . So having no farther
matter to wryte for this tyme I remitt yo' L. to
ye guyding of Almighty god Corke xij° Marche 1580

Yo' good L. as assured to command
as my may bee.

10 — Thomas Ormonde

Copia Vera
Edm: ffleu

Be it knowen to all men by these presentes that I
Edmund Epenser of kylcolman<del>…</del> the gyve unto
m' Henry the keping of all the meady wch I gave
in Ballygarin E of the wsshed E brakes warr
5 making any spoyle therwof E also doe ordeint
w' him that ye shall gave one goyst wth my
Barone of kilgardston for him self E ys outtaell ye
thyrd of watter And also wth the spare of my
yeures to repayre the castle of kilgardston after
10 suyd E in all thyse thyngs bythe god wyll be
god to him E ys

Edm: ffleu

25 Copy of Earl of Ormond's letter to Lord Grey
(conclusion), 13 March 1580. *Facile Elizabethan secretary*, with
signed attestation in *italic*, Spenser's holograph.
P.R.O., S.P. 63, vol. 81, no. 36, f. 79v, lower portion,
signed attestation raised.

horsemen *with* some footemen of the garrizon there pursued them, reskued the
pray and *present*ly slewe Thomas Browne, *with* one or ij other Horsemen, woundd
vlick Browne very sore, who is said to bee dead since and tooke iiij horses from
them. So having no farther matter to wryte for this tyme I com*m*itt yo*ur*
L*ord*ship to ye guyding of Almighty god. Cork xiij° march 1580
  Yo*ur* good L*ord*ship*'s* as assured to com*m*aund as any may bee, /
            Thom*as* Ormonde oss*er*y

            Copia vera
            Ed͞m: s͞p͞ser

26 Grant from Spenser to McHenry. *Facile Elizabethan
secretary*, holograph, *c.* 1589.
B.L., Add MS 19869.

Be it knowen to all men by these *present*es that I Edmund Spenser of kilcolman
esqu*ire* doe giue vnto m*ac* Henry the keeping*e* of all the wood*es* w*hich* I haue in
Balliganim & of the rushes & brakes *with*out making any spoyle thereof & also
doe coven*aunt* w*ith* him that he shall haue one house *with*in the bawne of
Richardson for him self & his cattell in tyme of warre. And also *with*in the
space of vij yeares to repayre the castle of Richardson afore sayd & in all other
thing*es* to vse good neigh bo*ur* hood to him & his
            Ed͟: s͞p͞ser

Notes

Although no poetic autographs have been
discovered, at least 59 documents are extant in
Spenser's hand. Five of them are in *italic*, the
rest are mainly in *Elizabethan secretary*, many of
them being letters written out on behalf of Lord
Grey, Lord Deputy of Ireland, whose secretary
he was for several years (*vide* R. M. Smith,
Studies in honor of T. W. Baldwin, ed. D. C.
Allen, 1958, 66 ff., who although mainly
concerned with Spenser's orthography,
contributes useful material on the
palaeographical aspect, provides two
facsimiles and summarizes the findings of
leading authorities on Spenser's hand). Three
distinct styles of writing have been distinguished
for Spenser: two for English (*secretary* and
italic) and a third for Latin (Greg, XXXIX–XL).
Other facsimiles are provided by H. R. Plomer
(*MP*, 21, 1923, 204 ff.). In the 19th century, no.
26 was sometimes considered a forgery
(ironically, by Collier among others) or to be in
the hand of a clerk, except for the signature. It
has now long been accepted as genuine, and
certainly bears a consistent and striking

resemblance to other documents in Spenser's
secretary hand, in general appearance, formation
of letters, spelling and other features (*vide FRHL*,
92; F. I. Carpenter, *Reference guide to Spenser*,
286–8; R. M. Smith, *op. cit.*, 71). It should be
added that the document shows thicker
penstrokes than is usual with Spenser, but this
may be attributed to the absorbency of the
paper.

Characteristics. A sloping, fairly delicate
secretary hand with small bodied letters and
extremely long descenders on *f* and long *s*, in
some cases going well below the succeeding line.
Plomer (*op. cit.*, 203) has also drawn attention
to *p* 'looking like a truncated *x*' (25, l. 1; 26, l. 2),
a 'pump-handle filial *o*' (?) and capitals *B*, *I*
and *E*. While *I* (26, l. 1) does not seem unusual,
the openness of the lobes of *B* resembling a
curtailed *3* is distinctive (25, l. 3; 26, l. 1), and
so is the extra top to italic *E* in the signature of
both examples. Letters *o* and *a* are often open,
the latter being frequently spurred in 25 (l. 6).
Four types of *r* are employed: a Greek *e* form
(25, l. 1, *horsemen*; 26, l. 8, *warre*), the

twin-stemmed or 'lyre' form (25, l. 4, *Browne*;
26, l. 3, *Henry*); the *2* form (25, l. 1, second *r* of
garrizon) and the *v* form (25, l. 4, *very*; 26, l. 4,
brakes). Among other distinctive letter forms
should be mentioned *g* with either a long, almost
diagonal tail (25, l. 7; 26, l. 4) or with a loop
crossing from right to left and up to the head of
the letter (25, l. 1; 26, l. 10). The attestation is
in Spenser's normal *italic* style, including the
foot serif for *r*, though *p* usually has a curved
tail.

Punctuation comprises the period, comma and
virgule.

Abbreviation includes the bar for *m* and *n*,
for general contraction (26, l. 1, *presentes*; and
spenser signatures) and for curtailment with a
colon (signature, *Edmund*); ℓ for *es*; *wᵗ* in various
compounds for *with* (e.g. *wᵗout* for *without*);
yoʳ for *your*; crossed *u* symbol (an early form of
c) for *ac* or possibly *c* (26, l. 3); *p* with a
reversed ' above for *pre*; ' for *er*, *ier* or *ire* (26,
l. 2, *esqu'*); *a* symbol for *au* or *a* (26, l. 5);
crossed *s* for *ser* (25, l. 10); and the punctum
for sigla (e.g. *L* for *Lordship*).

Right honorable. This poor man hath
been miserabli spoild as by the attestation
sent vnto you by the Embassadour you
may perceaue, there needes must be
sharp punishment vsed in such lyke
cases or els these men will take, an
euill tast of olr government.
I wryte to your honor at large
by an other and therefore in these
I will onely pray for your long
and happy lyfe.   Flushing
this 27 of november 1585.

your humble D

R. Sidney.

27   Letter to Sir Francis Walsingham, 27 November 1585.
Rapid italic, holograph.
P.R.O., S.P. 84, bundle 5, no. 63, f. 118.

Right honorable. This poor man hath been miserabli spoild[1] as by the
attestation sent vnto yow by the Embassadour yow maj perceau, there needes
must be sharp punishment vsed in such lyke caces or els these men will take an
Euill tast of owr gouernment.
I wryte to yowr honor at large by an other and therefore in these I will onely praj
for yowr leng and happy lyfe. At Flushing This 27th of nouember 1585.

Yowr humble *servant*[2]

Ph. Sidnej.

1. Apostrophe? deleted over *i*.   2. Transcribed as *son* by Feuillerat, *Complete works*, iii, 150.

Notes

The bulk of Sidney's holograph material lies in
his copious correspondence, concerning which
vide Feuillerat, *op. cit.*, iii, 73–183; C. S. Levy,
MP, 67, 1969, 177–81; *CBEL*, i, 1049–50;
facsimiles, Feuillerat, iii, frontispiece, Greg,
XLI. Other holographs include his 14 page
'Defence of the Earl of Leicester', an illustration
of which is given in *Major Acquisitions of the
Pierpont Morgan Library, 1924–1974*, 1974, no. 8;
and a solitary example of his poetry on the last
printed page of Jean Bouchet's *Les annales
d'Aquitaine, faicts & gestes en sommaire des Roys de
France & d'Angleterre*, 1557, in the Bibliotheca
Bodmeriana, Cologny, Geneva, reproduced by
Croft (14) who made the discovery. Also,
recently re-discovered is what could well be an
autograph *italic* inscription written when he was
about 12 in a copy of Belleforest's *Histoires
tragiques*, housed in King's School, Canterbury
(J. Robertson, *Lib.*, 5th ser., xxi, 1966, 326–8,
with facs.). Though the hand, understandably,
is not immediately recognizable as Sidney's, it
does contain letters characteristic of his early
handwriting, e.g. long *s* with a small curl at the
top and a wide curve at the bottom, and *t* with
a heavy horizontal foot-serif to the right.
Greg (XLI) discerned and illustrated three
stages in the development of Sidney's hand, from
the very formal, compact and spiky writing of a
letter of 1569, when he was 15, through an
intermediate more calligraphic stage, shown in
letters of 1577 and 1578, to the freer and more
flowing hand as illustrated here. A marked
characteristic of the three stages is also that the
hand becomes gradually broader and spreads
itself considerably. There is, too, a fourth and
tragic phase, shown in the letter written the day
before Sidney died of his battle-wound (Morton,
pl. I), a shakier and a more spidery hand,
though even there he takes the trouble to
indicate *u* by diacritic and to dot *i* carefully.
No examples of Sidney's *secretary* hand are
apparently extant.

General Characteristics.   A well spread
out and fairly free *italic* hand, written at some
speed, which seems to accelerate as the letter
progresses, when, too, blots are more in
evidence. Letter forms are somewhat
inconsistent, but *y* and *g* often have a very long,
looped tail running almost parallel to the line.
F, *T* and *Y* normally have a long cross-stroke
from left to right, *t* is made in one pen lift with a
low cross-bar, which, combined with a slight
curl serves for *to* (ll. 3, 8). Also to be noted are
the unusual spellings, with *u* for *v* in final
position (l. 4, *perceau*) and *j* for *y* (l. 4, *maj*, l. 10,
praj, and the signature, though elsewhere
normally *Sidney*).
Punctuation comprises the period for a major
pause and to end a sentence and paragraph,
and a comma, which seems to have the function
of a full stop. The only marks of **abbreviation**
are the curtailment indicated by punctum in
the signature (*Philip*) and the flourish joined to
initial *s* (l. 13) interpreted as *servant* (cf. note
1).

settinge on. but lettinge thes thinges pas for a whyle,
I must not forget to giue yowre lordship those
thankes, whiche ar due to yow. for this yowre
honorable dealinge to hir mage. in my behalf.
whiche I hope shall not be wythout effect.
the whiche attendinge from the court. I will
take my leaue of yowre lordship. and rest at
yowre Commandment. at my howse. this morning.

yowre lordships. assured.

Edward Oxenford

---

dd other with theyre (cowardly) flyght did only offend me
But thyne gaste denyed and now in that offer (face) yg[·]the
standest feelyng thy self with my damage (and savethe)
do thinge part of that pleasur belongs vnto the

Hope by one and one route round
The wordes of warre and of low fall
where peter seemed to be imprinted
In the ... (conqueror) or these two realms
... it wold make him boast that ...
for if from mortall eie often remote
virtue, which hath foand in vs, the ...
... (to of god) is able to ... in ... self
As a ... from raging ...
The ... in cold realms ...
At the ... tyde of the ... heated
Does quyte melt and resolue in to water
So the feare raging ... in the frosen hart
of peter then when the ...
... now and him his eies he ...
And ... into teares was resolued
... teares or ... word not ...
where at the ... season ...
for ... king of heauen ...
... him the graue which he ...
Yet all the ... the remnant of his ...
... was neuer ... but then he did ...
... the ... tell him how ...
I ... now ...

28 Conclusion of letter to Lord Burghley, July 1581.
Facile italic, holograph.
B.L., Lansdowne 33, f. 13.

settinge on. but lettinge thes thinges pas for a whyle, I must not forget to giue yowre lordship those thankes whiche ar due to yow. for this yowre honorable dealinge to her mage*sty* in my behalf. whiche I hope shall not be wythought effect. the whiche attendinge from the court. I will take my leaue of yowre lordship. and rest at yowre Commandment, at my howse. this morninge
yowre Lordships. assured.
Edward Oxenford

Notes
As with so many Elizabethan poets, no poetic autographs by the Earl of Oxford have yet come to light, but there is a considerable amount of his holograph correspondence extant, mainly in the British Library and Hatfield House (for other facsimiles see Greg, XXVIII). Oxford's hand, which is predominantly *italic*, is usually clear, fairly lightly penned, practical, and with the minimum of adornment, except for the signature where he permits himself a form of trellis-work above and below. (Noticeably, too, he uses a long *r* in the signature which is absent in the main body of his writing.) The hand is strikingly modern, and could pass for a near-contemporary script but for the occasional long *s*.
Punctuation, comprising the period and comma, is a little fuller than is common in correspondence of the period, but is somewhat haphazard. The only **abbreviation** is the unusual form of curtailment of *magesty* (l. 4).

St Robert Southwell (c. 1561–1595)

29 Draft of *Peeter Playnt*, c. 1592, 3rd page. *Facile Elizabethan secretary* mixed with *italic*, holograph.
Stonyhurst College, Lancashire, MS A. v. 4, f. 51.

All other with there (cowardly) flyght did onely offend me
But thow hast denyed and now[1] with the ⌈my⌉ other (foes) ghilty
standest feedynd thy eies with my damage (and sorows)
As though part of this pleasur belonged vnto the

5 Who by one and one could count
The wordes of wrath and of loue full[2]
Which peter seemed to se imprinted
In the holy gyre (compasse) [or] those two calme
eies, it wold make him brast that could vnderstand ([per] [con]ceiue) the*m*
10 for if from mortall eie often cometh
virtue, which hath force in vs, He which proueth ⌈(this)⌉ let him gesse
what an end diuyne (or of god) is able to worke in ma*n*s senses

As a feld of snow which frosen
The winter in close valew hiddyn laye
15 At the sprynge[3][t] tyde of the son heated
Doth quyte melt and resolue in to water
So the feare which [entred] ∧ [enterred was] in the frosen hart
Of peter then when the truth he conceled
When toward him his eies he turned
20 did quyte thow and into teares was resolued

He teres or weepyng were not as[4] riuer or torre*n*t
Which at the scorchyng hot season could euer dry vpp
for though Chryst kyng of heauen immayntena*n*t,
did retorne him the grace which he had lost
25 yet all the [he] remnant of his lyf
There was neuer nyght but therin he did wake
Herynge the cock tell him how vnfayful he had ben
and geu[y]ynge new teares to his old falt

1. *o* superscribed on *e*. 2. First *l* superscribed on *e*? 3. *n* superscribed on *r*. 4. *s* superscribed on *r*?

Notes
This first draft of a translation of part of Tansillo's *Le lagrime di San Pietro* comprises two leaves bound in with Southwell's papers and correspondence. See further M. Praz, *MLR*, xix, 1924, 273–90; J. H. Macdonald and N. P. Brown, *Poems of Robert Southwell*, 1967, lxxxvi–xciii, 103–7, 173–4, and frontis.; Croft, 19. The hand is remarkably small but fairly legible even allowing for corrections and interlineations. Though most of the letters are in normal *secretary* (including three forms of *e* and of *r*) less common forms include double long *s* in which the second *s* resembles a caret (l. 8), *y* with a curved bowl somewhat separated from the stem (l. 28) and *þ* with *italic* curves and serif. Completely *italic* letters are *c* (l. 1), *f* (l. 10, *for*), *H* (l. 21), *T* (l. 14) and possibly *O* (l. 18) and *r* (l. 22, *euer*).
Punctuation is generally lacking, save for one caret and the liberal use of brackets, seemingly employed to indicate alternative versions, e.g. l. 8, *gyre (compasse)*.
Abbreviation includes the usual bar for *m* and *n* (l. 9), crossed stem of *þ* for *per* (l. 9), concave loop through *þ* for *pro* (l. 11) and *w*[th] for *with* (l. 2).

Right worll. Mr Deane of westm. lately signified unto me
of his mties gracious inclination for my preferment, by reason
of yr worll favorable speeches in my behalfe. for the wch
5 ... I acknowledg my selfe most bound, So I humbly desyre
that as yu have layed the foundation, so you would
proceede to further yt to some effecte. I would be his
humble suppliant to his mtie ... neyther for personage, prebend
office or annuitye. but yf it maye nott dislike you ...
10 whereas I have bene now tenn yeares att westm. in a toyle
some ... without any hope of further rysing. that now
yt might please his most excellent mtie to directe his
mandatorye letters to the Deane and Chapiter of westm. to graunt
...

Psal. 6.

1. O doe not lord torment mee in thy wrath
Nor chasten mee in fury of thy choller
though many stripes my fault deserved hath
that in thy schoole am such a truant schollar

5 2. my naked soule too tender is, o god
too sensible of such a smarting rod

3. My perisht bones are in my body bruised
thy marrow with this maladie doth melt
let mercies oyle be to my wounds infused

10 4. Oh heale my soule of stripes so lately felt

5. for after death can none record thy storie
of all thy grace, thy goodnes, and thy glorie

6. My woefull daies I passe as wakefull nights
and of my griefe my bed a witnes beares
15 I weepe when I should sleepe with these affrights
in sighs distild I bathe my couche with teares

7. my beautie waste in sight of mine ill willers
and of my strength infeebled are the pillers.

30 Draft of letter to Lord Burghley (opening), *c.* March 1594. *Facile Elizabethan secretary,* holograph.
B.L., Add MS 36294, f. 24, upper portion.

Right *worshipful* Mr Deane of *westminster* lately signified vnto me of hir *majesties* gracious inclination for my preferment, by reason of *your* *worship's* fauorable speeches in my behalf. for the *which* as I acknowledg my self ⌈in all thankfullnes⌉ most bound, so I humbly desire that as *you* haue layed the foundation, [so] you would procede to further yt to some effecte. I would be an humble suppliant to hir *Majestie* neyther for personage, prebend office or annuitye ⌈delighting most in poore contentation⌉. but (yf it maye nott dislike you) that wheras I haue serued now xix yeares att *westminster* in a [most] toyle some [lyfe] ⌈place⌉, *without* any hope of farther rysing. that now yt might please hir most excellent *Majestie* to directe hir mandatorye *lettere*s to the Deane ant.[1] Chapiter of *westminster* to graunt

1. Apparently *ant.* though *and* seems intended.

Notes
This draft is contained in Camden's notebook, and has been dated by Greg (LXXIII), who provides five facsimiles of his hand, all from the British Library. The script is neat, small-bodied and compact, but there is the very noticeable characteristic of a heavy downstroke usually applied to the shaft of *d*. Camden is also partial to the high, hooked spur on open *a* (l. 6, *an*). Though there is a general impression of cursiveness, many of the letters are separate, necessitating a large number of pen-lifts in a rather compressed space.
Punctuation comprises the comma, looking like a short virgule, the period, used as a general factotum, and the colon.
Abbreviation relies heavily on curtailment, as might be expected in a draft (e.g. l. 1, *worshipful, westminster*). Superior letters are also used (e.g. l. 2, *m^{ties}* for *majesties*; l. 3, *y^r* for *your*), and the bar, linking *e* and for *n* (l. 11, *excellent*).

Sir John Harington (1561–1612)

31 Metrical paraphrase of Psalm VI. *Set Elizabethan secretary* with *hybrid italic* heading, holograph, *c.* 1600.
B.L., Egerton 2711, f. 104, upper portion.

Psalm 6.

1. O doe not lord correct mee in thy wrath
   Nor chasten mee in fury of thy Choller
   thowgh many strypes my fawlt deserved hath
   that in thy schoole am such a trewant scholler
5 2. my naked soule too tender is, o god
   too sensible of such a smarting rod.

3[1] My verie bones are in my body brused
   their marrow with this maladie doth melt
   let mercies oyle be to my wounds infused
10 4 Oh heale my soule of stripes so lately felt
5 for after death can none record the storie
   of all thy grace, thy goodnes, and thy glorie.

6 My wofull daies succeed as wakefull nights
   and of my greifs my bed a witnes beares
15 I weepe when I should sleepe with these affrights
   in sighs distild' I bathe my couche with teares
7 my beautie wasts in sight of mine ill willers
   and of my strength infeobled are the pillers.

1. Written over half-formed *2*?

Notes
Harington's paraphrases of the Penitential Psalms are in the same MS as the Wyatt autograph poems mentioned in no. 19. They cannot be dated with certainty, but K. E. Schmutzer (*PBSA*, 53, 1959, 243) thinks that 'the Egerton group were completed long before 1612, when Harington sent his completed psalter to James for revisions'. A date close to 1600, when Harington expressed his praise of the Countess of Pembroke's metrical paraphrases, seems a feasible one, and indeed, on purely palaeographical grounds a still earlier date would be justifiable. Harington's handwriting seems always to be of the highest quality whether in *secretary* or *italic*: carefully formed and with a refined sense of calligraphic artistry. (For further examples, including some from the holograph translation of *Orlando Furioso, vide* Greg, XLV, and *Collected Papers*, ed. J. C. Maxwell, 1966, 108; *EPA*, 4; Croft, 20. See also R. Hughey, *The Arundel Harington manuscript of Tudor poetry*, 1960.) Like Camden (no. 30), Harington uses heavy downstrokes for the back of *d*, and also for the shaft of *f* and *s* (noticeably not always at the same angle as might be expected from a set hand). By contrast to the thick downstroke are the hairline introductory strokes often to be found on initial minims, *t, v* and *w* (e.g. l. 1).
Punctuation is fairly carefully though lightly applied, combining the grammatical pause with the natural caesura of the verse: the comma for the short or intermediate pause, the period for the end of the poem.
Abbreviation, as might be expected of a fair copy, is infrequent, being limited to *y^e*: for *ye (the), y^t*: for *yat (that), w^{th}* for *with*, and the apostrophe, placed after the succeeding consonant to denote omitted and silent *e* (l. 16). The marginal numbers in the text relate to the psalm verse paraphrased.

Howbeit if some outcast Ismael, for want or of his owne dispose to lewdnes' sake
w[i]th pretext of dutie or relation, or to reduce himselfe to that he was not borne
unto by one wait intende y[ou]r L[ordshi]p to suspect me, I shall beseech in all humilitie
& in the feare of god that it will please yo[u]r L[ordshi]p but to reteine me as I shall
probe my self, and to repute them as they ar in deed. Cum totius iniustitiæ
nulla capitalior sit quam eorum, qui tum cum maxime fallunt id agunt ut viri
boni esse videantur. & for doubtles even then yo[u]r L[ordshi]p shalbe sure to breake
      their lewde desseigns, and see into the truthe; when but their lyued that
erein haue accused me shalbe examined & rypped vp effectually. For
maie I presume w[i]th paul to liue & shall set vpon of me came into the
       fyre he w[i]th the ignorant suspect me guiltie of the former. By which
And that for now I feare me I growe tedious & as wryting to a good that
that if I knewe time whom I hold vnfite accuse of that damnable of doing to
the dreadfull ma[jes]tie of god or of that other mutinous faction towrd the state
I wolde so willingly reveale them as I wolde requite yo[u]r L[ordshi]p better opinion of
me that neuer haue offended &c.

                                        yo[u]r L[ordshi]ps most humble in all duties

32 Ending of letter to Sir John Puckering, to be read by the Privy Council, late 1593. *Set Elizabethan secretary* with proper names and Latin quotations in *set Italic*, holograph? B.L., Harleian 6849, f. 218v. Termination and signature raised.

Howebeit if some outcast *Ismael* for want or of his owne dispose to lewdnes, haue with pretext of duetie or religion, or to reduce himself to that he was not borne vnto by enie waie incensd your lordships to suspect me, I shall besech in all humillitie & in the feare of god that it will please your lordships but to censure me as I shall prove my self, and to repute them as they ar in deed *Cum totius iniustitiæ nulla capitalior sit quam eorum, qui tum cum maximé fallunt id agunt vt viri boni esse videant*ur ffor doubtles even then your lordships shalbe sure to breake ⟨into⟩ their lewde designes and see into the truthe, when but their lyues that herein haue accused me shalbe examined & rypped vp effectually, soe maie I chaunce with *Paul* to liue & shake the vyper of my hand into the fier for which the ignorant suspect me guiltie of the former shipwrack And thus (for nowe I feare me I growe teadious) assuring Your good Lordship⟨s⟩ that if I knewe eny whom I cold iustlie accuse of that damnable offence to the awefull Ma*je*stie of god or of that other mutinous sedition towrd the state I wold as willinglie reveale them as I wold request your Lordships better thought*es* of me that never haue offended yow

> Your Lordships most humble in all duties
> Th Kydd

Notes
One of two surviving Kyd letters, it concerns charges of atheism levelled at him; the other (Harl. 6848, f. 154) contains his accusations against Marlowe. For further illustrations and discussion *vide* Greg, XV; A. D. Wraight, *In search of Christopher Marlowe*, 1965, 310 ff. Tannenbaum (*The Booke of Sir Thomas More*, 1927, 43–7) is sure both letters are holograph; Greg, *op. cit.*, seems to think they probably are; A. Freeman (*Thomas Kyd*, 1967, 27) feels they 'almost certainly' are not, apart from the signature. Bearing in mind the calligraphic beauty of the signature and that his father, being a scrivener, may have taught him how to write, it is not unlikely that the comely set hand of both letters is Kyd's. (It should also be noted that *italic d* of ll. 6, 7, is similar to those of the signature.)

Characteristics. Clear and squarish, but with generous loops sloping right for *f* and *s* and a compensating large infralinear loop sloping left for *h* and *y*. Initial letters often have a long, thin introductory upstroke. There are three forms of *e*: reversed, Greek, and one with curled headstroke; three kinds of *r*: twin-stemmed, *z* form, and backwards leaning Greek *e* type; and two forms of final *s*: sigma (l. 4, *as*) and a variant of the old *B* form or 'legal' *s*, comprising *c* + Greek *e* (l. 1, *his*)—cf. 15th-century form in, e.g., nos. 11 and 12. In the *italic* hand, ascenders have curled and clubbed finials.

Punctuation consists of an occasional comma.

Abbreviation in the *secretary* comprises mainly superior letters (e.g. l. 3, *yoʳ Lᵖˢ* for *your Lordships*) and ꝯ for *es* (l. 15, *thoughtes*). The *italic* contains a tilde standing on end for *m* (l. 6, *eorum*) and an elaborate form of the superior *2* symbol for *ur* (l. 7, *videantur*).

◉ Thomas Nashe (1567–1601?)

33 Letter to William Cotton, *c.* September 1596. *Facile/rapid Elizabethan secretary*, with proper names in *facile italic*. B.L., Cotton, Julius C. iii, f. 280, lower portion.

⟨haue⟩ sett for ye mott or word before it *Fah*, & dedicated it to the house of the shakerlies that giue for there armes three doggs turds reaking, ffor my parte I pitty him & [pri] pray for him that he may haue many good stooles to his last ending, & so I wold wish all his frends to pray, for otherwise it is to be feared, [that as] yat according as *Seneca* reports the last words *Claudius Cẹsar* was hard to speake were[1] *Hei mihi*[1] *vereor concacaui me* so he will dy with a turd in his mouth [if he reche ⟨it⟩ not] [at his last gaspe] & bee coffind vp in a iakes farmer tunne no other nosewise christian, for his horrible *per*fume being able to come nere him. well some men for sorrow singe as it is in the ballet of *Iohn Carelesse* in the booke of martirs, & I am merry when I haue nere a penny in my purse, God may moue you though I say nothing, in which hope that that which wilbee shalbe I take my leaue.

1. Superscription on illegible letters.

Notes
A good example of Nashe's vituperative gifts, the whole letter is reproduced with transcription and commentary in R. B. McKerrow, *Works of Thomas Nashe*, rev. F. P. Wilson, 1958, v, frontis., 192–6, and supplement, 80. For the identity of the recipient, William Cotton, M.P., *vide* E. M. Mackeness, *RES*, xxv, 1929, 242–6; C. G. Harlow, *N & Q*, Nov. 1961. Nashe's signature has long been obliterated, but Collier claimed that the top of an *N* was still visible when he transcribed the letter for his *History of English dramatic poetry* (1831), 303–6. Although the only mention of Nashe's name was added at the foot of the page, presumably by Collier, there is little doubt that this is a Nashe holograph. Unfortunately, the other known examples of his hand (Greg, XX) are too brief and too early (pre-1586) for a satisfactory comparison, but there are some similarities in both the *italic* and *secretary* examples (e.g. final *s* in *secretary*, ending in a left-handed hook (l. 3, *armes*). The handwriting seems to accord with the temperament of the man and the contents of the letter. The general impression is of scrappiness with numerous blots, several cancellations and some superscribed letters. The hand flows quite well, however, and is generally legible even though the minims tend to be ill-defined and the loops hang loose. The most distinctive features seem to be the wide right-handed arc shared by *h*, *y*, the ornamental curve on *G* (l. 15), and the Tironian sign for *and* (l. 4). Also distinctive is *g* looking like an elongated angular *8* leaning to the right.

Punctuation comprises mainly the comma and period, which seem sometimes interchangeable but are applied comparatively frequently and regularly, considering the general haste of the letter. A cedilla beneath *e* indicates *ae* (l. 8).

Abbreviation is fairly sparse, being confined mainly to superior letters (l. 16, *wᶜʰ*; l. 7, *yᵗ*) and crossed *p* for *per* (l. 11, *perfume*).

Wm Gammazley

Edmond Aphinsi

Christofer Marlow

John more

Enter the souldier wt a muskett

    Now ser. to you yt dares make a duke a Cuckolde
    and vse a counterfeyt key to his privye Chamber
Souldier thoughe you take out none but yor owne treasure
5   yett you putt in yt displeases him / And fill vp his rome yt
    he shold occupie. Herein ser you forestalle the markett
    and sett vpe yor standinge where you shold not: But you will
    saye you leaue him rome enoughe besides: thats no answere
    he to haue the Charte of his owne freeland/ yf it be
10   not to free yor neighbor to the anothour / now ser where he is
    your landlorde you take vpon you to be his / and will needs
    Enter by defaulte/ what thoughe you were once in possession
    yett dominion vpon you owne vnlawfull he ferayed you
    out againe. therefore your entrye is more Intrusion
15   this is againste the lawe ser: And thoughe I come not
    to keep possession as I wold I mighte. yet I come to
    keepe you out ser. you are wellcome ser haue at you
Enter minion
minion   Traytorouse guise ah thou hast mourthered me He kills him
20   Enter guise
Guise   Hold thee tale soldier take thee this and flye Exit
    thus far Inported occasiones
    that our greate sum of fraunce doth not afforte
    a fewe motion in the fermament
25   he that the kinge delyght and guises frownd
    revenge it henry yf thou liste ar darst
    I did it onely in dispyght of thee

84

34 Signatures of witnesses to the will of Katherine Benchkin. *Facile Elizabethan secretary*, autograph, November 1585.
Kent R.O., PRC 16/86.

Ihon marley
Thomas Arthur
Christofer Marley
Iohn moore

35 *Massacre at Paris* leaf, recto, version of scene xvii, ll. 806–20, *Facile Elizabethan secretary*, hand unknown, c. 1593, or forgery?
Folger Shakespeare Lib., S.b. 8.

Enter A[1] souldier with a mvskett[2]
    Now ser to you yat dares make a dvke a Cuckolde[3]
    and vse a Counterfeyt key[4] to his privye Chamber
souldier[5] thoughe you take out none but your owne treasure
5   yett you putt in yat displeases him / And fill vp his rome yat
    he shold occupie. Herein ser you fore stalle the markett
    and sett vpe your standinge where you shold not: But you will
    say you leave him rome enoughe besides: thats no answere
    hes to have the Choyce of his owne freeland / yf it be
10   not to free theres the questione / Now ser where he is
    your landlorde. you take vpon you to be his / and will needs
    enter by defaulte / whatt thoughe you were once in possession
    yett Comminge vpon you once vnawares he frayde you
    out againe. therefore your entrye is mere Intrvsione
15   this is againste the lawe ser:[6] And thoughe I Come not
    to keep possessione as I wold I mighte, yet I Come to
    keepe you out ser. yow are wellcome ser have at you
Enter minion   *He* Kills him
minion Trayterouse guise ah thow hast mvrthered me
20   *Enter guise*
Guise Hold thee tale soldier take the this and flye   *Exit*
    thus fall Imperfett exhalatione[7]
    which our great sonn of fraunce Cold not effecte
    a fyery meteor[8] in the fermament
25   lye there the Kinges delyght and guises scorne
    revenge it henry yf thow liste or darst
    I did it onely in dispight of thee

1. *A* altered from *S*.   2. *s* and probably *m* in *italic*.   3. *C* superscribed on loop and head of *k*.
4. *k* superscribed on *C*.   5. *r* altered from *t*?   6. *r* altered from *o*?   7. *h* superscribed on *a*.
8. 2nd *e* superscribed on *o*.

Notes

The only incontestable example of Marlowe's handwriting is his signature appended to the will of a neighbour, Katherine Benchkin, which was discovered in 1939. Written when he was 21, it is in a firm, fairly bold and formal *secretary*, with regular minuscules, except for the elaborate figure 8 ligature for *st*, and the rather short, thick shaft of *s*. The capitals are less common, *M* having a rather large third limb with a long loop, and *C* resembling two intersecting *italic C*'s. The *Massacre at Paris* leaf (sometimes called 'the Collier leaf') was supposedly found by J. P. Collier in a London bookseller's and first published by him in 1825. Though denounced as a forgery by Collier himself for a time (honestly or as a ruse), and later by Tannenbaum

(*Shaksperian scraps*, 1933, 177–86) it was till recently generally held to be a Marlowe holograph on palaeographical and literary grounds, e.g. J. Q. Adams (*Lib.*, 4th ser., xiv, 1934, 447–69, with facs. and impressive rebuttal of Tannenbaum); F. E. Boas (*Christopher Marlowe*, 1940, 168–71); and J. M. Nosworthy (*Lib.*, 4th ser., xxvi, 1946, 158–71), none of whom was aware of the signature (neither was F. Bowers, *Works of Christopher Marlowe*, i, 1973, 358, also frontis. and 390–1). The basis of comparison afforded by the signature has caused some scholars to deny the leaf holograph status (e.g. Croft, xiv, and very tellingly, R. E. Alton, *TLS*, 26 April 1974), but among those convinced that it is in the same hand as the signature are A. D. Wraight (*In search of*

Christopher Marlowe, 1965, 224–32, with facs.) and the former archivist to the city of Canterbury, Dr William Urry (*id.*, 227). It is extremely difficult to effect an adequate comparison if one specimen is a signature, thereby having few and possibly atypical graphs, especially when written in early manhood and predating the other example by at least seven years. Fortunately, the signature is at roughly the same level of formality as the leaf, and is not unduly embellished. Further, the idiosyncratic capitals might well be distinctive features of Marlowe's hand in general. At all events, it is hard to understand how Wraight can claim (230) that 'the character of both hands appears the same and the method of letter formation with the strokes of the quill changes very little'. The small similarity there is, is merely that shared by hands of the same species and level of script. In fact, the hand of the leaf seems far less certain and fluent, being uneven in inking and containing large numbers of irregularly detached letters; it also has a more pronounced slope to the right. The only noticeable but nevertheless faint and insignificant similarities are to be found in the reversed *e*, *f* and, very occasionally, *o*, the short, thick shaft of *s*, and *h* (l. 3, *chamber*). The following letters are consistently different: *a*, which is generally rounded in the leaf but is angular and split from the stem in the signature; *C*, having the conventional form in the leaf; *r* consistently a *v* form in the leaf and twin-stemmed in the signature; *y*, which differs both in the head and tail. Ties and links and the *st* ligature are also different. The evidence, such as it is, indicates that the leaf is not holograph, neither can the possibility of forgery be ruled out. Nosworthy (*op. cit.*, 161) thinks it unlikely that anyone before Collier would have had the motive to forge the leaf, and that the errors he made in two separate transcriptions are not a forger's trick but the result of cursory reading and unintelligent transcribing. However, his arguments cannot be accepted unreservedly, and Collier was capable of mistranscribing his own forgeries (cf. 39). Tannenbaum was surely right to be uneasy about the continual unevenness of inking, and the occasional retracing of letters (e.g. *s* of *guise*, l. 19). There is an incredibly large number of detached letters for a cursive script, and the slight tremulousness in the penstrokes, the blots and false starts may connote a forger's hesitancy. Also worrying is a lack of uniformity of character in the writing. On the other hand, the letter forms are in keeping with the period, though the very rudimentary *p* is uncommon, and if the leaf is a forgery it has a palaeographic subtlety and literary flair which are a little above Collier's usual standard. If it is genuine, then the further problems remain of whose hand it is and for what purpose it was written. It may have been copied from an authorial MS or prompt book of the play, at roughly the time of its performance, perhaps as an actor's part or as a memento of a skilful piece of bawdry. Whatever it is, it has gained a handsome home in the Folger Shakespeare Library, and pride of place as frontispiece in the most recent complete edition of the works of Christopher Marlowe.

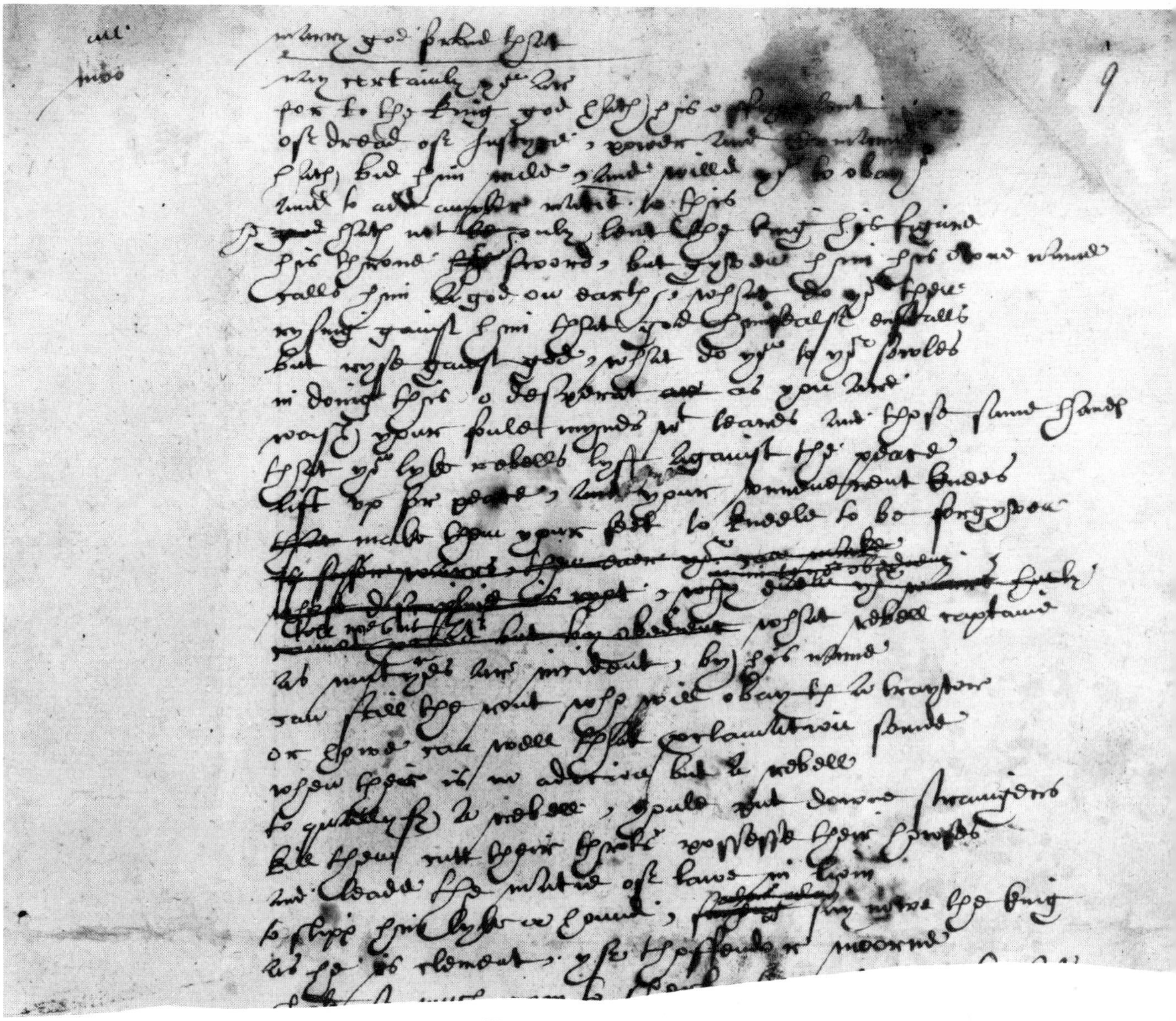

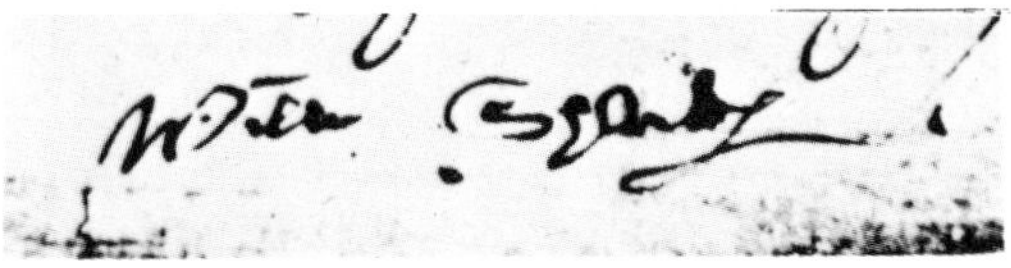

a.

b.

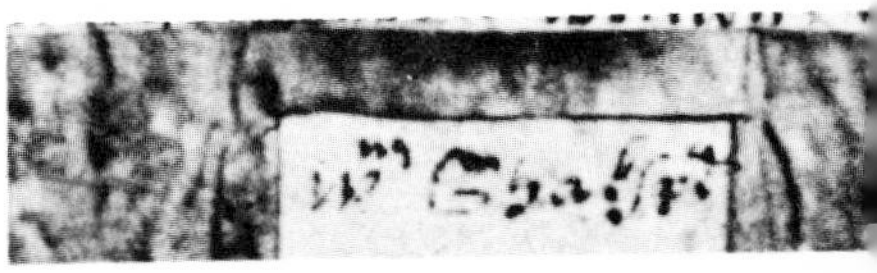

c.

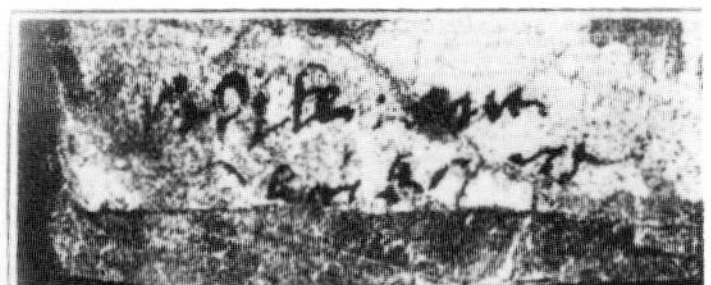

d.

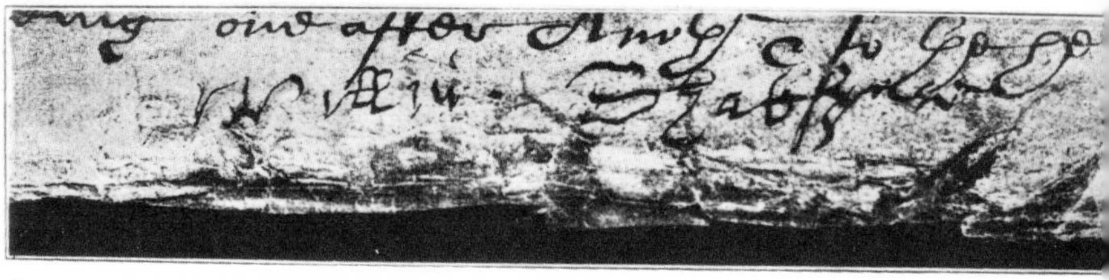

e.

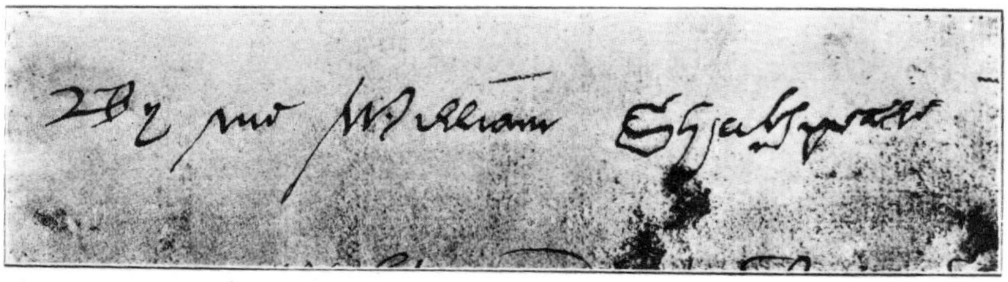

f.

36 *The Booke of Sir Thomas Moore*: revision of scene vi,
ll. 219–49. *Facile/rapid Elizabethan secretary*, holograph?
c. 1593.
B.L., Harleian 7368, f. 9, upper portion.

all   marry god forbid that

_____

moo   nay certainly you ar
      for to the king god hath his offyc lent
      of dread of Iustyce, power and Comaund
5   hath bid him rule, and willd you to obay
      and[1] to add ampler ma*jes*tie to this
      he [god] hath not [le] only[2] lent the king his figure
      his throne [his] &[3] sword, but gyven him his owne name
      calls him a god on earth, what do you then
10   rysing gainst him that god himsealf enstalls
      but ryse gainst god, what do you to yo*ur* sowles
      in doing this o desperat [ar] as you are.
      wash your foule mynds w*ith* teares and those same hand*es*
      that you lyke rebells lyft against the peace
15   lift vp for peace, and your[4] vnreuerent knees
      [that] make them your feet to kneele to be forgyven
      is safer warrs, then euer you can make
      whose discipline is ryot; why euem[5] your [warrs] hurly[6]
      cannot p*ro*ceed but by obedienc[7] what rebell captaine
20   as mutyes[8] ar incident, by his name
      can still the rout who will obay [th] a traytor
      or howe can well that p*ro*clamation sounde[9]
      when ther[10] is no adicion but a rebell
      to quallyfy a rebell, youle put downe straingers
25   kill them cutt their throts possesse their howses
      and leade the matie of lawe in liom
      to slipp him lyke a hound; [sayeng][11] say nowe the king
      as he is clement,. yf thoffendor moorne

1. *and*, superfluous minim. 2. *only* possibly prefixed by deleted *h*. 3. Transcription doubtful: possibly *th* replaced by *his* replaced by power and ampersand. 4. Word (yo*r* ?) interlined over caret before *your*, then deleted. 5. Usually transcribed *euen*. 6. *in* in to yo*r* *obedienc*, interlined and cancelled by Shakespeare. 7. l. 17 to *obedienc* cancelled Hand C, who has interlined *tell me but this*, 1st half l. 19. 8. *n* interlined Hand C? 9. *sounde* lacking a minim. 10. *r* altered from *ir*. 11. *alas alas* interlined by Shakespeare, deleted Hand C?

37 The Shakespeare signatures. *Rapid Elizabethan secretary*, authentic.

a. Bellot-Mountjoy lawsuit deposition, 11 May 1612, P.R.O.; *b.* conveyance of
Blackfriars house purchased by Shakespeare, 10 March 1613, London Guildhall;
c. mortgage deed of same, 11 March 1613, B.L.; *d, e, f,* signature on pp. 1, 2, 3, of
Shakespeare's will, 25 March 1616, P.R.O. Museum.

a. William Shak*per*   *b.* William Shaksper[1]   *c.* William Shaksper[2]
d. William Shakspere   *e.* William Shakspere   *f.* By me William Shakspeare[3]

1. *r* added later by Shakespeare, making bar unnecessary? 2. Graph above *e* usually transcribed as bar, here transcribed as *r*. 3. Medial *s* could be form of *italic s* or brevigraph for *es*.

Notes

The corpus of Shakespeare's undoubted holograph material is limited to six signatures, all executed in later life, the three on the will being written shortly before his death, when the hand is slightly shaky and tails off even in the final attesting signature. The signatures vary quite considerably. For example, the first two have two versions of the celebrated 'spurred *a*'; the 2nd, 3rd and possibly 6th have variants of *medial italic* long *s*, and there are varying degrees of abbreviation. In fact, as Greg observed (*TLS*, 1 Dec. 1927, repr. *Collected Papers*, ed. J. C. Maxwell, 1966), it is as difficult to descry the similarity of each to another as it is to establish their similarity to the only other serious candidate for holograph status, the three pages by Hand D in the revision to the play, *The Booke of Sir Thomas Moore* (cf. 40). The case for Shakespeare has been painstakingly stated by E. Maunde Thompson, e.g., in A. W. Pollard, *Shakespeare's hand in the Play of Sir Thomas More*, 1923, repr. 1968. Thompson's evidence has often been disputed (e.g. S. A. Tannenbaum, *The Booke of Sir Thomas Moore*, etc.; R. A. Huber, *Stratford Papers on Shakespeare*, 1961, 51–70). However, though the slender palaeographical proof rests mainly on 'general impression' and the spurred *a* with the horizontal continuation of the descender, feebly aided by *italic s* and forms of *p* and *k*, the case is generally held sufficiently proved with the support of linguistic, orthographic and stylistic evidence. Greg's summation (*op. cit.*) still seems appropriate: that (*a*) the case is stronger for similarity between the signatures and the revision than for dissimilarity; (*b*) the hand of the signatures more nearly parallels the revision hand than any extant dramatic document does; and (*c*) the revision was not written by any other dramatist of whose hand there is adequate knowledge. A useful summary of scholarship, together with revised readings is given by H. Jenkins in the repr. of Greg's Malone Soc. edition, 1961. See also, R. C. Bald, *Shakespeare Survey*, 1949; T. Clayton, *The Shakespearean addition*, 1969; *Riverside Shakespeare*, 2 vols., 1974, 1683 ff.; and esp. for revised dating, P. W. M. Blayney, *SP*, April 1972, 167–91. The MS was published in facsimile by J. S. Farmer, 1910, repr. 1970. For the unprepossessing claim of holograph for annotations in a copy of Hall's *Chronicles*, *vide* A. Keen and R. Lubbock, *The annotator*, 1954. **Characteristics of no. 36.** Though not especially distinctive or aesthetic, the hand is firm, even-stroked and very cursive, and ably combines boldness and freedom with compactness and economy. Particularly noticeable is the large number of different forms of letters, especially *a, b, g, h, p, s* and *t*, though this might be expected from a fairly rapid hand. Among the graphs to be noted is *g* with a tail which begins almost vertically and then ends in a strong though narrow anti-clockwise curve (l. 8, *gyven*), a tendency reflected sometimes in *h*; and *f*, the head of which ends in a dangling Greek *e* (l. 4, *of*). The firmness of the hand is also reflected in the **punctuation**, e.g. the large thick commas and the dots over *i*, and the debatable semicolons (ll. 18, 27). The **abbreviations** are common enough: *matie* surmounted by a bar (l. 6); *yo*r (l. 11, *your*); *w*t (l. 13, *with*), *p* with a concave curve through the stem for *pro* (l. 22, *proclamation*). For detailed illustration of letter forms and abbreviation *vide* Maunde Thompson, *op. cit.*, 57–112.

5

10

Sweete Nedde, nowe wynne an other wager
for thine olde frende and fellow stager.
Tarlton himselfe thou doost excell
And Bentley beate and conquer Knell
5 And nowe shall Kempe overcome aswell
The moneyed downe the plase the hope
Phillippes shall hide his head and hope.
ffeare not the victorie is thine.
You still is marchles Ned shall shine.
10 If fostius Richard foames and fumes
The globe shall haue but emptie roomes
If thou doost act, and Willes nowe playe
Shall be rehearst some other daye
Consent then Nedde, doe vt this graue
15 Thou cannot faile in anie case
ffor in the triall come what maye
All sides shall braue Ned Allin sayes

38 *Shakespeare's MS. catalogue of his books.* Forgery of Shakespeare's hand, *c.* January 1796.
U.C.L., Ogden collection, lower portion, last leaf.

Tamberrelayne	———————————————	1590
Tragedyes o Maryno ande Scylla	———————	1594
Tancredde ande Sysmunde	———————————	1592
Tom Tylesse ands Wyfe	———————————————	1561
5 Cobberres Prophecye	———————————————	1594
Orlandoe ffuriosoe	———————————————	1591
Maydes metamorpheses	———————————	1600
hystorye o Travayle	———————————————	1577
Dorastus ande ffawnya	———————————	1591
10 Mosieurre D Olive	———————————————	1601
Greenes Mamyllia	———————————————	1595

Notes
Ireland was first driven to forgery to impress and please his father with the discovery of works in Shakespeare's handwriting, which in time included the MS of *King Lear, Richard II* and parts of *King John* and *Othello.* His biggest success was not only in fabricating a completely new play by Shakespeare called *Vortigern,* but actually having it performed at Covent Garden (April 1796) though it met with derision. Ireland's father believed in the authenticity of the documents to the end and James Boswell was among those taken in; but the forgery was swiftly and devastatingly exposed by Edmund Malone (e.g. *Inquiry into the authenticity of certain miscellaneous papers,* 1796). Ireland himself 'revealed all' in his *Authentic account of the Shakespearian manuscripts,* 1796, and *Confessions of William Henry Ireland,* 1805, both works being best-sellers. Though his revelations are not fully to be trusted, they contain interesting and genuine information on how he set about the forgeries, the paper and ink he used and the models for his handwriting (e.g. *Authentic account,* 3–4, 10; *Confessions,* 37–42). See, further, J. Mair, *The fourth forger,* 1939; B. Grebanier, *The great Shakespeare forgery,* 1966; S. Schoenbaum, *Shakespeare's Lives,* 1970, 189–223. The catalogue of the books in Shakespeare's library, comprising seven leaves and now bound in green leather was sold at Sotheby's in 1801, and among its subsequent owners was C. K. Ogden, many of whose books and MSS were bequeathed, with this item, to U.C.L. It was forged around January 1796 in an effort to bolster an already tottering case. As usual, he had taken care not to use paper with a watermark, had employed his special ink mixture heated to age it, and had tried to make the paper look old by rubbing dirt over it and burning it, to the extent of leaving a charred hole on p. 8. This long spidery hand is so poor an attempt at forging a *rapid Elizabethan secretary* with *italic* mixture that it is not worth analysing apart from noting that reversed *e* is the only letter which closely approximates to the authentic script, and Ireland used his knowledge of the signature on Shakespeare's will to no purpose.

John Payne Collier (1789–1883)

39 Wager poem to Edward Alleyn from fellow actor. Collier forgery of *set Elizabethan secretary* mixed with *italic, c.* 1840.
Dulwich College, MS 1 (1st series) f. 8.

Sweete Nedde nowe wynne an other wager
ffor thine olde frende and fellow stager.
Tarlton himselfe thou doest excell
And Bentley beate and conquer Knell
5 And nowe shall Kempe orecome aswell
The moneyes downe the place the Hope
Phillipes shall hide his head and Pope.
ffeare not the victorie is thine
Thou still as macheles Ned shall shine.
10 If Roscius Richard foames and fumes
The globe shall haue but emptie roomes
If thou doest act, and Willes newe playe
Shall be rehearst some other daye
Consent then Nedde, doe vs this grace
15 Thou cannot faile in anie case
ffor in the triall come what maye
All sides shall braue Ned Allin saye

Notes
Collier is the most celebrated forger of Shakespearean documents, and the extent of his forgery may never be fully known. Part of his success came from his wide knowledge of Elizabethan literature and handwriting and his own literary gifts. Having general access to most collections in England, he was able to plant his own compositions written on 16th-century paper, or slip in postscripts. It is clear that he did this in the case of the present forgery, which he added to the Alleyn papers having based it on a genuine letter written to Alleyn on the subject of a wager. He himself transcribes it, a little inaccurately (e.g. l. 9, *shyne*; l. 10, *Rossius*) in *Memoirs of Edward Alleyn,* Shakespeare Soc., 1841, 13–14, commenting on the document and expressing surprise that Edmund Malone had not mentioned it, but assuming that it was to have been reserved for Malone's *Life of Shakespeare.* The forgery was detected by N. E. S. A. Hamilton (*An Inquiry into the genuineness of the manuscript correction in Mr. J. Payne Collier's annotated Shakspere,* 1860, 95) who describes it as 'the worst executed of all the fabricated documents' and refers to a 'very slight tremulousness . . . which betrays the fact that it was written slowly from an alphabet with which the writer was not too familiar'. Collier feebly replied by admitting that 'the reduplication of consonants and other points of orthography in it, might possibly rouse suspicion' in an otherwise genuine document (*Mr. J. Payne Collier's Reply,* 1860, 54). The most comprehensive account of the Collier forgeries is contained in C. M. Ingleby, *A complete view of the Shakspere controversy,* 1861 with many illustrations (esp. 266–9); see also S. Schoenbaum, *Shakespeare's Lives,* 1970, 332–61. Hamilton was right to note a tremor in the hand or rather a lack of steadiness, which is revealed in very uneven inking and a mottled effect in the strokes especially in the final lines. But Collier has managed to give the hand a uniformity of character (which the *Massacre* leaf, 34 seems to lack). Most of the letter forms are plausible except for *A,* which is not intended as an *italic* graph yet has a crossbar (ll. 4, 5, 17), *H* (l. 6), *K* (ll. 4, 5), *N* (l. 17) and *P* (l. 7, possibly intended as *italic*). Of the minuscules, *c* is unconvincing (l. 8) and *b* untypically linked to a succeeding letter (ll. 11, 13, 17).

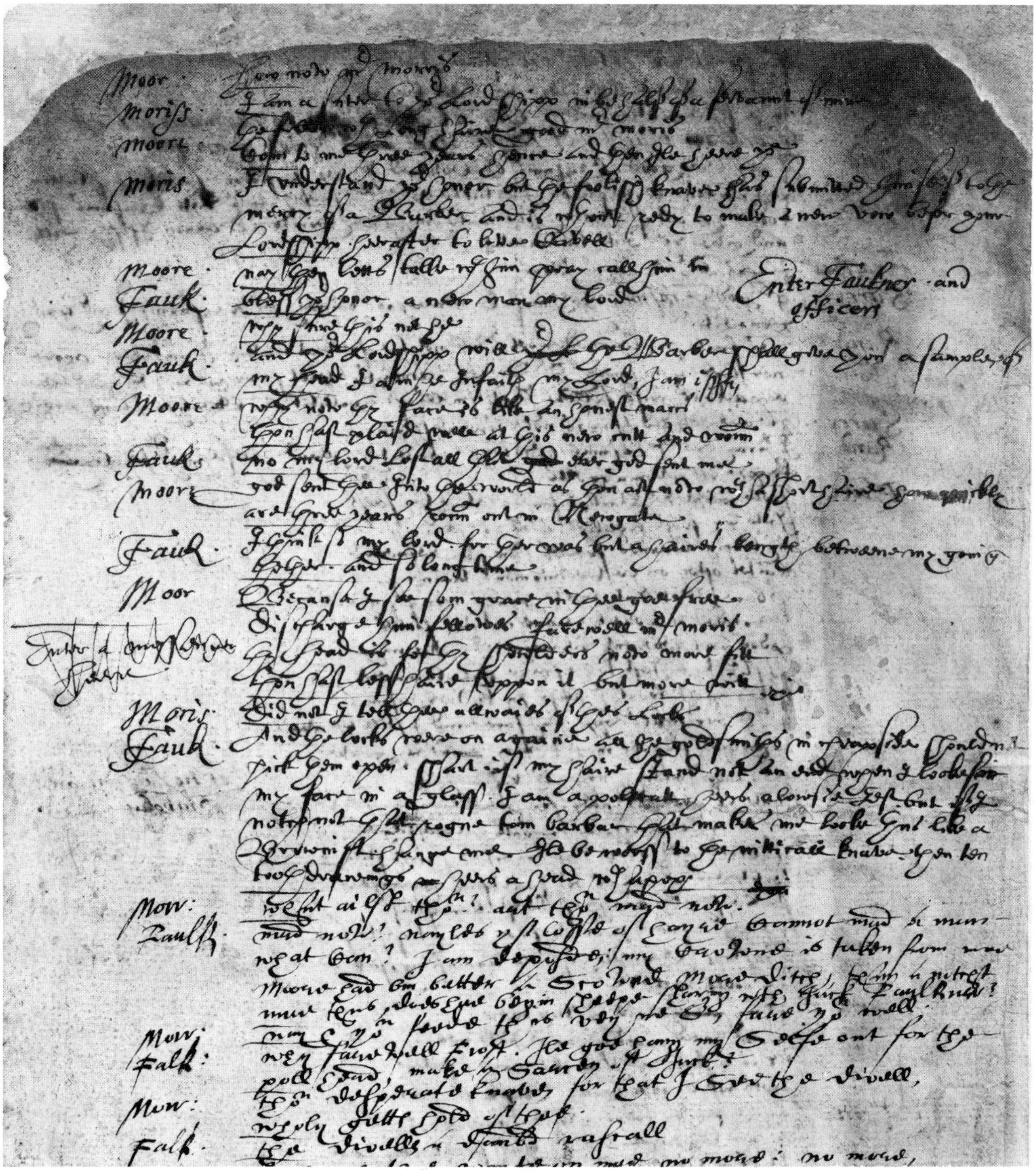

Moor: How now Morris

Moris: I am a sutor to yor lordshipp in behalf of a servant of mine

moore: The fellow wth long haire good mr moris
Come to me three yeares hence and then Ile heare you

moris: I understand yor honor but the foolish knave has submitted him self to the mercy of a barber and is without ready to make a new vow before yor lordshipp hereafter to live civill

moore: nay then lets talke wth him pray call him in

Enter Faulkner and officers

Fauk: blesse yor honor a new man my lord

Moore: why sure this is not he

Fauk: and yor lordshipp will the barber shall give you a sample of my head I am he in faith my lord I am ipse

Moore: why now thy face is like an honest mans
thou hast plaid well at this new cutt and wonne

Fauk: no my lord lost all that ever god sent me

moore: god sent thee into the world as thou art now
wth a short haire how quickly are three yeares
runn out in Newgate

Fauk: I thinke so my lord for there was but a haires length betweene my going thither and so long time

Moor: Because I see som grace in thee goe free
Discharge him fellowes farewell mr moris
Thy head is for thy shoulders now more fitt
thou hast lesse haire uppon it but more witt

Exit [illegible]

Moris: did not I tell thee allwaies of these lockes

Fauk: And the lockes were on againe all the goldsmithes in cheapeside should not pick them open shart if my haire stand not an end when I looke for my face in a glasse I am a polecatt heres a lowsie jest but if I notch not that rogue Tom barber that makes me looke thus like a Brownist hange me Ile be worse to the nitticall knave then ten tooth drawings heres a head wth a pox

Mor: what ailst thou art thou mad now

Faulk: mad now? nayles if losse of haire cannot mad a man what can? I am deposed, my crowne is taken from me. More had bin better a scowrd More ditch, then a notcht mee thus, does hee begin sheepe sharing wth Jacke Faulkner?

Mor: nay and yu feede this veine Sr, fare you well.

Falk: why fare well frost. Ile goe hang my selfe out for the poll head, make a Sarcen of Jacke?

Mor: thou desperate knave, for that I see the divell
wholy gett hold of thee.

Falk: the divells a damnd rascall

[illegible] no more: no more,

40 *Booke of Sir Thomas Moore,* addition IV, ll. 181–222.
Both hands: *facile/rapid Elizabethan secretary* with mainly
facile italic stage directions and speech headings, *c.* 1593.
B.L., Harleian 7368, f. 13v, excluding last 19 lines.

Moor.	How now m*aste*r morris
moriss.	I am a suter to yo*ur* Lordshipp in behalf of a servaunt of mine
moore.	the fellow w*i*th Long haire good m*aste*r moris
	Com to me three years hence and then Ile heere you
5 *moris*	I vnderstand yo*ur* honer but the foolish knave has submitted him self to the mercy of a Barber. and is without redy to make a new vow befor your Lordshipp. heerafter to live Civell
Moore.	nay then letts talke w*i*th him pray call him in *Enter Faukner and*
Fauk.	bless yo*ur* honor. a new man my lord. *officers*
10 *Moore.*	why sure this not he
Fauk.	and yo*ur* Lordshipp will [yo*ur* L] the Barber shall give you a sample of my head I am he Infaith my Lord, I am *ipse*,[1]
Moore.	why now thy face is like an honest mans thou hast plaid well at this new cutt and wonn[2]
15 *Fauk.*	no my lord Lost all that [god] ever god sent me
Moore	god sent thee Into the world as thou art now w*i*th a short haire. how quickly are three years ronn[2] out in Newgate
Fauk.	I think so my lord. for ther was but a haires length betweene my going thether. and so long time
20 *Moor*	Because I see som grace in thee goe free
Enter a messenger]	Discharge him fellowes farewell m*aste*r moris
[heere.]	thy head is for thy showlders now more fitt
	thou hast less haire vppon it but more witt
Moris.	Did not I tell thee allwaies of thes Locks ————— exit
25 *Fauk.*	And the locks were on againe all the goldsmiths in cheapside should not pick them open. shart. if my haire stand not an end when I looke for my face in a glass. I am a polecatt. heers. a lowsie Iest. but if I notch not that rogue tom barbar that makes me looke thus like a Brownist. hange me. Ile be worss to the nitticall knave. then ten
30	tooth drawings [w] heers a head w*i*th a pox ————— [exit]
Morr:[3]	what ailst thou? art thou mad now.
Faulk.	mad now.? nay les yf losse of hayre Cannot mad a man — what Can? I am deposde,: my Crowne is taken from mee Moore had bin better a Scowrd[4] More ditch, than a notcht
35	mee thus, does hee begin sheepe sharing with Iack *Faulkner*?
Morr:	nay & you feede this veyne S*i*r, fare you well.
Falk:	why fare well Frost.[5] Ile goe hang my Selfe out for the — poll head, make a Sarcen of Iack?
Morr:	thou desperate knave, for that I See the divell,
40	wholy gett*es* hold of thee.
Falk.	the divell*es* a dambd rascall

1. *I am ipse,* Dekker's hand.   2. Otiose looped bar.   3. Dekker's hand begins here.   4. *r* altered from *a*?   5. *Fro* in *italic.*

Notes

Five of the six hands in *The Booke of Sir Thomas Moore* have been identified as follows: S, the main author, Anthony Munday; A, Henry Chettle; B, Thomas Heywood?; D, Shakespeare? (*vide* bibliog. in 36) and E, Dekker (ll. 31–41 above). The sixth hand, C (ll. 1–30 above) was held by Greg to be a playhouse book-keeper's and the same hand as for the plot summaries of *The Seven Deadly Sins* (Dulwich Coll.) and *Fortune's Tennis* (B.L., Add MS 10449), though the similarities are not clearly proved and rely mainly on a comparison of *italic* samples and *set book-hand* headings (*DDR*, II, IV; *DDC*, 244; and *Lib.*, 4th ser., ix, where Tannenbaum's unlikely claim that C is Kyd is repudiated). Hand C may be that of a leading dramatist, and the resemblance it bears to Hand D (cf. 36) should not be completely ignored, since it has most of the same minuscule graphs, though its spurred *a* lacks the 'crucial' horizontal continuation of the descender (except perhaps in l. 29, *hange*) and final *f* has a reversed *c* finial rather than the dangling Greek *e* of Hand D's *f.* The apparent revisions of Hand C in no. 36 might be Hand D's written somewhat later.

Dekker's hand is easily identified not only by its spikiness, scratchy appearance and sharply angled duct, but by distinctive letter forms, e.g. *d* with a long, narrow, nearly horizontal loop, and the curved 6 form of final *s* (l. 36, *this*): cf. a Dekker receipt in the Henslowe fragment, B.L., Add MS 30262, f. 66v, Greg Xb. Resemblances can also be found between the *italic* speech headings and Dekker's two known forms of *italic* (described and illustr. Greg, IX) especially final *s* looking like *8* with a narrow squashed head (no example here). See, further, on Dekker's hand, Greg in A. W. Pollard, *Shakespeare's hand in the Play of Sir Thomas More,* 1923, 53–4.

Punctuation is rather sparse in Hand C (by contrast to Hand D), being limited to the occasional period and rare comma. Dekker employs frequent and varied punctuation: the period, comma, colon, question mark, and the dash (ll. 32, 37, possibly a line-filler). He also uses a combination of period and question mark (l. 32), and a comma and colon (l. 33) though in each case the second mark was meant to replace the first.

Abbreviation relies heavily in both hands on superior letters (occasionally unnecessary: l. 4, *yo*[u]); Dekker twice uses *ℓ* for *es* (ll. 40, 41).

Be it knowen vnto all men by thes presente
that I George Chapman off London gentleman
doe owe vnto mr Phillip Henshlowe off the
Pisse off st Saviours gentleman the some
off xld xb off lawfull money off England. In
wittnesse wherof I have hereunto sett my
hand this ~~present~~ xxiijth off october 1598

Geo: Chapman.

41 Acknowledgement of debt to Philip Henslowe, 24
October 1598. *Facile Elizabethan secretary*, signature *italic*,
holograph.
Dulwich College, Henslowe's Diary: MS 7 (1st ser.) f. 90,
upper portion.

Be it knowen vnto all men by thes presen*tes*
that I George Chapman of London gentleman
doe owe vnto mr phillip Henshlowe of the
p*ar*ishe of St Saviours gentleman the some
5 of x^{li1} x^s of Lawfull money of England. In
wittnesse whereof I haue herevnto sett my
hand this [present] xxiiijth of october i598
              Geo: Chapman.

$\left. \right\}$ x^{li1} x^s

1. Brevigraph for *libri*.

Notes

The volume of accounts and memoranda known
as Henslowe's Diary, from which plates 41–3
are taken, is generally considered to be the most
important extant document illustrating the
external history of Elizabethan drama. There
are editions by Greg (1904–7) and R. A. Foakes
and R. T. Rickert (1962). A particularly
fruitful source of dramatic holographs, it
contains two of the few undoubted examples of
Chapman's hand (the other being a stray leaf
from the Diary, B.L., Add MS 30262, f. 66,
dated 17th July 1599, Greg XII).
Characteristics. A strong hand, capable of
writing with some elegance even at speed,
especially when compared with many other
receipt entries. One of the most distinctive
features is the frequently split long tapering
shaft of *f* and long *s*, in some cases with the
ascender completely detached from the
descender (l. 5, *of*). Spurred *a* beginning in a
hook from the left (e.g. l. 1, *all*) is also
present, though not in the Shakespearean form
with the horizontal spur on the downstroke
which R. W. Chambers noticed in the
Chapman signatures in the B.L. (*TLS*, Aug.
1925). The Chapman *d* is almost as
characteristic as Dekker's (cf. no. 40), having a
small, often open body, a tall back and a
diagonal loop with a thick downstroke (ll. 3, 7).
The dramatist's name in the body of the text is
a form of signature, being nearly identical to the
secretary signatures in the B.L. MS, with the
exception already noted. The *italic* signature at
the end of the receipt is an eloquent example of
how different a hand can seem when employing
another script.
Punctuation comprises a period, dots
meticulously placed above *i* (including the
roman numeral mixed with arabic numerals in
the date), the colon in the curtailment of the
signature, and the brace enclosing the entry.
Abbreviation includes *es* brevigraph, *þ* with
convex looped arc for *par* and the bar for
contraction of *libri*.

5

...forty shillinge...
...1598

5

Receiued in earnest of patient Grissell
by vs Tho: Dekker, Hen: Chettle and Willm Hawton...
...the summe of 3 li. of good & lawfull mony, be...
...note sent from mr Robt Shaa: the 19th of
December 1599:

By me Henry Chettle.
W Haughton
Thomas Dekker

◉ Michael Drayton (1563–1631)

42 Receipt given to Philip Henslowe, 21 February 1599.
Rapid Elizabethan secretary, holograph.
Dulwich College, Henslowe's Diary: MS 7 (1st ser.), f. 31,
top portion.

I receued forty shilling*es* of mr
Phillip Hinslowe in part of vj^{li} for
the playe of willi*am* Longsword
to be deliu*erd* pr*esent* wi*th* 2 or three dayes
the xxjth of Ianuary / i598^2 /
      Mich^3 Drayton

      s
      xxxx^1

1. *xxxx* Henslowe's hand. 2. Old style dating. 3. Possibly *Mih.* Usual signature *Mi:* .

Notes

Drayton's hand survives in three inscriptions, some notes in legal documents, a stray signature, a recently discovered letter to Drummond of Hawthornden, 1620 (*Lib.*, 5th ser., xxi, 1966, 328–30, with fac.) and the above entry in Henslowe's Diary. Greg, VIII, provides three facs, including the inscription in the *Battle of Agincourt*, 1627. All the examples are in *secretary* unmixed with *italic* as late as 1627. Though even at its best, Drayton's hand is untidy and loosely written, there are three levels of formality discernible, from the fairly upright, moderately clear and medium-paced hand of the *Agincourt* inscription, through the more slanted, blotty and somewhat indistinct and elongated example of the Letter, to the thin, spidery, and threadlike example in the Diary. Present in varying degrees in all examples are long lines from left to right, usually on the ends of final letters, especially, *e*, *h*, *t* or *y*. The virgules too are long and thin and sometimes nearly horizontal (end of Letter). Long rules are also found accompanying the text, as in both the Letter and the *Agincourt* inscription. The *a* is often spurred (l. 2, and several times in the Letter) and *f* and long *s* sometimes have a split shaft. A particularly distinctive graph is final *r* looking like an elongated roman *c* with or without a shaft (l. 2, *for*, cf. Letter).

Punctuation comprises two virgules and a brace; in other examples Drayton uses a wide range and is especially partial to the colon.

Abbreviations used are ℰ for *es*; open *a* symbol with headstroke for *ia*; ' for *er* and for *re* when above *þ*; and *wth* for *with*.

◉ Henry Chettle (1560?–1607?)

43 Receipt given to Philip Henslowe, 19 December 1599.
Facile Elizabethan secretary mixed with *italic*. Chettle's holograph with signatures of William Haughton and Thomas Dekker.
Dulwich College, Henslowe's Diary: MS 7 (1st ser.), f. 31,
bottom portion.

Receiued in earnest of patient Grissell
by vs Tho*mas* dekker, Hen*ry* Chettle and willi*am* Hawton
the sume of 3.^{li1} of good & lawfull money, by
a note sent from mr Rob*ert* Shaa: the 19th of
5 December. 1599:──────

      3.^{li1}

      By me henry chettle.
      W̄^{2} Haughton
      Thomas Dekker.

1. Brevigraph for *libri*. 2. Possibly superior crossed *i* above *W*.

Notes

From Henslowe's Diary it can be seen that Chettle participated in writing 45 plays, though only five have survived (H. Jenkins, *Henry Chettle*, 1934, 1), and he also contributed 71 lines to *The Booke of Sir Thomas Moore* (Hand A, cf. nos. 36, 40). *Patient Grissell*, mentioned in the above receipt, is one of the extant plays, written in collaboration with William Haughton and Thomas Dekker, who have also signed the above receipt, Dekker's elaborate and elongated signature almost swamping the other two. The surviving holographs of Chettle comprise six entries in the Diary (facs. Greg, VII), the *Thomas Moore* passage, and 12 lines of a play in Alnwick Castle (Jenkins, *op. cit.*, 55, who provides notes on the handwriting, 55, 95–6). His hand is not especially distinctive and tends to vary, but is generally somewhat angular, clearly written and quite heavily inked. A recurrent feature is the use of *italic* capitals in an otherwise *secretary* script: *C*, l. 2; *G*, l. 1; *H*, l. 2; *R* and *S*, l. 4 (cf. *Moore*, Hand A). However, despite using *italic* capitals for his name in the text, Chettle has minuscule *secretary* initials for the signature. Other notable features are an occasional *m* with a long third minim (l. 2, *william*) and *e* so closely looped to the top that it sometimes lacks an eye (l. 1, 2nd *e* of *Receiued*; l. 2, 2nd *e* of *dekker*.

Punctuation comprises the period, comma, colon and brace.

Abbreviations are either curtailments indicated by period or colon, or simple contractions with a bar above.

but to all ye world, and talk with the Clarke. And in the end, this Councell as the others
also did, safeguarded by them the rights of all princes fro any prjudice by any Acte
donne, ore omitted then. So, no Councell wytnessinge any precedency in the french before
nor any forfeyture beinge on ye Spa: part here, and the Spa: haveinge donne here the last
5 Acts of precedency, sittinge first, and speakinge first, as longe as he stayd, the matter seems
at least Res integra on the Spa: side. though yt shall scarse light upon any french
ma, but considers ys as Rem Contestam. Not upon these Councelles, but upon the beleif of
Pius 4, against Charls 9 for Phil: 2. But to yt Valdesius says, yt was not donne Judi-
cally: An Appeal was put in: The case nor pties are not now ye same, Spaine beinge
10 encreasd by Portugall. And ye Spanish legat at Rome then, was by ye kings expresse com-
mandemt remisse in yt, because france had solemnly made hys protestacion then of departinge fro the Romane Churche, except yt were pronounced for hym. But before
or after this Valdesius meddles with no Opposition; I thinke because he respects no
other Judge. Therfor he remembers not ye decree of ye Venetian state 1558. Nor yt at
15 Vienna since, where hys party was so stronge, and yet the Emperor did no more but forbid intermeetinges: Nor that in Poland Monluc had yt after. Allmost all ye french
offer thys for ye Issue, yt before 58 at Venice yt was never askt, and Valdesius
makes ye quarrell I know not how old, for hys words are mille saeculis. But before
58, I have observd one summe of differinge, at Calais 1521, when the point was when
20 their yt then belongd to ye Spanish, Charls beinge then Elect Emp: and K: of ye Ro:
for wth that yt essentiale circumstance it seems no offer had been then made on
yt part. And though Valdesius profes liberality, to give more then theyr Suitors
aske, (as indeed he ys often more submiss, then hys Nation useth to bee, in armes or
Argumt, when they have reasonable assurance of Conquest,) yet it is easy to remem-
25 ber som of many such Circumstances for ye french, as he swells up for ye Spanishe.
As ye Clement gave 100 dayes indulgence to any wth prayd for ye french k: and Innoce:
4 added to wth ys in The: Agn:. and many tymes ye Gr: k: hath gonne laterallity wth the
Emp: But there are such heaps of these, on both sides, as it wyll I thinke
ever remaine unfixed. for since in H 2 of fra: hys tyme, ye pope would not judge for
30 hym, since Phil: 2, could never requyre yt, in all H 3 hys bravery against Rome, nor
in H 4 hys grovellinge to creepe into ye Churche, nor in such a Succession of Cosen Emperors, I know not when he should hope for yt. St I have both held ye booke
longer then I ment and held yow longer by thys letter, now I send it backe. But yt
yt are a Hall and free doer of benefits, I presume are also an easy pardoner of unmali-
35 cious faults.

ys affectionate frinde & servant

293

J. Donne.

44   Letter to Sir Robert Cotton, 1602. *Facile italic,* holograph.
B.L., Cotton Cleo., F. vii, f. 293, lower portion.

but to all ye world, and satt with the Clarke. And in the end, this Councell, as the others also did, safeguarded by Decree, the rights of all princes from any pr*e*iudice, by any Acte donne, or omitted there. So, no Councell wytnessinge any pr*e*cedency in the french before, nor any forfeyture beeinge on ye spa*niards'* part here, and the spa*niard* hauinge donne here the last Acts of pr*e*cedency, sittinge first, and speaking first, as longe as he stayd, the matter[s] seems at least Res integra on the spa*niards'* sid*es*. though yow shall scarse light up*on* any french ma*n,* but considers yt as Rem Confectam. Not up*on* these Councells, but up*on* the Decisio*n* of pius 4, [against] [for] Charls 9 [for] ⌐against⌐[1] phili*p* 2. But to y*at* Valdesi*us* says, It was not donne Iuridically: An Appeal was put in: The case, nor p*ar*ties are not now ye same, spaine beeinge increased by portugall: And ye spanish legat at Rome then, was by ye kings expresse Commandem*ent* remisse in yt, because fraunce had solemly made hys p*r*otestaci*ons* there, of departinge from the Romane Churche, except yt were pronounc*d* for hym. But before or after these, Valdesius meddles w*i*th no opposition; I thinke because he respects no other Iudge. Therfore he remembers not ye Decree of ye Venetia*n* state i558. Nor y*at* at Vienna since, where hys party was so stronge; and yet the Emperor did no more, but forbid intermeetings: Nor that in poland Monluc had yt after. Allmost all ye french offer thys for ye Issue, y*at* before 58 at Venice yt was never askd, and Valdesius mak*s* ye quarrell, I know not[2] how old, for hys words are, mille sæculis. But before 58, I haue obserud one tyme of Differinge. at Calais i52i. where the point was whether yt then belongd to ye spanish, Charls beeinge then Elect Emp*er*or and k*i*ng of ye R*o*mans for w*i*thowt y*at* Essentiall Circumstance, it seems no offer had been then made on y*at* part. And though Valdesius profes liberality, to giue more then theyr Autors aske, (as indeed he ys often more submis, then hys Nation useth to bee, in armes or Argum*ent,* where they haue reasonable apparence of Conquest,) yet it is easy to remember hym, of many such Circumstanc*es* for ye frenche, as he swells up for ye spanishe. As y*at* Clement gave i00 Days indulgence to any w*h*ich prayd for ye french k*i*ng and Innoc*ent* 4 added io w*h*ich ys in Tho*mas* Aquin*as.* and many tymes ye fr*ench* k*i*ng hath gonne lateraliter with the Emp*er*or. But there are such heaps of these, on both sides, as it wyll I thinke [re] euer remaine p*er*plexd. for since in H*enry* 2 of fra*n*ce hys tyme, ye pope would not iudge for hym, since phili*p* 2, could neuer p*r*ocure yt, in all H*enry* 3 hys brauery against Rome, nor in H*enry* 4 hys grouelinge to creepe into ye Churche, nor in such a succession of Cosen Emperors, I know not when he should hope for yt. *s*ir I haue both held yo*ur* booke longer then I ment, and held yow longer by thys letter, now I send it backe. But yow y*at* are a r*e*all and free doer of benefits, I p*r*esume are also an easy pardoner of v*n*malicious faults.

Yo*ur* affectionate frinde & seruant

I: Donne.

1. Corrections possibly in different hand. 2. Apostrophe before *how*?

Notes

Donne's holographs comprise mainly letters, two Latin epigrams in the fly leaves of books, a receipt, and, since its identification by Croft in 1970, the 'Letter to the Lady Carew and Mrs Essex Rich', the only example of his English poetry in his own hand, which fetched the staggering sum of £23,000 at Sotheby's, and is now in the Bodleian. Reproduced many times, among the best facs. are those by the Scolar Press, 1972, and Croft, 25, with a description of the handwriting. For other facs. and refs. *vide* G. Keynes, *A bibliography of John Donne*, 1973, 183–4, App. IV, L.53, L.161, esp. good on sources of holograph letters; *FRHL*, 93; Greg, XLVIII; *EPA*, 7; R. C. Bald, *John Donne*, 1970, pl. viii and ix; and N. Barker, *BC*, 22, 1973, 487–93, and *TLS*, 20 Sept. 1974, with extensive palaeographical discussion and a caution against precipitate identification.

Characteristics. A firm, compact, unobtrusive and very cursive hand, even if there are often gaps between letters, especially after Greek *e*. It is generally upright, with a slope appearing only sporadically and at an irregular angle. Traces of *secretary* are to be seen in *t* with the crossbar linked to the foot by a drawn-back loop, and in *y*, normally in the combination *yt*, in which the tail curves to the right and then ascends to form a link (ll. 17, 32). There are at least three varieties of *y*, however, all visible in l. 17, the other two with a tail ending in a little curl to the left or in a loop crossing the tail. Many other letters appear in two or three forms. For example, *d* usually has an arched back, but it can also have a looped stem (l. 6, *side*) or a vertical one (l. 2, *preiudice*) and there are many permutations of all three; *e* is generally the Greek form, leaning slightly backwards, but is also in regular *italic*; *f* may be straight with a small curved head and separate cross-stroke (l. 34, *free*) or like a bow with a large lower loop intersecting it (l. 25, *for*) or in regular curved *italic* form (l. 2, *safeguarded*); *p* always has a long shaft both above and below the body, but it may have a closed narrow bowl or an open and squarish one (both forms, l. 13, *opposition*). The most characteristic Donne letter forms have been well tabulated by Croft and Barker (*TLS*, 20 Sept. 1974), who itemise 18 main points, though not all of them hold perfectly true here: e.g. *N* is not regularly a large minuscule (l. 7) but a distinctive *H* form of *roman N* (ll. 14, 16, 23), nor is *R* here (ll. 6, 7, 10) really as Barker describes it. To their list of distinctive graphs might be added *D*, which with its small body and high, projecting shaft resembles *b* (ll. 7, 14, 19, 26); *ff* with a long, thin 1st shaft with two tiny loops, a bow-shaped 2nd shaft with a wide top loop, and a common, separately made cross-stroke (ll. 17, 21); a usually open-head *g*; *k* with a long, looped, linking tail (l. 32, *booke*; l. 33, *backe*); and the long, thick, virgule-like commas almost invariably below the line.

Punctuation, sensitively applied, displays the usual range, including two semicolons corresponding quite closely to modern usage (ll. 13, 15).

Abbreviation. Extremely varied forms of the bar for *m* and *n* are employed, including the arch (upright or sideways) and the tilde (sometimes linked to *o*, as in l. 7, 1st *upon*). Crossed *p* stands for *par/per*; *p* with a concave bar for *pro*. A colon represents curtailment, usually confined to proper names; and the normal superior letters are employed, including *pᵣ* for *pre* and, less commonly the *9* symbol with a straight back for *us* (l. 8).

I finding during pleasure a willingness in
you to conferre with me in that great busines
concerning the Unyon, I doe now take yt
occasion to expresse my boldnesse, to
desire that now wyth your offred leaue,
for both the tyme as to leisure is
more lyberall, and as to the busines
yt self is more urgent. Wherefore yt
will leke you to come to me to Grayes Jnn
or to appoynt me whear to meete wyth
you If any undifferent land leaue yt
to yr respecte, and accordingly desire
to hear from you. So I remayne

yr poore louing ffrend

Fr. Bacon

Grayes Jnn this ffr
of Sept. 1604

45 Letter to Sir Robert Cotton, 8 September 1604. *Facile*
Elizabethan secretary mixed with *italic*, holograph.
B.L., Cotton Jul. C. iii, f. 10.

Sir finding during parlam*ent* a willingness in yow to Conferre w*i*th me in this
great service Concernyng the vnion, I doe now take hold thearof to excuse my
boldness, to desire that now w*hi*ch yow offred then, for both the tyme as to
Leasure is more liberall, and as to the service it self is more vrgent, whether it
will like yow to Come[1] to me to Graies I⟨nn⟩ or to appoynt me whear to meete
w*i*th yow I am indifferent, and leaue it to yo*ur* choise,[2] and accordingly desire to
hear from yow So I remayne

             Your very loving ffrend
               Fr. B̄acōn

Graies Inne this 8th
*of Sept*ember *1604*

1. Otiose bar. 2. Upstroke on *i* beginning of long *s*?

Notes

A large amount of Bacon holograph material survives, much of it in the B.L. and the P.R.O. Though most of it is correspondence, there are quite a few examples from his other writings, including the celebrated Memorandum Book (B.L., Add MS 27278). The best guide to holograph material is still the unrivalled complete edition of Bacon's works by J. Spedding and R. L. Ellis, though there is no comprehensive list in any one place and it is a question of working through all fourteen volumes, the 1st seven of which begin in 1857, and the 2nd set, entitled *Life and Letters of Francis Bacon*, in 1861 (the above letter being transcribed in iii, 1868, 217). For facs. *vide* FRHL, 24; Greg, LXXVI–VII; T. J. Brown, *BC*, 15, 1966, 184–5; J. G. Crouther, *Francis Bacon*, 1960, 48. Most of Bacon's correspondence is in *secretary* mixed with *italic*, but he widely used *italic* of varying degrees of formality and style, ranging from cramped jottings, often with heavy admixture of *secretary* (e.g. B.L., Add MS 27278, f. 13v), to a bold and somewhat eccentric *italic*, as in his letter to King James, 23 March 1623 (repr. Morton, pl. II). This contains heavy angled tops of shafts and stems, and an extremely unusual *M*, the 1st part of which looks like omega dwarfed by the 2nd part

resembling a tall, narrow unbarred *A* with a thick head angled to the right. Bacon's signature, in whatever form of designation, is usually in *italic*.

Characteristics. The *secretary* of the body of the letter shows a fluency and elegance often lacking in Bacon's less formal *italic*. It does however contain several *italic* graphs: an elliptical *C* (l. 2, *Conferre*; l. 3, *Concernyng*), a bold *f* with balanced arcs at the ends of its shaft (l. 6, *for*) alternating with varied forms of *secretary f*; and short *s* when doubled (l. 1, *willingness*; l. 4, *boldness*). A touch of *italic* is also to be seen in the stem and tail of *k* (l. 3, *take*). Among the distinctive *secretary* letters are several variants of spurred *a*: a small-bodied open *a* with the descender of the spur retracing the path of the ascender and projecting below the body (l. 5, *that*; l. 12, *accordingly*); a larger and more rounded body with introductory ascender from the left (l. 11, *and*) or from the right (l. 12, *and*). Yet another spurred *a* ends with the descender projecting in the Shakespearean horizontal stroke to the left at the top of the body (l. 7, *and*), and sometimes the spur is linked to the preceding letter (l. 1, *parlament*). Other notable *secretary* letters are *g* with a slight headstroke and a long tail moving

diagonally to the left and ending in a small downward curl (l. 2, *great*); *o* in the combination *to*, looking like a small *v* (ll. 9, 10); and *v* (often used medially as well as initially) with a tall and frequently looped first arm, and the rest of its body resembling a minute *w* (l. 8, *vrgent*). Another form of *v* is smaller and made in two strokes, but this may be due to altering it from another letter (l. 7, *service*). Three types of *r* appear: the *v* form (l. 2, *great*), the left-shouldered Greek *e* form (l. 1, *during*), and the twin-stemmed *r* (l. 2, *service*). The dating of the letter is in a *facile italic* but with *e* and *t* uniformly in *secretary*.

Punctuation is mainly a frequently applied comma, with the period used only for curtailment (l. 17, *Sept.*). It is also remotely possible that there are two or three semicolons instead of commas (l. 5, after *then*; l. 7, after *liberall*; and l. 8, after *vrgent*), but the supposed upper point is probably only an unintentional fleck of ink.

Abbreviation relies mainly on superior letters: *m^t* for *ment* (l. 1), *wth* for *with* (l. 2); *w^{ch}* for *which* (l. 5); *yor* for *your* (l. 12); and there is also a superfluous use of raised *r* in *o^r* (l. 10, *or*). The bar is otiose in both instances (l. 9 and signature).

agayne mounted, into three triumphant Chariots,
ready to come forth. The first foure were
drawne wth Eagles, (whereof I gaue the reason, as
of the rest, in Fames speech) they st Torchbearers
attending on the chariot sides, and foure of the
Hagges, bound before them. Then follow'd the se=
cond, drawne by Griffons, wth theyr Torch=bearers,
and foure other Hagges. Then the last, wh was
drawne by Lions, and more eminent (wherin her Ma tie
was) and had sixe Torch=bearers more, (peculiar to her)
wth the like number of Hagges. After wh, a full
triumphant Musique, singing this Song, while they
rode in state, about the stage.

Song.

Helpe, helpe all Tongues, to celebrate this wonder:
The voyce of FAME should be as loud as Thonder.
    Her House is all of echo made,
      Where neuer dies the sound;
    And, as her browes the cloudes invade,
      Her feete do strike the ground.
Sing then good Fame, that's out of Vertue borne,
For, Who doth fame neglect, doth vertue scorne.

Here, they alighted from theyr Chariots, and daunc'd
forth theyr first Daunce; then a second, immedi=
ately following it: both right curious, and full of
subtile, and excellent Changes, and seem'd performd,
wth no lesse spirits, then those they personated. The
first was to the Cornets, the second to the Violins.
After wh they tooke out the Men, and daunced the
Measures; entertayning the time, almost to the space
                                  - of

46 Presentation copy of *The Masque of Queenes*, 1609,
ll. 710–38. *Set mixed hand*, holograph.
B.L., Royal, 18A, xlv, f. 19v.

THE MASQVE OF QVEENES.

agayne mounted, into three triumphant Chariots, ready to come forth. The
first foure were drawne with Eagles, (wherof I gaue the reason, as of the rest,
in Fames speech) theyr ∧ [4] Torchbearers attending on the chariot[1] sides, and
foure of the Hagges, bound before them. Then follow'd the second, drawne [with]
by Griffons, with theyr Torch = bearers, and foure other Haggs.[2] Then the last,
which was drawne by Lions, and more eminent ([3]Wherin her Majestie was) and
had six Torch = bearers more, (peculiar to her) with the like number of Hagges.
After which, a full triumphant Musique, singing this Song, while they rode in
state, about the stage.

Song.

Helpe, helpe all Tongues, to celebrate this wonder:
The voyce of FAME should be as loud as Thonder.
Her House is all of echo made,
Where neuer dies the sound;
And, as her browes the cloudes invade,
Her feete do strike the ground.
Sing then good Fame, that's out of Vertue borne,
For, Who doth fame neglect, doth vertue scorne.

Here, they alighted from theyr Chariots, and daunc'd forth theyr first Daunce;
then a second, immediately following it: both right curious, and full of subtile,
and excellent Changes, and seem'd performd, with no lesse spirits, then those they
personated. The first was to the Cornets, the second to the Violins. After which
they tooke out the Men, and dauncd the Measures; entertayning the time, almost
to the space
– of

1. *t* superscribed on *r*. 2. comma altered to period and following *T* altered from *t*. 3. bracket
superscribed on comma.

Notes

No holographs of Jonson's plays have survived,
but his other works are quite well represented,
including poems, epigrams, letters and a
complete masque in a fair copy presented to
Prince Henry, an excerpt of which is illustrated
here. A near-complete list of holographs is given
in C. H. Herford and P. Simpson, *Works of Ben
Jonson*, ix, 1950, 3–4, who also provide facs. of
Jonson's hand, i, 56, vii, 290, viii, 178, and an
edition of the masque, vii, 267–317. A
meticulous facs. of the whole masque even
including an approximation to the colour of ink,
edited by G. Chapman, was published in 1930.
For other facs. *vide* Greg, XXIII–IV, Croft, 27;
FRHL, 94; *Cat. of Royal MSS in B.M.*, pt. 1,
103; EPA, 8; *The Connoisseur*, viii, 36; Morton, 3.
Characteristics. Jonson's hand is aptly
described by Maunde Thompson (*Shakespeare's
England*, 1916, i, 293) as a 'delicate example of
literary calligraphy'. Its special achievement is
the way in which it harmoniously blends
secretary and *italic* to form an integrated hand in
its own right, conveniently described as *mixed*,
though without any perjorative connotation. It
is true that *italic* graphs are in the majority, and

certainly almost entirely dominate the capitals.
The general smallness and lightness of touch of
the writing are also more suggestive of *italic*,
but therein lies part of the success of
integration. The following *secretary* graphs are
present: spurred *a* with the horizontal end to the
spur, but with descender starting from the
right (l. 2, *agayne*); *b* with indented bowl
forming a point with the bottom of the shaft
(l. 7, *bound*); tall and wide-looped *d* (l. 6, *and*);
reversed *e* (l. 3, *come*) alternating with Greek *e*;
h (occasionally after *g* and more rarely
elsewhere), with a long linking tail and little or
no body (no example here, but *vide*
Dedicatory Epistle, 4th line from end, *nights*); *r*
either twin-stemmed (l. 4, *drawne*) or in ornate
Greek *e* form when in superior position (l. 5,
*they*ʳ); *t* usually with short introductory ascender
and linking loop from base (l. 5, *the*); and a
simplified form of minuscule and capital *w* (l. 11,
was; l. 23, *Who*). These graphs exist side by
side with their *italic* counterparts, except that
there is no purely *italic e*. At least one letter
exists in hybrid form: *þ* with introductory *2*
stroke to the bowl as in *secretary*, but with an

italic tail which often loops over itself. In other
examples of Jonson's *mixed* hand the *secretary*
right-angled *c* is quite common, e.g., *Epitaph on
Cecilia Bulstrode* (l. 13) and accompanying
letter (ll. 4, 8), Houghton Library, Harvard
(Croft, 27).
Punctuation is extremely meticulous and
almost the full range of modern marks are to be
found in the MS. Occurring here are the
period, comma, semicolon, a double hyphen
for compound words and syllabication, brackets
(actually used for parenthetical material rather
than for emphasis, as is more common in
dramatic manuscripts), the apostrophe for
unvoiced *e*, and the caret. Key nouns are
underlined, and in order to keep the text within
the margins, liberal use is made of the double
hyphen at the end of the line. Also to be noted
are the running title and catchword prefixed by
a dash.
Abbreviation, as might be expected in a
presentation copy, is not very frequent, being
mainly confined to the commonest superior
letters, e.g. *w*ᶜʰ for *which*. The superior position
of *r* in *they*ʳ (l. 5) is otiose.

Egypt, supposed to be made by ye mud & slyme brought
downe by ye river nilus, being in tyme but a bay
of ye mediterran sea, & was therfore as it
someth called by Stephanus Potamitis, who with
Dionysius genes it thes other names following
Aeria Aetia, Ogygia, Hephestia, Myara, & Melambolos,
Appollodorus calls it Melampodū for ye fertilitie
It was also called Thebæ as Aristotle & Herodotus
witnes The scriptures call it Mesraim, Honorius
Augustodunensis affirms yt it had ye name of
Enxea: other call it Chus. but most authentiously
Cham, of Cam ye sonn of Noe. wth Cam first possest
it, ps: 77, 104. 105.

Joseph: call it
Mersin. l.1.r.12.

As if love could find a quill   ...hemera her could indyte
drawn from an angels wings   to please all other seuns
or did the muses singe   but lote & was experi
yat proke wanton's noill.   herrole rem only write

The coast of octob[er] att night, rising out of bed being in a
great sweat by reason of a suddayne gust & much rla-
mor in ye shipp before they could get downe the sailes
J tooke a violent cold wth suche me into a burning
fever then wth never man indured any more violent
nor never more suffered a more furious that an ungraint
able drough[t] for ye first 10 dayes J never voyd abo[ut]
any sustenance that now & then aftewed prune
but dranck every houre day & night, sweat so[me]...

47 Ralegh's notebook for his *History of the World*: Egypt.
Set/facile mixed hand, holograph, *c.* 1610.
B.L., Add MS 57555, f. 24, upper portion.

Ægypt, supposed to be made by the mud & slyme brought downe by the river
nilus / being in tyme but a bay of the mediteran Sea / & was therfore as it semeth
called by Stephanus Potamitis, who with Dionysius geues it thes other names
followinge / Aeria Aetia, Ogygia, Hephestia, Myara, & Melambolos / Appollodorus
calls it Melampodum for the fertilitie / It was also called Thebæ as Aristotel &
Herodotus witnis / The Scriptures call it Mesraim, Honorius Augustodunensis
affirms yat it had the name of Euxea: other call it Chus. but most awntiently
Cham, of Cam the sonn of Noe. which Cam first possest it, psalm 77., 104. 105.
[margin] Josephus call it Mersin. l. 1. c. 12.

48 Ralegh's notebook, end fly leaf, last two stanzas of
Now we haue present made (*c.* 1597). *Facile mixed hand*,
holograph, *c.* 1610.
B.L., Add MS 57555, f. 170v, bottom of page.

If love could find a quill   perchance hee could indyte
drawn from an angells winge   to pleas all other sence
or did the muses singe [yat]   butt loves & woes expenc
that prety wantons will.   Sorrow can only write

49 Journal of 2nd voyage to Guiana: entry from Oct.–Nov.
1617. *Facile mixed hand*, holograph.
B.L., Cotton, Titus B. viii, f. 172, middle portion.

Thursday mornig we had agayne a duble rainebow which putt vs in feire[1] yat yat[2]
the raines would never end, from wensday 12 to thursday 12 we made not above 6:
Leagues having allwayes vncumfortable raines & dead calmes
The last of october att night rising out of bedd being in a great sweat by reason
of a suddayne gust & much clamor in ye shipp before they could gett downe the
sailes I tooke a violent cold which cast me into a burnig fever then which never man
indured any more violent nor never man suffered caret [a] more furious heat & an
vnquenchable drough, for ye first 10 dayes I never receaved any sustenance but
now & then a stewed prune but dranck every houre day & night, & sweat so
strong . . . my shirts thrise every day & thrise

1. 1st *e* superscribed on *a*? 2. *yat*, dittography.

Notes

A large number of Ralegh holographs have
come to light in recent years, including poems in
the Hatfield House MSS and the Ralegh
Notebook, another of the distinguished
discoveries by Walter Oakeshott (*vide The Queen
and the Poet*, 1960, 17–20). For facs. *vide* Greg,
LXXIV, LXXV; *EPA*, 2; Croft, 13; *FRHL*,
20; P. Edwards, *Sir Walter Ralegh*, 1953, 96–7;
Oakeshott, *op. cit.*, 119, 141, 223. A few examples
of Ralegh's *secretary* hand are extant (e.g. letter
to Leicester, 1581, B.L., Harl. 6993, f. 5, repr.
Greg, LXXVa) but from about the last decade
of the 16th century onwards he used mainly
italic, though with sufficient *secretary* forms to
constitute the *mixed hand*. Various attempts have
been made to date Ralegh's works after 1590
by means of assigning chronological phases to
the different styles of his writing, but this has
recently been discounted as a satisfactory method
(e.g. by Croft) and certainly it seems especially
difficult in Ralegh's case when particular
circumstances such as imprisonment and
sickness also place their own marks upon the
hand. Neither can the date safely be gauged
by the relative frequency of *secretary* graphs,
since the hand of 1617 (no. 49) contains as
many, proportionately, as that of *c.* 1610 (nos.
47, 48). The Notebook provides some of the
raw material and the illustrations used in
Ralegh's *History of the World*, the 1st example
here containing notes on Egypt. It also
includes, on a fly-leaf (excerpt in 2nd
illustration) a 32-line poem to Cynthia
(representing Queen Elizabeth) as a type of
epilogue, which Oakeshott thinks was
probably composed around 1599, though he
feels that this copy, like the rest of the Notebook
should be dated *c.* 1610 (80, 119, 205–9). The
Journal relates to his last and disastrous voyage
to Guiana in 1617, the excerpt being written
just before and after Ralegh had contracted the
sickness to which many in his fleet had
succumbed. His recovery is indicated by the
clearer firmer hand, though a darker ink has
aided the clarity.

Characteristics. As can be seen from the
three examples, Ralegh's *mixed hand* can vary
considerably in size and general appearance.
The main entries in the Notebook are in a
small, fairly formal, thick and quite rounded
script, though from l. 11 onwards and in the
marginalia a thinner nib is used and the
writing is more cursive. In the poetic extract,
the hand is less formal and even smaller,
especially when Ralegh is attempting to cram the
last stanza into the bottom right-hand margin.
In the top section of the Journal extract, the
writing is quite bold and squarish. It becomes
more compressed and a little more angular
when Ralegh takes up the pen afresh. Despite
these differences, the illustrations contain
basically the same graphs. They share, for
example, the same *secretary* letters: the right-
angled *c* (47, l. 4, *called*; 48, l. 1a, *could*; 49,
l. 8, *could*); reversed *e* (47, l. 1, *the*; 48, l. 1a,
love; 49, l. 1, *duble*); two-stroke *e* looped at the
top (47, l. 1, *be*; 48, l. 4a, *prety*; 49, l. 8, *before*);
h with little or no body and a linking tail (47,
l. 1, *the*; 49, l. 15, *houre*), and double-looped *h*
(47, l. 4a, *that*; 49, l. 15, *shirts*), no. 49 also
containing the set form (l. 3, *thursday*); *r* in its *v*
form (47, l. 2, *river*; 48, l. 2a, *drawn*; 49, l. 6,
october); *t* either uncrossed (47, l. 2, *the*; 49, l. 2,
the) or with cross-stroke formed by a loop
from the base (47, l. 3, *it*; 49, l. 9, *tooke*—a word
typical of Ralegh's more cursive hand); *w* in
the *n+v* form (47, l. 4, *who*; 49, l. 7, *sweat*); and
y with a linking tail to the right (47, l. 10, *yt*;
48, l. 4a, *prety*; 49, l. 7, *by*). The three
illustrations also share a hybrid *h*, with the
stem not quite reaching the line and the body
ending in a short unlinking tail (47, l. 5, *thes*;
48, l. 1b, *he*; 49, l. 10, *then*).

Punctuation. The most noticeable feature
is a long virgule which seems to serve as a
general factotum, though it is usually an
alternative to the period and the comma. The
colon is quite common, being generally for
curtailment (47, l. 13, *ps:*; 49, l. 4, *L:* for
Leagues). Ralegh is careful to punctuate his
references, using the point for curtailment of
line and *chapter* and to enclose numerals (47,
ll. 12, 13, margin).

Abbreviation includes the bar for *m*, *n* (47,
l. 7), the regular *secretary* *p* with crossed stem for
per (48, l. 1b) and superior letters: y^t (*that*), *ye*
(*the*) and w^{ch} (*which*).

So

The busines of this letter is to thanck you
for yours as for news this place yeilds
none, becaush all things here hang in suspence
but nothing is done and only matters of fact
~~bought noth change~~ are reale marks of
change. your frends here present Sr
Harry Nevile and Sr Robert Killigrew
salute and Jo commend my loue to
you whois Debt Bou it self in all offices
and uppon all occasions You Debt often
Yourselues So taking my leaue J will

London the xxmth   Your assured frend
of February   Tho: Overbury.

Desspotris what away at an hundred peeces, and
much reputaçon: who indeed the supreme physital
did all, almost without these.. J neuer saw
the king look better, then some houres since
J saw him; Only his leggs are not yet returned to their
due & strength. W s. Since my returne J haue
twise read in generall rumor, laud my Dignities
sued for; yet still J rub out; and hope for as much
health as J haue yet. J long to heare of my
Pew-fellowes of the Synode. Whose returne J wish
happy & speedy. If my duty & thanks may be
represented to my good lady. J haue done.
Who shall neuer ceasse to be
Yor Lops truely deuoted
Jos: Hall:

Walton.
Apr. 25°

Sir Thomas Overbury (1581–1613)

50 Letter to Sir Dudley Carleton, 24 February 1613.
Rapid italic, holograph.
P.R.O., S.P. 14, lxxii, f. 83, signature and termination raised.
Reduced by ⅓.

*s*ir
The busines of this letter is to thanck you for yours as for
news this place yeylds none, beecause all things here hang in
suspense but no thing is ⌈done,⌉ and only matters of fact
⌈beegett reall changes⌉ are reall marks of chang. your frends
here present *s*ir Harry Neuill and *s*ir Robert Killigrew
salute and I commend my loue to you which shall shew it
self in all effects and vppon all occasions that shall offerr
themselus so taking my leaue I rest

London the xxiiijth	Your assured frend
of February	Tho Overbury.

Notes
Overbury is a much neglected writer, though his character-writings ran to
many editions in the 17th century. Like Ralegh he wrote much of his
extant holograph material while in the Tower, where he was murdered by
poison in 1613. Most of the letters written from the Tower (as this one
was) are preserved in the B.L. (Harleian 7002) or in the P.R.O., among
State Papers Domestic, James I. No comprehensive edition of his works
has appeared since A. Grosart's in the last century, and his complete
correspondence has never been published. Facs. are extremely rare, and
Greg, strangely enough, does not provide any.
Characteristics. An immediately recognizable hand because it is
usually long, thin and spiky, the impression conveyed mainly by the shafts
of *b, f, h, l* and long *s*, and the tails of *p* and *y*. Loops are very
uncommon, being confined mainly to *g* and to the double-looped long *s*
(which alternates with an unlooped variety) and even so, they are generally
narrow. Many letters are so elongated that they lose any shape in their
bodies, as in the *h* of *shall*, l. 11; and the lack of horizontal definition
tends to make some words resemble a succession of barely decipherable
scratches (e.g. l. 10, *which*). Among other distinctive features is the
frequent habit of reducing the head of *italic e* and the arm of *italic r* to a
detached dot (l. 6, *reall*). In *ll* the second *l* is often reduced in size
and shape to a form resembling a *c* (l. 11, *shall*; cf, however, l. 8,
Killigrew). No purely *secretary* graphs are to be found in the hand, but
there are two forms common in *secretary* also: Greek *e*, and *v* form of *r*
(l. 8, *Killigrew*).
Punctuation comprises two periods and two commas in the shape of
small left-to-right obliques, one of them with a slight tail (l. 5,
interlineation). The only **abbreviation**, apart from the curtailed
signature, is *sʳ* for *sir*.

 Joseph Hall (1574–1656)

51 Letter to Sir Dudley Carleton, 24 April 1619. *Facile
italic*, holograph.
P.R.O., S.P. 14, cviii, no. 72, lower portion.

Despotine went away w*ith* an hundred peeces, and much
reputa*tion*: Tho indeed the supreme physi*tian* did all,
almost w*ith*out these. I neuer saw the king look better, then
some houre since I saw him; Only his leggs are not yet
returned to their vse, & strength. ·/· Since my. returne I
haue ∧ ⌈bene⌉ twise dead in generall rumor, and my
dignityes sued for; yet still I rub out; and hope for as much
health as I haue lost.[1] I long to heare of my Pew-fellowes of
the Synode whose returne I wish happy & speedy. If my
duty & thanks may be ⌈con⌉ presented to my good Lady. I
haue done. who shall neuer cease to be
Yo*ur* Lordshi*ps* truly deuoted
Ios: Hall:

Walth*am*
Ap*ri*lis 25°

1. *l* altered from partly formed *s*?

Notes
Like Overbury, Hall has been somewhat neglected, and no complete
edition of his works has been published this century. His holographs
comprise mainly letters housed mostly in the P.R.O. among State Papers
Domestic, the Bodleian, Tanner MSS, and in the B.L., Harleian MSS,
from which Greg takes two examples (LXXIX). The correspondence is
printed in P. Wynter's edition of Hall's works, x, 1863.
Characteristics. Hall's hand is an unremarkable but workmanlike
form of *italic* which is very similar to the later English hands of the 17th
century, though it is not quite so round (it becomes rounder and more
open in examples of his hand dating from the fourth decade of the
century, e.g., letter to Sancroft, Harleian 3783, f. 101, Greg, LXXIXb).
The general effect of the writing is misleadingly blotchy because of the thin
absorbent paper he used for this and other letters around 1619 and the
corrosive quality of the ink. There is, however, a marked difference
between the heaviness of the downstroke and the almost feathery lightness
of the upstrokes so that the ink does not flow evenly, giving them a dotted
appearance. Among the few unusual features of the hand are the
horizontal stroke occasionally linking words (l. 14, with other examples
in the upper portion of the letter not illustrated here), and *d*, usually in
initial position, which begins with a tiny upstroke and then a right-angled
bend before descending almost vertically to form the stem (l. 3, *did*;
l. 7, *dead*; l. 12, *done*). Though the script is predominantly *italic*, there
are examples of *secretary* in *k* (l. 11, *thanks*) and possibly *t* (l. 10, *the*).
Greek *e* is used throughout.
Punctuation includes an unusual form of paragraph mark comprising
a virgule enclosed by periods (l. 6).
Abbreviation. A tilde form of bar indicates *ti* or *ci* (more commonly
i in *cion* suffixes); and the superior letters are *wᵗ* (*with*), *yʳ* (*your*), *Loᵖˢ*
(*Lordships*), and, earlier in the letter, *wᶜ* (*which*) rather than the usual *wᶜʰ*.

Roome for a little prose, like a Sermon; There were certaine Bookes
Maddame that Sir Thomas Beamont menntioned, and as shee tolld mee,
ffrom my Ladishyp, which shall bee very shortely sent downe, and
some others to attende them. I am sure yow will doe my service to
my Lord: So I commytt yow to yor Closett, maddame
                                        All at yor noble service
                                                    John Fletcher

Chorus

Is, is there nothing cam withstand
        The hand
Of Time: but that it must
Be shaken into dust?
Then poore, poore Israelites are wee
        nor yee
But cannot shunn the Graues captiuitie.

Alas Good Browne! that Nature hath
        No bath
Or vertuous herbes to stay me
To boyle thee yong againe.
Yet could shee (kindly) but back command
        Thy brand
Her self would else ere thou shouldst be Inmaned.

But (ah) the golden twine by stroke
        Is broke.
And now the Almond Tree
With teares, with teares wee see
Doth bowe hye and with itt fall
        Do all
The daughters dye, that oner were musicall.

Thus yf weake builded man cann saye
        A day
He liues tis all, for why
He's sure at night to dye.
For fading man in fleshly lome
        Doth rome
Till he his graue find, His eternall home.

Then farewell, farwell man of woe
        Till when
For as the mourners meet
Guild visagd in the street
To speake of this our brittle birth
        In earth)
wee meet with Thee triumphant in our mirth.

                                        Trinitoll halls
                                            Exequies.

52 Letter to the Countess of Huntingdon: conclusion and address, *c.* 1619–20. *Set/facile Elizabethan secretary* mixed with *italic*. Signature, interlineation *maddame*, and address holograph.
H.L., HA 1333, text *recto*, address *verso*.

Roome for a Little prose, lyke a Lenvoy;
There were certaine Bookes *Maddame*[1]
that *Sir* Thomas *Beamont* mencioned,
and (as hee told mee) ffor your
Ladiship, *w*hich shall bee very shortely
sent downe, and some others to attend
them. I am sure yow will doe my
service to my Lord: so I commytt yow
to your Closett.[2] ⌈maddame⌉
   All at your noble service./
    Iohn Fletcher[3]
To the ∧ Excelent[4] and best Lady the
Countess of Huntington[5]

1. Beginning of *s*? before *dd*. 2. *C* superscribed on *s*. 3. *F* superscribed on *f*. 4. *c* superscribed on *e*. 5. *t* superscribed on *d*.

Notes
Fletcher is yet another prolific dramatist whose extant holograph material is pitifully small, in this case 13 words comprising the insertion *maddame* (l. 5), the signature and the address. The rest of the letter, mainly in verse, is in the hand of an unknown scribe. There is little doubt, however, that Fletcher is the author. As F. Bickley, who discovered the letter, points out (*HMC, Hastings MSS*, ii, 1930, 59), 'the easy flow of the verse and the reference to a member of the Beaumont family both point to this conclusion'. Bickley dates the letter *c.* 1620, though it could be considerably earlier or a little later. A facs. of the whole letter is given in Greg, XCIII.
Characteristics. The scribe writes a small, neat *secretary* typical of the late Elizabethan and early Jacobean period. There are the calligraphic features of introductory strokes, the simple oblique spur on *a*, indentation on *b* and *l*, a certain pointedness, as on minims, suggestive of the engrossing *secretary*, a very elegant twin-stemmed *r* and the most formal types of *e*, the Greek and the two-stroke *t* form (l. 1, *were*). Two graphs are consistently *italic*: *f* and long *s* which are of the very cursive long figure *8* variety. Two words, both connected with proper names or modes of address, are also in *italic* (l. 2, *Maddame, Beamont*), though, inconsistently,

Thomas and two modes of address are left in *secretary*. The scribe seems to be copying from Fletcher's rough draft and has made and corrected two minor errors while doing so (*vide* nn. l. 2). The **punctuation**, also probably copied from Fletcher's, is very full and fairly careful, and comprises the period, comma, colon, semicolon, brackets and the period *cum* virgule for ending the letter. It is possible, as Greg suggests (*loc. cit.*), that some marks were added by a later hand, e.g. the thick periods in ll. 4, 5.
Abbreviation consists entirely of superior letters: *S*[r] (*Sir*), *w*[ch] (*which*), *yo*[r] (*your*) and otiose raising of *w* in *yo*[w].
Fletcher's hand is in a fairly rapid *italic*, so carelessly written that there are 3 errors in the 13 words (nn. 4, 5, 6), one of them, incredibly, in the signature, when Fletcher decides at the last moment to use a capital rather than minuscule *f*. He has also inserted a caret but has forgotten to interlineate anything (presumably he intended to write *most*). There is no doubt that his hand is not the same as that in the body of the text: a comparison of *Maddame*, l. 2, with the interlineated *maddame* shows a clear difference in the formation of each *italic* graph.

⚙ Robert Herrick (1591–1674)

53 *Elegy on the death of John Browne*, 1619. *Facile italic*, holograph.
B.L., Harleian 367, f. 154, divided into 2 cols.

   Chorus
Is, is there nothing cann withstand
   The hand
Of Time: but that it must
Be shaken into dust?
5 Then poore, poore Isralites are wee
   who see
But cannot shunn the Graues captiuitie
   S S[1]
Alas Good Browne /. that Nature hath
   No bath
10 Or virtuous herbes to strayne
 To boyle thee yong againe
Yet could she (kind) but back command
   Thy brand
Hir self would dye ere thou shouldst be
   vnmand.
   S S
15 But (ah) the golden Ewer by stroke
   Is broke.
And now the Almond Tree
With teares, with teares we see
Doth lowly lye, and with its fall
20   Do all
The daughters dye, that once were
   musicall.
   S S

Thus yf weake builded man cann saye
   A[2] day
He liues tis all, for why
He's sure at night to dye.
25 For fading man in fleshly lome
   Doth rome
Till he his graue find, His eternall home.
   S S
Then farwell, farwell man of men
   Till where
30 (For vs the morners meet
Pa'ld visagd in the street
To seale vp this our britle birth
   In earth)
We meet with Thee triumphant in our
 mirth.

35   Trinitall hall,
   Exequies.

1. The ornaments dividing the stanzas have been standardized as *S S*. 2. *A* superscribed on ?

Notes
Until very recently, Herrick's holographs were limited almost entirely to a few begging letters to his uncle, written while he was an undergraduate at Cambridge, 1613–16, and even these seem to have been unknown to Greg. Now Croft (32, 33) has discovered some of his holograph poetry: the elegy on John Brown, Fellow of Caius, reproduced here, and examples in what appears to be Herrick's commonplace

book, sold to the University of Texas at Austin in 1965. However, while Croft is convinced that portions of the commonplace book are in Herrick's hand, N. K. Farmer, *PBSA*, 66, 1972, 1–34, feels that the palaeographical evidence is inconclusive. Initially, at least, the long, spiky and hurried hand with unusual graphs (e.g. *th* resembling a fat *6* with a looped bowl) looks different from the small compact hand of the poem, but Croft seems to have demonstrated the case sufficiently.
Characteristics. This is an especially small example of Herrick's hand, and not a particularly pleasing one. The penstrokes are too thick in places, giving a blotchy impression, and supralinear loops are often proportionately too large, somewhat unbalancing the whole and congesting the space between the lines (which all slope downwards). Elements of *secretary* are present in that one of the three forms of *d* has an open bowl and looped stem (l. 21, *dye*), and there is a reversed *e* which alternates with Greek *e*. There are also touches of *secretary* in *b* and *W*. Among distinctive *italic* graphs is *r* with a foot serif, resembling a rounded *italic x*. Notable points of **punctuation** are the question mark (with top reversed), brackets (generally for emphasis, but cf. last stanza), the apostrophe (ll. 25, 32), and the virgule with a period, seemingly as a pronounced pause but possibly representing an exclamation mark (l. 8). There is no **abbreviation.**

Actus Secundi Scæna prima.
Enter Wh: Q. Pawne w[i]th a booke in her
hand.

Wh: Q. p.   and now agen it is thy daughters duty
to obaye your Conste Vowes command in all things
w[i]thout exception, or expostulation,
tis the most generall Rule that ere I read of,
yet when I thinke your boundlesse vertue is
Goodnes and Grace, tis gentlie worthie
and then it appeares nott to haue thy power
of thy dispenser as vnvertuous spirits

Enter Bl: Bb: p.

Bl: Bb: p.   Misse said vppont, twas the most modest Key
that I could vse to open my Intrade,
what litle or no paynes goes to some people,
hss! a sealed Note, vnsure to is?
to thy black Bishops pawne togge, pow? to mw?   (eee!
strange, who subscribes it?   the   Black King?   what would
thy letter?

Pawne?   sufficientlie holie, but vnmoa humble appli=
tique;   hau had late intelligence from our most indust
trious Servant famous in all parts of Europe, our
Knight of thy black house, that you saw at this instant
in chardge thy white queenes pawne, and were likelie
by thy carriage of your Game to entrap and take
her, these are therefore to require you by thy burning

54 *A game at chesse*, 1624: II, i, 1–21. *Facile mixed hand*,
holograph.
Trinity College, Cambridge, MS O.2, 66, f. 10.

Actus Secundi Scæna prima.
_____

Enter wh*ite* q*ueen*s pawne with a booke in her
hand.
_____

White q*ueen*s p*awn*   and here agen it is the daughters dutie
5 to obaye her Confessors command in all things
without exception, or expostulation,
tis the most generall Rule that ere' I read of,
Yet when I thinke how boundlesse Vertue is
Goodnes and Grace, tis gentlie reconcilde
10 and then it appeares well to haue the power
of the dispenser[1] as uncircumscribd _____   Enter B*lack* B*ishop*s p*awn*
B*lack* B*ishop*s p*awn*   shee's[2] hard uppon't, twas the most[3] modest Key
that I could use to open my Intents,
15 what litle or no paynes goes to some people,
hah? a Seald Note, whence this?
to the black Bishops pawne these, how? to mee?
strange, who subscribes[4] it? the Black King? what would ∧ ⌈hee?⌉[5]
_____
the letter
(∵)
20 Pawne! sufficientlie holie, but unmeasureablie poli=
tique; we had late intelligence from our most indus=
trious Seruant famouc in all parts of Europe, (our
Knight of the black house, that you haue at this instant
in chace, the white queenes pawne, and uerie liklie
25 by the carriage of youre Game to entrap and take
her, these are therefore to require you by the burning

1. *n* altered from *r*. 2. Cancelled apostrophe after *h*? 3. *st* altered from *de*. 4. 2nd *s* altered from *c*.
5. *hee*? bracketed to indicate connection to line below.

_____

Notes

Middleton's *Game at chesse*, an allegorical play satirizing King James' Spanish policy, ran for nine consecutive performances before being banned, while three editions, probably all secretly printed, appeared in swift succession. It was also widely distributed in MS, six copies still being extant. One of these, illustrated here, is entirely holograph, another (H.L., EL.34, B.17) is partly so, while three in all have holograph title-pages. See further R. C. Bald's edition, 1929, esp. 26–43, addend. and facs. 27, 33, 34, 39; J. W. Harper's edition, 1966, xxv–vi; Greg, XCIV.
Characteristics. Middleton seems to have used two main hands. For formal writing he had a fairly bold and elegant *italic* with few cursive elements, among its distinctive features being an occasional hybrid *h* with *italic* body and *secretary* but unlinking tail; *f* and long *s* with the bottom of the shaft clubbed, and *y* with a very long elliptical tail (*vide* facs. Bald,

op. cit., 33). For more general purposes he employed a *mixed* hand which by its general appearance might seem to be mainly *italic*, but in fact has a greater frequency of *secretary* graphs, even in the stage directions, with the act and scene division being the only purely *italic* words on the page. Generally speaking, Middleton uses *italic* forms for the capitals (*A*, l. 1; *C*, l. 5; *E*, l. 22; *G*, l. 9; *K*, l. 18; *N*, l. 16; *P*, l. 20; *R*, l. 7; *S*, l. 1), and though *B* seems an exception to the rule, it is at least in the simplest *secretary* form, the *L+3* variety which closely resembles *italic* (ll. 12, 13, 18). The minuscules, by contrast, are predominantly *secretary*, with the following main *italic* exceptions in their order of frequency: uniformly, *k* (l. 17, *black*); often, *f* (l. 11, *of*), long *s*, looped and unlooped (l. 11, *dispenser*), *t* (l. 8, *vertue*); occasionally, *c* (l. 17, *black*), *e* (l. 6, *expostulation*), *p* (l. 25, *entrap*), *r* (l. 7, *generall*), and short *s* looking like *r* (l. 12,

shee's). Other letters, like the minims, are 'neutral', e.g. *b*, *I/J* and to some extent *g*. One of the most easily recognizable features is the consistently long oval loop of *h*; there is also an occasional final *t* with a long foot serif running parallel to the cross-stroke (l. 23, *instant*).
Punctuation includes the period, comma, colon, semicolon, brackets, liberal use of question mark (formed of inverted comma above period) and apostrophe (n.b. position in *ere'*, l. 7), and one instance of an exclamation mark (l. 20). Also used are double hyphens (l. 20), speech rules, and a device of a bracketed triangle of points (above l. 20). Rather unusually, speakers' names are not given in the margin, but in the text.
Abbreviation consists of curtailment indicated by period or colon (ll. 2, 4).

55 *The Captives, ll. 292–335. Rapid Elizabethan secretary*
mixed with *rapid italic,* holograph, 1624.
B.L., Egerton, 1994, f. 54, upper portion.

no lardger then[1] our ffull stretcht conscienses /
lett mee once more Imbrace thee. exnt. ⌐ cleare[2]

Actus [2 s], I *scena* 2[a].

	Chaire[2]	Enter An abbot with his Covent off ffryars, amongst them[3]
5		Fryar Ihon, and ffryar Ritchard.
	Abbatt,[4]	As I have heare priority off place. *Iack: Gibsen*[2]
		boathe by our patrons ffavour and your voyce /
		so giue mee leave to arbitrate amongst you
		without respect off person /
10	ff: Ihon[1]	wee acknwledge you
		our princ and cheiffe /
	ff Richard:	and to your ffatherly
		and grave aduyse humbly[5] submitt our selves
	Abbott.	Knwe then in this small covent[6] wch Consysts.
15		only off 12 in nober ffryars I meane.
		and vs the abbat: I have ffownde amongst[3] you
		many and grosse abuses: yet ffor the present
		I will Insist on ffewe. quarrells, debates.
		whisperinge supplantinges.[7] private callmnyes:
20		these ought not bee in such a brother hoodd[8]
		off these ffryar Ihon and you ffryar Richard are.
		accusd to bie mst guilty ever Iarringe /
		and opposite to peace.
	ff Ihon	The ffawlts in him /
25	ff Richard	as in all other thinges so even in this
		hee[9] still is apt to wronge mee
	ff [Abbot] Ihon	hee that ffyrst giues th'occation ffyrst Complaines
		It ever was his ffashion /
	ff Richard	never myne
30		I appeale to the whole covent
	Abbot	mallyce rooted
		I ffinde is woondrous hard to bee supprest.
		but knwe where consell and advise prevayle not
		the ffayrest meanes that I can woork your peace
35		I'l take vpon mee my authority /
		and where I ffinde in you the least contempt
		I shall severely punishe /
	ff Ihon	I submitt
	ffry Richard	I yeeld my selff to your grave ffather hoodd
40	Abbott	Consider soonnes. this cloysterd place off oures.
		Is but newe reard the ffownder hee still lyves
		[a noble] A souldier once/ and eminent in the ffeild
		and after many battayles nwe retyrd
45		in peace to lyve [contemplatiue] a lyff Contemplatiu⟨e⟩
		mongst many other charitable deedes.

1. otiose bars above final *n* and *u* omitted in transcript. 2. Hand of book-keeper. 3. minim
lacking. 4. *a* rewritten. 5. Two minims lacking. 6. Apostrophe? after *e*. 7. superfluous minim.
8. Possibly *headd*. 9. Blotted.

Notes
The only certain examples of Heywood's hand
are the four signatures attached to a Chancery
deposition, 3 October 1623 (facs. Greg, XCVIII),
but there is little doubt that two plays in B.L.,
Egerton 1994, *The Captives* and *The Escapes of
Jupiter,* are not only of his authorship but also
in his abominable hand, *The Captives* being his
foul-papers. By no means the same certainty of
hand or authorship applies to Hand B in the
Booke of Sir Thomas Moore, which predates the
Egerton examples by over thirty years, even
though it anticipates the typical form of
Heywood illegibility (cf. H. Jenkins's summary,
Malone Soc. repr. of Greg's ed. of the More
play, 1961, xxxv–vi). See further concerning the
holograph plays, Greg, XXII; *DDC,* 202 ff.,
284–7; *DDR,* pl. 7; Greg, *Collected Papers,* ed.
J. C. Maxwell, 1966, 156–83; *The Captives,* ed.
A. Brown, Malone Soc., 1953, esp. v–xiii, with
facs.; A. Low, *N. & Q.,* July 1968, 252–3.
Characteristics. Heywood's hand is
probably the least legible of all those extant in
Elizabethan dramatic documents, and it is
doubtful whether a perfect transcription of it
will ever be possible. Not only is it extremely
small, thick-stroked and rapidly written, but it
pays such scant attention to distinguishing its
individual letters, that deciphering them is often
a matter of sheer guesswork combined with a
shrewd interpretation of context. The only
exceptions are the three stage directions inserted
by a book-keeper (n. 2) in a clear though thin-
stroked *mixed* hand. Heywood uses mainly
secretary in the body of the text. However, among
minuscules, three *italic* graphs are common
alternatives to *secretary* forms: *c* (l. 27,
occation), cursive *d* with a curved back (l. 10,
acknwledge) and cursive *s* which almost
completely ousts sigma from final position.
Italic capitals also predominate (l. 14,
Consysts; l. 14, *Knwe*; l. 21, *Richard, R*
resembling a *b* with a foot-serif; l. 24, *The*).
For act and scene headings and directions,
Heywood usually employs a rapid *italic,* but in
this illustration they are mainly in a *mixed* or
entirely *secretary* hand. Distinctive features
(summarized Brown, *op. cit.*) include the almost
invariable doubling of *f*; the frequent
disappearance of vowels before *w* and *v* and
occasionally *s* (l. 43, *nwe*; l. 22, *mst*); a shortage
or surplus of minims (cf. nn. 3, 5, 7); and the
occurrence of an otiose bar over final *n* and
even *u* (cf. n. 1; l. 10, *you*). Little or no
distinction exists between *l* and *t* and
between Greek *e* and left-shoulder *r*; while
there is a general lack of differentiation of *a, e,
o, u* and the *v* form of *r*.
Punctuation, which is moderately adequate,
includes very short speech-rules, the virgule
used mainly as period and comma, the colon,
and the apostrophe for contraction and
elision (l. 35, *I'l*; l. 27, *th'occation*).
Abbreviation is generally by curtailment,
with or without colon (l. 25, *ff Rich:*) and by
common contractions, e.g. *wth,* with normally
superior letters often on the line (l. 14, *wch*).

    busines alonge with em that deserues your eare
    it beeinge for the safetie of the republicke
    and quiet of the prouinces. they are ful
    of goulde, I haue felt theire bountie

5 Flaminius: such are wellcome.
    giue them admittaunce. in this darious plaie

Ent: Chrisalus of state, and policie, thinges not properlie
Geta: Syrus: but may bee vsefull — . now friendes what designes
Demetrius: carries you to mee?

10 Geta: my most honor'd lord
Syrus: may it please youre mightinesse.
Flaminius: let one speake for all
    I cannot brooke this discorde.
Chrysalus: as our duties
    comaundes vs noble Roman, hauinge discouerd
15   a dreadfull danger with swift nimble winges
    of speede approchinge to the state of Rome
    wee thoughte it fit you shoulde haue the first notice
    that you may haue the honor to preuent it.
Flaminius: I thanke you. but instruct mee what forme it beares
20   the danger that you speake of.
Chrysalus: it appeares
    in the shape of Antiochus:
Flaminius: how? is hee
    rose from the dead?
25   alas hee neuer died
Chrysalus: hee at this instant liues the more the pittie
    hee showlde suruiue to the disturbance of
    thinges close, and politiequely counsailed, in the gettinge
30   possession of his kingedome wh hee woulde
    recouer, simple as hee is, the playne
    and downe right way of iustice.
Flaminius: very likelye.
    but how are you assured this is Antiochus
35   and not a counterfaite? answer that

56 *Believe as you list*, ll. 612–46. *Facile mixed hand,*
holograph, 1631.
B.L., Egerton 2828, f. 9, upper portion.

buisnesse alonge with em that deserues your eare
it beeinge for the safetie of the republic*que*
and quiet of the provinces. they are full
of golde, I haue felt their bountie

5 *flaminivs*:[1]   such are welcome.

Enter chrisalus[3]   gieue them admittance. in this various play[2]
Geta : Syrus :   of state, and policie, theres noe propertie   [*Enter* ∧ [*Demetrius*]]
Demetrius :   but may bee vsefull—. now freindes what designe[s]   [*Calistus.*]
                          carries you to mee?   [*Chrysalus. Geta*]

10 *Geta :*   my most Honor'd lord   [*Syrus.*][4]
Syrus :   may it please your mightinesse.[5]
flaminivs :   let one speake for all
                          I cannot brooke this discorde.

Chrysalus :   as our duties

15   com*m*andes vs noble Roman, havinge discover'd
                          a dreadfull danger with the nimble winges
                          of speede approchinge to the state of Rome
                          wee houlde it fit you shoulde haue the first [honor] notice
                          that you may haue the honor to prevent it.

20 *flaminivs :*   I thancke you. but instruct mee what forme weares
                          the danger that you speake of.

Chrysalus :   it appeares
                          in the shape of [*Dom Sebastian*] ∧ [*King*] *Antiochus*[6]:

flaminivs :   how! is hee

25   rose from the dead?

Chrysalus :   alas hee never died *Sir*
                          Hee at this instant liues the more the pittie
                          Hee showlde surviue to the disturbance of
                          Romes close, and politic*que* counsailes, in the gettinge

30   possession of his kingedome *which* hee woulde
                          recover, simple as hee is, the playne
                          and[7] downe right way of iustice.

flaminivs :   very likelye.
                          but how are you assur'd this is Antiochus

35   and not a counterfaite? answer that?

1. *v* superscribed on *s*. 2. *y* superscribed on *c*. 3. Directions in adapter's hand. 4. Interlineation, caret, and all deletions in adapter's hand. 5. *sse* altered from sigma *s*. 6. Cancellation caret, interlineation and *Antiochus*: in adapter's hand. 7. Same hand, finer nib.

Notes

The Massinger holograph material is especially valuable as well as comparatively extensive because it includes a complete play, *Believe as you list*, not only in the hand of its author but with the autograph licence of the Master of the Revels (6 May 1631) and the revisions and markings of the playhouse adapter ('Ihon') to convert it into a promptbook. Also extant are a presentation copy of a printed play, *The Duke of Milan*, with MS verse epistle and holograph corrections (V. and A., Dyce Collection) and Massinger's own set of eight printed copies of his plays with his holograph corrections in six of them. In addition, there is a letter from Massinger to Philip Henslowe in Dulwich College. See, further, Greg, XIV; *DDC*, 293–300, *DDR*, pl. 8; Greg, *Collected Papers*, ed. J. C. Maxwell, pp. 110–48; *Believe as you list*, ed. C. J. Sisson, Malone Soc., 1927, with intro. and facs.; J. E. Gray, *Lib.*, 5th ser., v, 1950, 132–9; A. K. McIlwraith, Lib., 5th ser., vi, 1951, 213–16. A complete facs. of *Believe as you list* was published by J. S. Farmer, 1907, repr. 1970.

Characteristics. Massinger's hand has been harshly described as awkward and untidy because the letters 'tend to be disproportionately sized and irregularly aligned' (Sisson, *op. cit.*, xiii). Yet not only does it appear to be well above average in clarity among dramatists' hands in the period, but it could also be considered pleasing if not artistic, especially in its use of elongated curves (e.g. tails of *secretary h*, *italic* long *s* and Greek *e*), and though many of the letters are often detached, it has a general impression of continuity and of smoothness (partly aided by a slightly blunt pen). Sisson also implies criticism of the mixture of the hand in so far as he can discover no system in it and feels that the English forms came more naturally to him. Again it is difficult to accept these observations because there was no one system of mixing letters in the period, and Massinger's method seems harmonious and convincing, even if graphs of the two scripts are freely interchanged. Prominent among the *secretary* letters are: *a*, sometimes detached from its stem (l. 32, *and*), *d* with open bowl and tall upright stem, reversed *e* and set two-stroked form (l. 18, *wee*), *g* with bulbous tail (l. 32, *right*), *h* with long oval tail, *p* with introductory 2, twin-stemmed and left-shoulder *r*, *q*, long *s* and sigma, *t* and *v*. *Italic* graphs include *c* and *g* (both predominant), *h*, simple *p*, *r* with foot-serif, long *s* (predominant), set and cursive *s*, and *t* with foot-serif. Many other letters are 'neutral', with Greek *e* being especially common. Capitals are usually *italic* (but cf. *secretary R*, l. 17), and the exclamation mark (l. 24).

Punctuation, as Sisson and Greg have noticed, is sporadic and light. Especially to be noted is the sideways arch above the period to form the question mark (ll. 9, 25, 35).

Abbreviation, also very light, comprises a tilde for *m*, *n* (l. 15), *q3* for *que* (ll. 2, 29), *S*ʳ (*Sir*, l. 26), and *w*ᶜʰ (*which*, l. 30).

Easter-wings.

Lord who createdst man in wealth & store
Though foolishly he lost ysame
Decaying more and more
Till he became
Most poore.
Wth thee
O lett mee rise
As larks harmoniously
And sing this day thy victories
Then shall my fall further ye flight in mee

Easter-wings

My tender age in sorrow did begin
And still with sicknesses and shame
Thou didst so punish sinne
That I became
Most thinn
With thee
Lett mee combine
And feele thy victorie
For if I imp my wing on thine
Affliction shall advance the flight in mee

Roma. Anagr. ⎰ Oram Maro
          ⎱ Ramo Armo
          Mora Amor.

5   ROMA tuum nomen quam non pertransiit Oram
Cum Latium ferrent secula prisca iugum.
Non deerat vel fama tibi, vel carmina famae
Unde Maro laudes ducit ad astra tuas.
At nunc exucco similis tua gloria Ramo
10   A veteri trunco & nobilitate cadit.
Laus antiqua & honor perijt: quasi scilicet Armo
Te deiecissent tempora longa suo.
Quin tibi tam desperata Mora nulla medetur
Quam Fabio quondam sub duce nata salus.
15   Hinc te olim gentes miratae odere vicissim
Et cum sublata laude recedit AMOR.

Urbani VIII Pont. Respons.

Cum Romam nequeas, quod aves, evertere, nomen
Invertis, mores carpis & obloqueris:
Te Germana tamen pubes, te Graecus & Anglus   5
Arguit, exceptos, quos pia Roma fovet:
Hostibus hac etiam patiens imitatur Jesum,
Invertis nomen. Quid tibi dicit? Amor.   10

Respons. ad Urb. VIII

Non placet Urbanus noster de nomine lusus   10
Romano, sed res seria Roma tibi est:
Nempe caput Romae es, cuius mysteria velles
Esse iocum soli, plebe stupente, tibi:
Attamen Urbam deleto nomine, constat
Etiam satur & gravis sit tibi Roma iocus.   15

57 'Easter-wings' (*The Temple*). *Set mixed hand*, unknown
scribe, with holograph *facile italic* corrections, *c.* 1631–2.
London, Dr Williams's Library, MS Jones B 62, ff. 27v, 28.

The Church.

Easter-wings.

Lord who createdst man in wealthe[1] & store
    Though foolishly he lost ye same
5   Decaying more and more
           Till he became
             Most poore.
             With thee
           O lett mee rise
           harmoniouslie
10   As Larks [doe by degree]
          victories.
    And sing this day thy [sacrifice]
Then shall my fall further ye flight in mee.

The Church.

Easter-wings

    My tender age in sorrow did beginn
    And still[2]
    [Yet thou] with sicknesses and shame
        Thou
        [Dayly] didst ∧ [so] punish sinne
          That
           [Till] I became
           Most thinn.
          With thee,
        Lett mee combine
      And feele thy victorie.
    ffor if I impe my wing on thine
Affliction shall advance ye flight in mee.

1. *a* altered from *e* by scribe. 2. All interlineations and cancellations holograph.

58 *Lucus*, XXV, XXVI, XXVII (late 1623). *Set/facile italic*, holograph, *c.* 1631–2.
London, Dr Williams's Library, MS Jones B 62, ff. 113v, 114.

Lucus

            ⎧ Oram. Maro
Roma. *Anagramma* ⎨ Ramo. Armo
            ⎩ Mora. Amor.

5 Roma tuum nomen quam no*n*
    pertransijt Oram[1]
Cum Latium ferrent secula prisca
    iugum.
Non deerat vel fama tibi, vel
    carmina famæ
Vnde Maro laudes duxit ad astra
    tuas.
At nunc Exucco similis tua gloria
    Ramo
10 A veteri trunco & nobilitate cadit.
Laus antiqua & honor perijt: quasi
    scilicet Armo
Te deiecissent tempora longa suo.
Quin tibi tam desperatæ Mora[2] nulla
    medetur
Quâ, Fabio quonda*m* sub duce nata
    salus.
15 Hinc te olim gentes miratæ odere
    vicissim
Et cum sublatâ laude recedit Amor.

Lucus

Vrbani VIII Pon*tificis* Respon*sum*

Cum Romam nequeas, quod aues,
    euertere, nomen
Invertis, mores carpis & obloqueris:
Te Germana tamen pubes, te Græcus
    & Anglus
Arguit, exceptos, quos pia Roma
    fovet:
Hostibus hæc etiam parcens imitatur
    Iesum,
Invertis nomen. quid tibi dicit?
    Amor.

Respon*sum* ad Vrb*anum* VIII

Non placet vrbanus noster de nomine
    lusus
Romano, sed res seria Roma tibi est:
Nempe Caput Romæ es, cuius
    mysteria velles
Esse iocum soli, plebe stupente, tibi:
Attamen Vrbani delecto nomine,
    constat
Quam satur & svavis sit tibi Roma
    iocus.

1. All the words of the anagram are in bolder *italic*. 2. *Mora* superscribed on *null*?

Notes

The chief source of Herbert holographs is the Jones B 62 MS illustrated here, a small volume containing *The Temple*, in which the corrections alone are in his hand, and Latin poetry entirely written out by him. The MS is thought to be the 'little book' which according to Isaac Walton, Herbert asked, on his death-bed, to be given to Nicholas Ferrar. Among other holographs are a memorandum, 'Reasons for Arthur Woodnoth's living with Sir John Danvers' (Ferrar Papers, Magdalene College, Cambridge) and a Latin letter to Lancelot Andrewes (B.L., Sloane 118, ff. 34–5). For facs. *vide* Greg, XLIX; *EPA*, 10; F. E. Hutchinson, *Works of George Herbert*, 1941, frontis.; Croft, 34. **Characteristics of Herbert's hand** (58 and corrections 57). The writing is fairly compact, firm, often heavily inked, with words regularly spaced but with letters, especially the minims, irregular in their slope (the middle leg of *m* often being angled to the left). It is fairly cursive even though restrained in the use of loops and with some unlinked letters, especially those succeeding *d* and *i*. The graphs are all *italic* except for *e*, which although most commonly in Greek form, is quite often a set *secretary* two-stroke *e* (58a, l. 12, all three in *deiecissent*), or, when Herbert is writing more cursively, a reversed *e* (no example here but *vide* f. 75, l. 9, *stone*, repr. *EPA* and Croft). Capitals are of a fairly simple nearly *roman* form, but sometimes with a loop (58a, l. 5, *Roma*). Among the minuscules to be noted is *d*, which is regularly of the cursive curved stem variety, and an occasional almost straight *s* in the ligature *st* (58a, l. 8, *astra*). Digraph *æ* is usually written as *a* with a sign resembling an inverted comma immediately above it (58a, l. 8, 15). It should be noted that double *i* is written as *ij* which is fairly common practice with Latin, whereby the last of a group of *i*'s is always tailed. Herbert's **punctuation** is fairly meticulous with liberal use of the colon, and includes a circumflex accent on *a* (58a, l. 14, *Quâ*). His **abbreviation** has some distinctive features, notably the brevigraph for *m* and *n* which is a hook on the end of a tall, wavy ascender above the preceding vowel (58a, l. 5, *non*; l. 14, *quondam*), and a large ampersand resembling a *G* clef leaning backwards (58a, l. 10; 58b, l. 4). **The hand of the scribe** is a good example of a successful attempt at a *set mixed hand*. It has the impression of being chiefly if not entirely *italic* at first glance, because supralinear strokes are unobtrusive (especially on *g* and *p*) and because *h* (particularly noticeable in *secretary*) is predominantly *italic*. The main *secretary* graphs include *c*, two-stroke *e*, twin-stemmed *r*, *g* with short-angled and clubbed tail, *k*, *p* without linking-stroke (hybrid?), sigma *s*, *w* and *y*. The most constant *italic* forms are *f*, *h*, the minims, long *s* and short cursive *s*, and *t* with foot-serif. The capitals are predominantly *secretary*, other letters are 'neutral' or, like *d*, somewhat hybrid. The scribe's **punctuation** is sparser than Herbert's, though probably based on the author's. His **abbreviation** is confined here to superior letters: *w^{th}* and raised *e* in *y^e* (*the*).

& fruitlesse curiosity of knowing, had then a naturall desire of honour wch I thinke possesses the brest of every scholer aswell of him that shall as him that never shall obtaine it (if this be altogether bad) w^d would quickly oversway this flegme & melancholy of bashfulnesse, or that other humor, & prevaile wth me to preferre a life that had at least some credit in it before a manner of living much disregarded, & discountenanc't, there is besides this, as all well know, about this time of a mans life a strong inclination, bee it good or no, to build up a house & family of his owne in the best manner may to wch nothing is more helpfull then the setling early into some credible Employment, & nothing more crosse then my way, which my wasting youth would
peculiar conceit may you in charitie thinke could hold out against the long knowledge of a contrarie command from above & the terrible seasure of him that hid his talent therfore count grace to grace or nature to nature, there it will be found more obnoxious temptations to bad as goine, preferment ambition more winning presentments of good, & more presse affections of nature to encline not counting expect outward causes as expectations & murmurings of friends scandals taken & such like, then the bare lot of nations, loud vessell so that it be that wch you suppose it had by this bin round about begirt & overmaster'd whether it had proceeded from vertue, vice, or nature in me Yet that you may see that I somtime suspicious of my selfe, & doe take notice of a certaine belatednesse in me from the bottom to shew you some of my night-ward thoughts since they come in fitly in a Petrarchian stanza. &

How soone hath Time the suttle theefe of youth
Stolne on his wing my three & twentith yeere
my hasting days fly on wth full careere
but my late spring no bud or blossome shew'th
Perhapps my semblance might deceave ye truth
that I to manhood am arriv'd so neere
& inward ripenesse doth much lesse appeare
that some more tymely-happie spirits indu'th
Yet bee it lesse or more, or soone or slow
it shall be still in strictest measure eben
to that same lot however meane or high
toward wch Tyme leads me, & the will of heaven
all is if I have grace to use it so
as ever in my great task-maisters eye

116

59 'Letter to a friend' and Sonnet VII (MS of Milton's
Minor Poems). *Rapid italic*, holograph, *c.* 1633.
Trinity College, Cambridge, MS R.3.4, p. 6, lower portion.

& fruitlesse curiosity of knowing, and then a naturall desire of honour, [& repute]
wh*ich* I thinke posseses[1] the brest of every scholar aswell of him that shall as ∧ [of]
him that never shall obtaine it (if this be altogether bad) wh*ich* would quickly
over sway this flegme & melancholy of bashfullnesse, or that other humor, &
[induce me] prævaile with me to præferre a life that had at least some credit in it,
[&] some place given it before a manner of living much disregarded, &
discountenanc't, there is besides this, as all well know, about this tyme of a mans
life a strong inclination, beit good or no, to build up a house & family of his
owne in the best manner ∧ [he] may, to wh*ich* nothing is more helpfull then the
early entring[2] into some credible employment, & nothing more crosse then my way,
which my wasting youth would [praesently bethinke her of &] [never brooke,
but] kill one love with another, if that were all; but what delight or what peculiar
conceit, may you in charitie thinke, could hold out against the long knowledge of a
contrarie com*m*and from above, & the terrible seasure of him that hid his
talent, therfore com*m*it grace to grace or nature to nature, there [is] will be
found ∧ [on the other way] more obvious temptations to bad as gaine,
præferment ambition [[& the like]] more winning præsentments of good, &
more prone affections of nature to encline ∧ [& dispose] [to the other side, then
the bare love of notions could resist] not counting [expect] outward causes as
expectations & murmurs of freinds scandals taken & such like, then the bare
love of notions could[3] resist, so that [the wh*ich*] if it be that wh*ich* you suppose, it
had by this bin round about begirt, & over master'd whether it had proceeded
from vertue, vice, or nature in me, Yet that you may see that I am somtyme
suspicious of my selfe, & doe take notice of a certaine belatednesse in me[4]
[selfe], I am the bolder to send you [a peice] some of my nightward thoughts
∧ [some while since] since they come in fitly, [∧ [packt]] made[5] up [for] in a
Petrachian stanza. [wh*ich* if you please, you may reade]

How soone hath Time the suttle theefe of Youth
    stolne on his wing my three & twentith yeere
    my hasting days fly on with full careere
    but my late spring no bud or blossome shew'th
Perhapps my semblance might deceave ye truth[6]
    that I to manhood am arriv'd so neere
    & inward ripenesse doth much lesse appeare
    that some more tymely-happie spirits indu'th
Yet be it lesse or more, or soone or slow
    it shall be still in strictest measure even
    to that same lot however meane or high
toward wh*ich* Tyme leads me, & the will of heaven
    all is if I have grace to use it so
    as ever in my great task-maisters eye

1. 2nd *e* possibly altered from *s*. 2. The *2* below *entring* and *1* below *early* indicate reversed word
order. 3. *l* and *d* confused, bowl of *d* being attached to *l*. 4. *e* superscribed on *y*. 5. Rule under
made seems to imply stet. 6. 1st *t* superscribed on *f*?

Notes

More holograph material of Milton survives
than of any other major English poet prior to
the 18th century. It includes the famous and
now very fragile Trinity MS of his Minor
Poems, with *Comus*, *Lycidas* and most of the
Sonnets, repr. in facs. by W. A. Wright, 1899,
and more recently by Scolar Press, 1972.
Another important MS is his commonplace book
(B.L., Add MS 36354) containing mainly
holograph entries between 1630 and 1650, facs.
ed. by Royal Soc. of Literature, 1876. Further
B.L. examples are pages from Milton's Bible

(Add MS 32310) and from the album of
Christoph Arnold (Egerton 1324, f. 85); and
the Bodleian contains an inscription from a
printed book (F.56 h.) and a Latin ode (MS
Lat. Misc.). For sources *vide* F. A. Patterson,
The works of John Milton, 18 vols., 1931–8,
esp. vol. 18. For a discussion of the MSS,
transcr. and facs. *vide* S. L. Sotheby,
Ramblings in elucidation of the autograph of Milton,
1861; J. H. Hanford, *PMLA*, xxxvi, 251 ff. and
xxxviii, 1923, 290 ff.; H. Darbishire, *Lib.*, 4th
ser., xiv, 1934, 229–35; *FRHL*, 95; Greg, LII,

LIII; Morton, pl. 4; R. Mohl, *Complete prose of
John Milton*, Yale ed., 1952, and *John Milton
and his commonplace book*, 1968 esp. 1–10; Croft,
47; H. E. Fletcher, *John Milton's complete
poetical works in photographic facsimile*, 4 vols.,
1943–8. The illustration here is the first of two
drafts of a 'Letter to a friend', the second (on
the next page of the MS) omitting the sonnet.
The letter is dated *c.* 1633 by most critics (e.g.
W. R. Parker, *John Milton*, 1968).

Characteristics. Mainly on the basis of the
commonplace book three distinct forms of
Milton's handwriting have been descried
(Sotheby, *op. cit.*, 105 nn., 108 nn., pl. xiv, xv
and xxv, and subsequent writers, cf. Mohl, 2nd
work cited, 6). The early examples are in a
small, neat hand with a fine nib. This changes
to a somewhat larger writing with a short,
thick and blunt nib. The later hand, before
blindness impares it, is in a freer hand with
flourishes written with a fine nib again. The
dating of these three hands has been effected by
Hanford (1st article cited) and a sharp dividing
line has been placed in the year 1639, when,
after his return from Italy he appears to have
given up the Greek *e* for the Italian. The present
example, which has some similarity to the
Herbert examples written at about the same
time (nos. 57, 58), is either in or approaching
the second stage of Milton's writing described
above, and also employs Greek *e* exclusively. It
is so heavily inked to the point of blotchiness, so
irregular in the size and lineation of letters and
with such little space between lines, that it
could hardly be described as comely, and one
can understand why Lamb was so upset when
he saw the MS for the first time and lamented
how unlovely the draft of *Lycidas* seemed by
comparison with the 'full-grown beauty' of its
printed pages. Still, one would not wish, as he
did, that the MS had been thrown into the
River Cam. Particularly variable in size and
slope is the Greek *e* as can easily be seen by
running the eye along any line of the text.
Other graphs vary considerably too, *b*, *d* and *s*
providing good examples. Among distinctive
letter forms are an occasional *þ* with a curl to
the left of its tail (l. 11, *peculiar*), and a spurred *a*,
especially for the indefinite article (ll. 1, 7, 20,
22), presumably a relic of *secretary*. Neither of
these characteristics is common in Milton's
hand as a whole, however.

Punctuation is somewhat loose and
sporadic, but when it appears it is firmly made
and clearly visible.

Abbreviation is chiefly the bar for *m*, *n*
(ll. 12, 13) and superior letters, *w^{ch}* (l. 3), *w^{th}*
(l. 4), with the raising of *e* in *y^e* (l. 27) for *the*.
The nota for *and* is ℰ.

and advice but by adoption and donation of this House
and that all the rights of the people should be specifyd
and indorsed upon that Donation. But we know well
enough what they mean. A Petition from some thousands
in the City to their purpose hath been brought in, & they say
they are trying to promote another in the Strand, but laid
by to be read at the end of this debate in which nothing
is to intervene. They have held us to it all this weeke
and yet little nearer. It was propounded on our side seeing
the whole bill stuck so, that before the Commitment of it
it should be voted in the house as part of it that his Right
is Protector &c: and not to passe but with the whole bill
But all we could gaine hitherto is that their shall be a
previous vote before the Commitment, but yt that should
be it is yet as farre of as ever, For they speak eternally to
the question, to the orders of the house, and in all the
tricks of Parliament. They have much the odds in speaking but it is to be hoped that our justice our affection
and our number which is at least two thirds will weare

him out at the long runne. That is all that I can
tell you at present but that I am
Whitehall Febr: 111
1658 Sir your most humble servant
Andrew Marvell

Sir this is all the account I can give you of any writers of Jesus
College. The name of the place where my Brother lyes buried,
I doe not know; butt tis a village upon the Thamis side within
wzor being onwards or 6 miles of Oxford, & without doubt well knowne to the
University. My Cousin Walleoffe presents you with her reall affections
& respects, & would be very glad to see you in these parts. Sir John
with his son & Lady are come well home from London. I begge
yr pardon for all this trouble & remaine with all integrity Sir
your most affectionate and
Honored Cousin,
faithfull servant
JVaughan.

Newton Juxta 7th
—73

I sent you word
by Sr Ro: Moray
morning before yt

Dear Sr

Andrew Marvell (1621–1678)

60 Final section of letter to George Downing, 11 February 1659. *Set/facile round hand*, holograph.
B.L., Add MS 22919, f. 78, lower portion. Reduced by ⅓.

and advice but by adoption and donation of this House and that all the rights of the people should be specifyd and indorsed upon that Donation. But we know well enough what they mean. A Petition from some thousands in the City to their purpose hath been brought in (& they say they are trying to promote another in the Army) but laid by to be red at the end of this debate in which nothing is to intervene. They haue held us to it all this weeke and yet litle nearer. It was propounded on our side seeing the whole bill stuck so, that before the Commitment of it it should be voted in the house as part of it that his Highn*ess* is Protector &c: and not to passe but with the whole bill But all we could gaine hitherto is that their shall be a previous vote before the Commitment but y*at* that shoulde be it is yet as farre of as euer For they speak eternally to the question, to the orders of the house, and in all the tricks of Parliament. They haue much the odds in speaking but it is to be hoped that our justice our affection and our number which is at least two thirds will weare them out at the long runn. This is all that I can tell you at present but that I am

  Whitehall Febru*ary* 11.   Sir, Your most humble Serv*ant*
   1658[1]   Andrew Marvell

1. Old style dating.

Notes

Although no holographs of Marvell's poetry are known to exist, a great deal of his correspondence survives, the bulk of it written by Marvell as M.P. for Hull, including 294 letters to the Hull Corporation, preserved in the Guildhall, Hull, and 69 connected with Trinity House, Hull, where they are still housed. There are also many miscellaneous letters, one of the most important being to Oliver Cromwell (Soc. of Antiquaries, London). The bulk of them are in the B.L. (Add MS 22919), East Riding R.O., Bodleian (Carte Papers, see also instructions to Sir Philip Meadows, Rawl. A. 58, ff 380–7), John Rylands Lib. Manchester, Pierpont Morgan Library, and Osborn Collection, Yale. For sources *vide Poems and letters of Andrew Marvell*, ii, *Letters*, ed. H. M. Margoliouth, rev. P. Legouis and E. E. Duncan-Jones, 1971, 358–93, facs. of Cromwell letter betw. 304 and 305. Another facs. is given in Greg, LVII.

Characteristics. A fine and very early example of the English *round hand*, with the roundness, clarity, smoothness and cursiveness which look forward to the copperplate of the 19th century. Though large and bold (even when reduced by ⅓ here) it is nevertheless controlled, evenly sloped (at roughly 30° from the perpendicular) and well-proportioned. If there were more space between the lines, as in the Cromwell letter, the elegance of the hand would be all the more apparent. One of the notable features is the balancing of long, oval loops above and below the line, the tops of *b*, *h* and *l* being offset by the tails of *g* and *y* and the split shaft of *p*. The balance is further reflected in the double loop of *f*. To loop all the shafts and stems would have exaggerated the roundness of the hand: *d* rarely has one, and *b*, *h* and *l* are sometimes without. Long *s* is so shortened that it looks like a double-looped cursive short *s*, thus contributing to the modern appearance of the hand; but by contrast *u* and *v* are not yet fully normalized (l. 8, *haue*), and *y* occasionally appears for *th* in the abbreviated relative.

Punctuation is light and a little erratic.

Abbreviation is mainly contraction with superior letters: *Highn*[s] (l. 11), *Serv*[t] (termination) and *y*[t] (for *that*, l. 14).

Henry Vaughan (1622–1695)

61 Conclusion of letter to Anthony Wood, 7 July 1673. *Facile mixed hand*, holograph. Marginalia and underlining by Wood.
Bodleian, MS Wood F.39, 227 v.

S*ir* this is all the account I can give you of any writers of Jesus College. The name of the place, where my broth*er* lyes buried, I doe not know; butt tis a village[1] vpon the Thames side within 5 or 6 miles of Oxford, & without doubt well knowne to the vniversity. My Cousin Walbeoffe pr*e*sents you with her real affections & respects, & would be very glad to see you in these parts. Sir John with his[2] Son & Lady are come well home from London. I begge yo*ur* pardon for all this trouble & remaine with all integritie

          Honoured Cousin,
 Newton Julie 7th.   Y*our* most affectionate and
   —73   faithfull servant
          H Vaughan.

1. U*n*derlining by Wood, who adds the marginal note: *I sent you word where, being informed by Sir Rob*er*t Moray ye morning before he dyed* . 2. *is altered from* er.

Notes

Nine letters form the main corpus of Vaughan's holograph material. Seven of these, addressed to John Aubrey and Anthony Wood between 1673 and 1694, are housed in the Bodleian. Of the remaining two, both official letters, one is in Lambeth Palace Library (MS 1027, Brecon, f. 36v) and the other in the National Library of Wales (Welsh Papers, Bundle 178). For trans. and sources *vide* L. C. Martin, *The works of Henry Vaughan*, 2nd ed., 1957, 687–99; facs. in Greg, LIX.

Characteristics. A delicate, pleasing and very cursive hand, small-bodied with proportionately tall shafts and tails (especially the back of *d* and tail of *y*). By contrast with Marvell's style, this is a traditional *italic*, with sufficient *secretary* forms to make it a *mixed* hand. The main *secretary* letters are reversed *e* (l. 2, *the*) and two-stroke *e* with the head separated from the stem (l. 1, *writers*), left-shouldered *r* (l. 2, *buried*), *t* (l. 3, *tis, the*), *w* (l. 3, *know*) and *y* (l. 2, *my*). An occasional *secretary h* appears (l. 3, *within*), there are traces of *secretary* in the angular *b* (l. 2, *brother*), while *d* sometimes appears to be a hybrid with open body and looped stem (l. 7, *London*, l. 11, *and*). Of the *italic* letters, especially to be noted is *p* with open body, typical of later *italic* hands.

Punctuation is in general meticulously applied.

Abbreviation comprises superior letters (*S*[r] and *yo*[r]) and large ampersand, &.

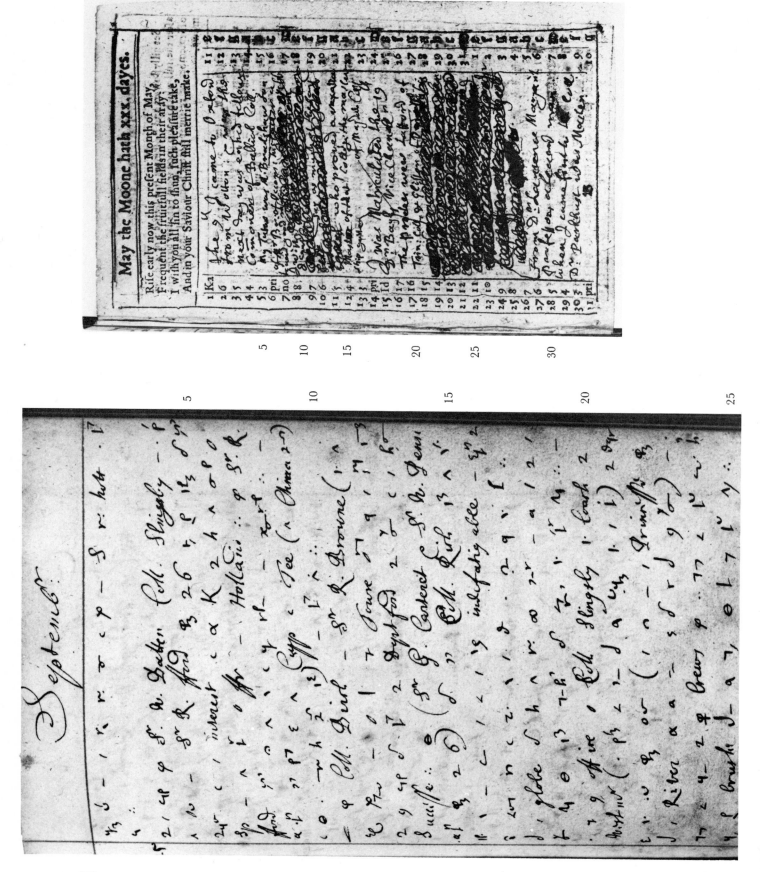

120

62 Entries in Langley's *New almanack*. *Rapid italic*, holograph 1637, cancelled and rewritten 1660.
Balliol College, Oxford, PRT. 670 a. 13, sig. B 1.

the 9th I came to Oxford from Wotton: & was the next day was entred fellow Com*m*oner of Balliol Coll*ege*: My Tutor was M. Bradshaw son of Mr B*r*adshaw of Occom: his father a learnd good man [Mr Higham and Mr Webb ⟨...⟩[1] came with me][2] I wish I coud say as much of the son who proved a vexatious Master of that Coledge: the mastership gotten From Dr. Laurence Margarit Professor, a learnd man: when I came first to the Coll*ege* Dr. Parkhust was Master: of Magdal*ene* Coll*ege*.[3]

[9 of this mounth I came to Oxford]

[the 10 of this mounth I was entred]

I was Matriculated the 19th Dr. Bayly Vice Chanellor

The Procters were Lafford of Trin*ity* Coll*ege*, & Glisson of Oriel.

[19 of this month I was matriculated

coram Rich*ard* Bayly Vice Chancelor of Oxford 1637 cost 2 Shill: vid in St Mary's church Proctors were Lafford of oriel coll the Senior proctor & Glisson of Trinity Coll*ege* the Iunior proctor.]

1. Two or three words obliterated. 2. All cancelled passages were written in 1637. 3. The different sections of this passage are linked, from ll. 10–12, 16–29, 29 back to 16 *via* 18.

Notes
Evelyn's extremely copious diary encompasses four MS volumes, three of them holograph, the property of the Evelyn family of Wotton. A quantity of other Evelyn material survives, including his Notes for *Elysium Britannicum* (B.L., Add MS 15950) and two printed almanacs (in a collection of five in Balliol) containing his diary entries in the 1630s, which he rewrote in part in 1660. These are Dove's *A new almanacke and prognostication*, 1630, and Thomas Langley's *A new almanack and prognostication*, 1637, from which an illustration is given here. See, further, E. S. De Beer, *The diary of John Evelyn*, 6 vols., 1955, esp. i, intro, 44 ff., 75–7, with facs. i, 76, 93; ii, 211; iii, 215, 351, 574, 628; v, 402. For other holograph sources and facs. *vide* G. Keynes, *John Evelyn*, 1968, *passim*, facs. 10, 11, 16, 17, 247–9. De Beer (i, 48) notes that Evelyn at first wrote so badly that his father

made him take a special course in handwriting when he was 14. Even by his late twenties his writing was still poor, and it is only by 1660 that the mature Evelyn hand appears, remaining constant until it degenerated in his final years. De Beer also distinguishes three main types of hand: a well-formed clear letter hand of reasonable size, a book hand which is a formal variant of the letter hand, and a small note hand, malformed and close to illegibility.
Characteristics. The present illustration is a good example of Evelyn's note hand. It is basically *italic*, which Evelyn learned as a boy, with one or two *secretary* forms, the reversed *e* being an obvious example (l. 17, *the*). Speed and the necessity to cram the page have obviously impaired legibility, especially between ll. 7 and 16. Many letters are badly formed or incomplete and there is a general insufficiency of strokes (e.g. l. 7, *learnd*, l. 18, *Chanellr*). A particular cause of confusion is the frequent openness of *a* and *o*, while the thickness of the nib results in a lack of distinction among linear letters (e.g. *e* and *r*). The 1637 passages are too heavily cancelled to give an idea of his hand at that time, but the following leaf of the almanac (sig. B2) contains three lines, showing it to be spidery and clumsy, with additional *secretary* graphs: *d* and *p*.
Punctuation is more common than might be expected, with the period and the colon frequently indicating curtailment.
Abbreviation includes the bar for *m*, *n* (l. 4) and superior letters (l. 29, *Dr*.). Innumerable words are curtailed when space is short.

⊛ Samuel Pepys (1633–1703)

63 *Diary*, extract from entries for 24 and 25 September 1660. Shorthand with plain text in *facile italic*, holograph.
Magdalene College, Cambridge, Pepys, *Journal*, vol. i.

September

growing[1] *late and the room very full of people and so very* hott *I went home* ∴.
25 *to the office where* Sir William *Batten* Collonel *Slingsby and I sat a while and* Sir Richard *fford coming to us about some business we talked together of the* interest *of this* Kingdom *to have a peace with* Spain *and a war with* ffrance *and* Holland ∴. *where* Sir Richard *fford talked like a man of great reason and experience* ∴. *and afterwards did send for a* Cupp *of* Tee (*a* China[2] *drink) of which I never had drank before) and went away* ∴.
then came Collonel *Birch and* Sir Richard *Browne (by a former appointment and with them from* Towre *wharf in the barge belonging to our office we went to* Deptford *to pay off the ship* Successe ∴. *which (*Sir George[3] *Carteret &* Sir William *Penn afterwards coming to us) we*

did Collonel[3] *Rich being a mighty busy man and one that is the* most *indefatigable and forward to make himself work of any man that ever I knew in my life* ∴. *at the* globe *we had a very good dinner and after that to the* pay *again which being finished we returned by water again* ∴. *and I from our* office *with* Collonel[3] *Slingsby by* Coach *to* Westminster (*I setting him down at his lodgings by the way) to* enquire *for my* Lord's *coming thither (the* King *and the* Princesse *coming up the* River *this afternoon as we were at our pay) and I find him gone to* Mr. *Crews, where I find him well only had got some* brush *upon his foot which was not well yet* ∴.

1. Transcription of shorthand and expansion of contractions indicated by italics. 2. *n* altered from *a*. 3. Initial letter superscribed on S.

Notes
The *Diary*, or 'Journal' as Pepys referred to it, runs from 1 January 1660 to 31 May 1669, and comprises six volumes. The most recent edition (in progress) is by R. Latham and W. Matthews (*vide* esp. i, 1970, xlii–lxvii, and facs. facing xlv, xlviii, l, c–ciii). Holograph material is abundant at Magdalene College, Cambridge (*vide* J. R. Tanner, *A descriptive*

catalogue of the naval mss. in the Pe*p*sian library, 1903–23), the Bodleian (esp. Rawlinson MSS), the B.L. and P.R.O. The correspondence is especially copious (ed. by J. R. Tanner, 1926 and 1929). for other facs. *vide* Morton, 5; R. Ollard, *Pepys*, 1974, 51, 292–3, 320.
Characteristics. Apart from a scattering of words, mainly proper names, in an *italic* longhand, the diary is in a shorthand derived mainly from Thomas Shelton's *Tachygraphy*, first published under the title *Short writing*, 1626. In addition to containing 300 symbols for basic words and affixes (e.g. l. 2, — = *and*; / = *the*; 3 = *ing*), it comprises simple lines and curves which stand invariably for consonants in any position and vowels in initial location. A medial vowel is indicated by the position of the following consonant against the preceding consonant: for *a* above, *e* top right, *i* middle right, *o* lower right, *u* below; and a final vowel is shown by a dot in one of the same five positions (*vide* Latham and Matthews, *op. cit.*, xlviii–liv). The longhand words are typical of Pepys' *facile* hand generally, though a little less carefully formed than in his correspondence. They contain almost sufficient *secretary* forms to qualify as mixed: *c* (l. 15, *Rich*), possibly *d* (l. 8, *fford*), reversed *e* and long *ss* (l. 22, *Princesse*), with apparently hybrid forms in *ff* (esp. when used for capital, l. 7, *ffrance*) and left-shouldered *r* (l. 11, *Birch*). As with Marvell's hand, the *p* has a split stem.
Punctuation is sparse to avoid confusion with the shorthand symbols. A pyramid of points acts as a major pause, and parentheses are common.
Abbreviation is by superior letter (*Sr*) and by curtailment with or without point or colon.

Rob: Hutchinson at the white heart in st Peters
in norwich drunk a gallon of Brandie
burnt & sweetned in the month of June 75
in the space of 14 howers. yet drunk
it Got fell into a feuer & complained of
an extroordinarie burning in his stomack
butt recouered, in 7 dayes, with a great
loathing of brandie after. There was
april 76. Another man w.ch drunk w.th him
drunk also a gallon of brandie burnt for his share
& went into ye countrie not after
ward and seemed not to suffer any more
then in a burning heat in his stomack
for some dayes. hee drunck a good
quantitie of beer after hee had made
an End of his gallon of brandie

And I the said John Bunyan all and singulor the a
said goods chattels and premises to the said elizabeth my wife
her executors administrator and asignes to the use aforesaid
against all people do warrant and forever defend by these
presents. And further know ye that I the said John
Bunyan haue put the said elizabeth my wife, in
peaceable and quiet possession of all and singulor the afore
said premises, by the deliuery into her at the ensealing
heerof one cornered peece of siluer commonly called two
pence fixed on the seal of these presents
In witnes wherof I the said John Bunyan haue
hereunto set my hand and seall this 23 day of december
in the first year of the reigne of our souraigne lord
King James the second of England &c in the year
of our lord and sauiour Jesus Christ 1685

sealed and deliuered in the
presence of us whos names
are here under written

                                    John Bunyan

64 Notes on brandy drinking (Commonplace Book).
Rapid mixed hand, holograph, *c.* 1680.
B.L., Sloane 1843, f. 32v.

Rob*ert* Huchenson at the wheat sheaf[1] in st peters in norwich dranck a gallon of Brandie burnt & sweetend in the month of Iune 1675 in the space of [14] 14[2] howers. hee drank it hot, fell into a feuer & complained of an extroordinarie burning in his stomack[3] butt recouered, in 7 dayes, with a great loathing of brandie after. [Anoth] hee [w] is aged 56. Another man who drank with him drank also a gallon of ∧ [burnt] brandie for his share & [r] road home into the countrie [not] after it. and seemed not to suffer any more then a burning heat in his stomack for some dayes. hee dranck a good quantitie of beere after hee had made an end of his gallon of brandie

1. *s* altered from *c*? 2. otiose bar above *14*.   3. *c.* possibly superfluous stroke of *k*.

Notes

There are no known holographs of Browne's major works, but a considerable number survive of his minor works, notebooks and correspondence. The chief sources are the B.L. (especially Sloane MSS), the Bodleian (e.g. Rawl. D.58, D.191) and the Castle Museum,

Norwich. See, further, G. Keynes, *A bibliography of Sir Thomas Browne*, 1968, *passim*; *Works of Sir Thomas Browne*, rev. 1964, iii, iv (*Letters*); facs. Greg, LXXXIX.
Characteristics. The present example was written when Browne was well over 70 (an

entry preceding the brandy item refers to a book published in 1678). Nevertheless, it is not very different from his earlier hand (e.g. letter to Dugdale, 1658, illustr. Greg) except that it is a little less formal, being his note hand. As usual, it is heavily inked and with a suspicion of scratchiness as if an angled pen were being used to write a rounded script. Though it does have something of the look of a *round* hand, it has (like the spelling) general features which are more characteristic of the beginning of the 17th century, especially in the graph *h* which is invariably *secretary* with a thick curved tail, either with a body (l. 15, *hee, had*) or, unusual even for a *mixed* hand, completely without (l. 9, *Another*). The graph of *e* is predominantly Greek, with occasional *secretary* two-stroke form (l. 1, *wheat sheaf*). Particularly distinctive graphs are *d* with the end of the loop of the curved back running parallel to the line, and *k*, which looks like the body of a gothic *C* with a diagonal from right to left touching the lower arc (ll. 2, 4, *drank*, with a variant, l. 13, *stomack*). The **punctuation**, comprising period, colon and caret, is moderately adequate. There is no **abbreviation** other than *ꝯ* for *and*.

 John Bunyan (1628–1688)

65 Deed of Gift, 23 December 1685, concluding paragraph.
Facile italic, holograph.
Bunyan Meeting Museum, Bedford. Reduced by $\frac{1}{6}$.

And I the said Iohn Bunyan all and singuler the aforesaid goods chattels and premises to the said Elizabeth my wife her executors administrator and asignes to theese aforesaid against all people do warrant and forever defend by these presents. And further know ye that I the said Iohn Bunyan have put the said Elizabeth my wife, in peacable and quiet possession of all and singuler the aforesaid premises, by the delivrye vnto her at the ensealing hear of one coyned peece of silver commonly called two pence fixed on the seal of these presents

In wittnes wherof I the said Iohn Bunyan have herevnto set my hand and seall this 23[d] day of December in the first year of the reigne of our souraigne lord King Iames the second of England &c in the year of our lord and saviour Iesus christ 1685

sealed and delivered in the
presence of vs whos names   Iohn Bunyan
are here vnder written[1]

1. Signatures of four witnesses omitted here; also the cancelled beginning of Bunyan's signature [*Ioh*] which he began to write again immediately below his completed signature.

Notes

Bunyan holographs are few, being mainly limited to the Deed of Gift illustrated here, and seven passages in the Church Book of Bunyan Meeting, written between 1672 and 1683.

Other possible holographs and signatures have sometimes been called in question. See, further, J. Brown, *John Bunyan*, rev. F. M. Harrison, 1928, esp. 122, 216–17, 230, 338,

415–38, 469–75; F. M. Harrison, *Supplement to Bib. Soc. Trans.*, no. 6, 1930 for 1932, xxv–vi, 65–71; J. Godber, *Bedfordshire Magazine*, vi, 1957, 47–9; *BC*, 8, 1959, 427 (a possible autograph); T. J. Brown, *BC*, 9, 1960, 53–5. A facs. of the Church Book of Bunyan Meeting, intro. by G. B. Harrison, was published in 1928. The Deed of Gift was made by Bunyan in place of a will in case he was again imprisoned and his property confiscated. He then hid it so successfully that it was not found until two years after his death.
Characteristics. A fairly bold, rounded hand, a little more careless and larger than in the Church Book (cf. facs. T. J. Brown). It is markedly irregular in letter and word formations, and the minims are drawn out and splayed. While basically *italic*, it anticipates something of the appearance of *round* hand at its more negligent. Though nearly all the graphs are from the more cursive type of *italic* (e.g. *d* and the double-looped medium-sized *s*), *e* is exclusively of the reversed *secretary* form. One of the most variable letters is *r*, which can be the *v* type (l. 9, *hearof*), or the low-shouldered form with a foot-serif (l. 13, *souraigne*), or possibly as a variant of the twin-stemmed variety, like a rounded *italic* x (l. 8, *her*). The left-shouldered type is also present (l. 13, *first*), while a form of the regular *italic* r makes an occasional appearance (l. 15, *lord*). **Punctuation** is very light, comprising an occasional period and comma and line fillers (top, ll. 6, 10) to prevent unauthorized additions. There are no **abbreviations**.

Heroique Stanza's,
Consecrated to the glorious ~~it Military~~ memorie
Of his most Serene & Renowned Highness
OLIVER

5 Late Lord Protector of this Common-wealth. &c.
Written after the Celebration of his Funeralls.

And now 'tis time; for theire officious hast
Who would before have borne him to the sky
Like Eager Romans, ere all ritds were past
10 Did let too soone the sacred Eagle fly.

2

Though our best notes are treason to his fame
Joynd with the loud applause of publique voice,
Since Heav'n what praise wee offer to his name
15 Hath render'd too authentiq by its choise;

Posterity. I have consulted the Judgment of my Unbyass'd friends, who have
Some of them the honour to be known to you, & they think there is nothing
which can justly give offence, in that part of the Poem. I say not this, to
cast a blind on your Judgment (which I could not do, if I indeavourd it) but
5 to assure you, that nothing relateing to the publique shall stand, without your
permission. For it were to want Common Sense, to desire your patronage, &
resolve to disoblige you: And I will not hazard my hope of your protection
by refusing to obey you in any thing, which I can performe with my Conscience, or
my honour; So I am very confident you will never impose any other terms on Mee.
10 My thoughts at present are fix'd on Homer: And by my translation of the first
Iliad; I find him a Poet more according to my Genius than Virgil: and consequently
I may do him more justice, in his fiery way of writing; which as it is liable
to more faults, so it is capable of more beauties, than the exactness, & sobriety
of Virgil. Since 'tis for my Countryes honour, as well as for my own, that I am
15 willing to undertake this task; I despair not of being encourag'd in it, by your favour
who am Sir
                    Your most Obedient Servant
                                              John Dryden.

66 'Elegy on Oliver Cromwell': title and opening stanzas.
Set/facile round hand, holograph, 1659.
B.L., Lansdowne 1045, f. 101, upper portion.

Heroique Stanzas,

Consecrated to the glorious [& happy] memorie
Of his most Serene[1] & Renowned Highness

OLIVER

5 Late Lord Protector of this Common wealth. &c.
Written after the Celebration of his Funeralls.

And now t'is time; for theire officious hast
Who would before haue borne him to the Sky[1]
Like Eager Romans, e're all rites were past
10 Did let too soone the sacred Eagle fly.

2

Though our best notes are treason to his fame
Ioyn'd with the loud applause of publique voice,
Since[1] Heav'n what praise wee offer to his name
15 Hath render'd too authentiqʊe by its choise;

1. Uncertain whether *S* or *s* intended.

67 Lower half of letter to Charles Montague, later Earl of
Halifax, October 1699. *Facile round hand*, holograph.
B.L., Add MS 12112, f. 373, lower portion.

Posterity. I have consulted the Iudgment of my Unbyassd friends, who have
some of them the honour to be known to you; & they think there is nothing
which can justly give offence, in that part of the Poem. I say not this, to cast a
blind on your Iudgment (which I cou'd not do, if I indeavourd it) but to assure you,
that nothing relateing to the publique shall stand, without your permission.
For it were to want Common sence, to desire your patronage, & resolve to
disoblige you: And ∧ ⌈as⌉ I will not hazard my hopes of your protection by
refusing to obey you in any thing, which I can perform with my Conscience, or my
honour; so I am very confident you will never impose any other terms on Me. My
thoughts at present are fixd on Homer: And by my translation of the first Iliad;
I[1] find him a Poet more according to my Genius than Virgil: and Consequently
hope I may do him more justice, in his fiery way of writeing; which as it is liable
to more faults, so it is capable of more beauties, than the exactness, & sobriety of
Virgil. Since tis for my Country's honour, as well as for my own, that I am
willing to undertake this task; I despair not of being encouragd in it, by your
favour who am Sir
                    Your most Obedient Servant
                    Iohn Dryden.

1. *I* superscribed on &. The preceding semicolon apparently replaces uncancelled comma.

Notes
Dryden provides a further example of a recent
discovery of an important poetic holograph, in
this case, as with Sidney, Donne and Herrick,
the first of any consequence. The find, an
unsigned fair copy of the Cromwell elegy, was
reported by A. M. Crinò (*TLS*, 22 Sept. 1966,
879), who later transcribed it with facs. in
English Miscellany, xvii, 1966, 311–20. This
holograph augments the rather scanty material
in his hand in the form of revisions to his *State
of Innocence* (Harvard College) and
correspondence in the B.L. For discussion and
facs. of Dryden's hand *vide* FRHL, 101; T. J.
Brown, *BC*, 1, 1952, 180; Croft, 53; facs. of the
earliest Dryden letter, 23 May 1653, *Works of
John Dryden*, ed. E. N. Hooker and H. T.
Swedenberg, i, 1956, betw. 8 and 9. For
sources *vide* H. Macdonald, *John Dryden*, 1939
and 1967. The correspondence was edited by
C. E. Ward, with a facs., 1942, repr. 1965.
Characteristics. Dryden's hand has been
described as influenced by the cursive baroque
Italian style (T. J. Brown, *op. cit.*), which was
undoubtedly important in the development of
the English *round hand*. Three phases have been
discerned in Dryden's writing, first an upright
and ornate schoolroom script, then a plainer,
sloping and very cursive style of the 1680s, and
finally an upright, simple and slow hand of his
last years (*id.*). While there are examples to
support this helpful chronological division, it
does not appear to be an invariable one. Some
differences of style seem more explicable in
terms of degrees of formality while the slope of
the middle period sometimes holds good for the
early and late ones, as the present illustrations
show. It is certainly clear, however, that the
hand becomes more halting and the slope a
little intermittent by 1699, and there is nothing
of the gliding delicacy which characterizes the
poem. On the other hand, the letter forms have
changed remarkably little over the forty years.
For example, the curved back of *d* is much the
same, so are the general proportions of *f* with
cross-stroke drawn back in a bow behind the
shaft (66, l. 3, *Of*; 67, l. 10, *first*) or of the more
formal *italic f* (66, l. 7, *officious*; 67, l. 13, *faults*).
Both use not only *italic e*, but *secretary* reverse *e*
(66, l. 9, *Eager*; 67, l. 10, *the*) and versions of the
two-stroke variety (66, l. 6, *written*; 67, l. 1,
friends, have). Both have further traces of
secretary, e.g., *W* (66, l. 8, *Who*) and *w* (67, l. 15,
willing). Another shared characteristic is the
tendency to have an upward curl on stems (cf.
P, 66, l. 5, *Protector*; 67, l. 11, *Poet*). However,
67 develops this characteristic on the stem of *p*,
which in 66 is quite straight and unadorned.
Punctuation is extremely full, and while still
not conforming to modern practice, it
establishes some pattern of three degrees of
pause from comma, through semicolon, to
period. The apostrophe is used liberally for the
possessive (67, l. 14), unvoiced *e* and *l* (66,
l. 11; 67, l. 4), and for ellision, in the case of *tis*
(66, l. 6) the apostrophe coming after the *t*
rather than before, as sometimes happens in the
period. Apart from elision, the only other
marks of **abbreviation** are *qȝ* for *que* (66, l.
15), & and &c (*etc.*).

◉ Select Bibliography: 1375–1700

Works are listed only once, but if they are also relevant to another section of the Bibliography, the number of that section is given in brackets at the end. Items not included under section 6 which contain extensive facsimiles are followed by (f). An asterisk signifies that the entry is considered especially useful in the context of this book. Individual authors are dealt with in the appropriate places in the text. References to manuscript collections and collectors are touched on in the Introduction (especially notes 11 to 24), and are comprehensively listed in the *New Cambridge bibliography of English literature*, i, 1974, 985–1006.

1. Bibliographies and general reference

Christopher, H. G. T., *Palaeography and archives: a manual for the librarian, archivist and student*. London, 1938.

Johnston, E., *Writing, illuminating and lettering*. New impr., London, 1965. (f, 2)

Madan, F., *Books in manuscript*. 2nd ed., rev., 2nd impr., 1927. (2, 3, 4)

Prou, M., *Manuel de paléographie latine et française*. 4th ed., rev. A. de Boüard. Paris, 1924. (f)

Thompson, E. M., *Introduction to Greek and Latin palaeography*. Oxford, 1912. (f)

Turner, E. G., Barbour, R., Brown, T. J., 'Palaeography', *Encyclopaedia Britannica*, 1971 ed. (f, 4)

University of London Library. The palaeography collection, ed. J. Gibbs. 2 vols., Boston, 1968.

Valentine, L. N., *Ornament in mediaeval manuscripts: a glossary*. London, 1965.

*Watson, G., *New Cambridge bibliography of English literature*, i, 600–1660. Cambridge, 1974, 209–20, 927–38, 985–1006.

2. Writing materials: parchment, paper, implements

Briquet, C. M., *Les filigranes*. 4 vols., 2nd ed., Leipzig, 1923, repr. New York, 1968.

Bühler, C. F., 'Watermarks and the dates of 15th century books', *Studies in Bibliography*, ix, 1957. (9)

Churchill, W. A., *Watermarks in paper in Holland, England, France in the seventeenth and eighteenth centuries*. Amsterdam, 1935. (9)

Clapperton, R. H., *Paper: an historical account of its making from earliest times down to the present day*. Oxford, 1934.

'The history of paper-making in England', *Paper-Maker*, xxii, 1953.

Heawood, E., 'Papers used in England after 1600', *Library*, 4th ser., xi, 1931. (9)

Watermarks mainly of the 17th and 18th centuries. Hilversum, 1950. (9)

Hunter, D., *Papermaking: the history and technique of an ancient craft*. Rev., London, 1947.

Jones, L. W., 'Pricking manuscripts: the instruments and their significance', *Speculum*, xxi, 1946. (9)

Labarre, E. J., 'The study of watermarks in Great Britain: English index to Briquet's *Watermarks*', *The Briquet album: a miscellany supplementing Dr Briquet's Les filigranes*. Hilversum, 1952. (9)

Saxl, H., 'The histology of parchment', *Technical studies in the field of fine arts*, viii, William Hayes Fogg Art Museum, Boston, 1939.

Shorter, A. H., *Paper mills and paper makers in England, 1495–1800*. Hilversum, 1957.

Stevenson, A. H., 'Chain indentations in paper as evidence', *Studies in Bibliography*, vi, 1954. (9)

'Paper as bibliographical evidence', *Library*, 5th ser., xvii, 1962. (9)

'Tudor Roses from John Tate', *Studies in Bibliography*, xx, 1967.

Thompson, D. V., 'Mediaeval parchment-making', *Library*, 4th ser., xvi, 1935.

The materials of mediaeval painting. New Haven, 1936, repr. New York, 1956.

Ustick, W. L., 'Parchment and vellum', *Library*, 4th ser., xvi, 1936.

3. The manuscript book

Bennett, H. S., 'The production and dissemination of vernacular MSS in the 15th century', *Library*, 5th ser., i, 1947.

Bühler, C. F., *The 15th century book: the scribes, the printers, the decorators*. Philadelphia, 1960.

Deansly, M., 'Vernacular books in England in the 14th and 15th centuries', *Modern Language Review*, xv, 1920.

Destrez, J., *La pecia dans les MSS universitaires du xiiie et du xive siècle*. Paris, 1935.

Grant, J., *Books and documents*. New York, 1937.

Harthan, J. P., *Bookbindings*. HMSO, 2nd ed., rev., London, 1961.

Hobson, G. D., *English bookbinding before 1500*. Cambridge, 1929.

Ivy, G. S., 'The bibliography of the manuscript book', *The English library before 1700*, ed. F. Wormald and C. E. Wright. London, 1958.

Millar, E. G., *English illuminated manuscripts of the xivth and xvth centuries*. Paris, 1928.

Nixon, H. M., 'English bookbindings', *Book Collector*, i, 1952– (in progress).

Oldham, J. B., *Blind panels of English binders*. Cambridge, 1958.

Plant, M., *The English book trade*. 2nd ed., London, 1965.

Pollard, H. G., 'Notes on the size of sheet', *Library*, 4th ser., xxii, 1941.

Putnam, G. H., *Books and their makers during the Middle Ages*. 2 vols., New York and London, 1896, repr. New York, 1962.

Wilson, R. M., 'The contents of the mediaeval library', *The English library before 1700*, ed. F. Wormald and C. E. Wright. London, 1958.

4. Handwriting

Bischoff, B., *Lieftinck, G. I., Battelli, G., *Nomenclature des écritures livresques du ixe au xvie siècle*. Paris, 1954. (f, 9)

Brown, T. J., 'English literary autographs' (1650–1950), *Book Collector*, i–xiv, 1952–64. (f)

Byrne, M. St Claire, 'Elizabethan handwriting for beginners', *Review of English Studies*, i, 1925.

Crous, E., Kirchner, J., *Die gotischen Schriftarten.* Leipzig, 1928. (f)

Day, L. F., *Penmanship of the 16th, 17th and 18th centuries.* London, 1911. (f)

de la Mare, A., *The handwriting of the Italian humanists,* i, fasc. i, Oxford, 1973. (f)

*Denholm-Young, N., *Handwriting in England and Wales.* Cardiff, 1954. (f)

Fairbank, A. J., *A book of scripts.* Rev. and enlarged, Harmondsworth, 1968. (f)

*Wolpe, B., *Renaissance handwriting,* 1960. (f, 2, 5)

*Heal, A., Morison, S., *The English writing-masters and their copy-books, 1570–1800.* Cambridge, 1931, repr. Hildesheim, 1962. (f)

*Hector, L. C., *The handwriting of English documents.* 2nd ed., rev., London, 1966. (f, 2, 7, 8)

Jenkinson, H., 'Elizabethan handwritings: a preliminary sketch', *Library,* 4th ser., iii, 1923. (f)

'English current writing and early printing', *Trans. of Bibl. Soc.,* xiii, 1915.

The later court hands in England. 2 vols., Cambridge, 1927. (f)

*Johnson, C., Jenkinson, H., *English court hand, 1066–1500.* Oxford, 1915. (f)

Lowe, E. A., *Handwriting: our Medieval legacy.* Rome, 1969 (repr. from *The legacy of the Middle Ages,* ed. C. G. Crump and E. F. Jacob. Oxford, 1926).

Massey, W., *The origin and progress of letters.* London, 1763.

McKerrow, R. B., 'The capital letters in Elizabethan handwriting', *Review of English Studies,* iii, 1927.

Morison, S., 'Early humanistic script and the first roman type', *Library,* 4th ser., xxiv, 1944. (f)

*Parkes, M. B., *English cursive book hands, 1250–1500.* Oxford, 1969. (f)

Ryder, J., *Lines of the alphabet in the 16th century.* London, 1965.

Schulz, H. C., 'The teaching of handwriting in Tudor and Stuart times', *Huntington Library Quarterly,* v, 1943.

*Simpson, G. G., *Scottish handwriting, 1150–1650.* Bratton Press, 1973. (f)

Steinberg, S. H., 'Mediaeval writing-masters', *Library,* 4th ser., xxii, 1942.

Stiennon, J., *Paléographie du Moyen-Age.* Paris, 1973. (f)

Strange, E. F., 'The early English writing-masters', *Bibliografica,* iii, 1897.

*Tannenbaum, S. A., *The handwriting of the Renaissance.* London and New York, 1931. (f, 6, 7)

Thompson, E. M., 'Handwriting', *Shakespeare's England,* vol. i. Oxford, 1916.

Ullman, B. L., *The origins and development of humanistic script.* Rome, 1960. (f)

*Van Dijk, S. J. P., 'An advertisement of an early 14th century writing master at Oxford', *Scriptorium,* x, 1956. (f)

Wardrop, J., 'Civis Romanus sum', *Signature,* n.s., xiv, 1952. (f)

The script of humanism. Oxford, 1963. (f)

5. Copybooks

*Anon., ed. B. Wolpe, *A newe booke of copies* (1574). Oxford, 1962.

Ayres, J., *The accomplish'd clerk.* London, 1673?

*Baildon, J., de Beauchesne, J., *A booke containing divers sortes of hands, as well the English as the French secretarie.* London, 1570.

Billingsley, M., *The pen's excellencie, or the secretarie's delighte.* London, 1618.

Clement, F., *The petie schole, with an English orthographie.* London, 1587.

Cocker, E., *The pen's transcendencie: or faire writing's labyrinth.* London, 1657.

Cresci, F. C., *Essemplare di piu sorti lettere* (1560 and 1578), ed. and transl. A. S. Osley. London, 1968.

Da Carpi, U., *Thesauro de scrittori* (1535), intro. by E. Potter. London, 1968.

Davies, J., *The anatomie of fair writing.* London, c. 1620.

Fugger, W., *Wolffgang Fugger's handwriting manual* (1550), transl. F. Plaat, London, 1960.

Gery, P., *Gerii viri in arte scriptoria quondam celeberrimi opera.* London, 1659.

Hondius, J., *Theatrum artis scribendi* (1594). Nieuwkoop, 1969.

*Ogg, O., *Three classics of Italian calligraphy* (works by Arrighi, Tagliente and Palatino). New York, 1963.

*Yciar, J. de, *Arte subtilissima* (1550), transl. E. Schuckburgh. London, 1958, 2nd ed., 1960.

6. Facsimiles

Brouwer, H., *Atlas voor Nederlandsche palaeographie.* The Hague, 1946.

*Croft, P. J., *Autograph poetry in the English language.* 2 vols., London, 1973. (4)

*Dawson, G. E., Kennedy-Skipton, L., *Elizabethan handwriting.* Rev., London, 1968. (4)

Fairbank, A. J., Dickins, B., *The italic hand in Tudor Cambridge.* Cambridge, 1962.

Hunt, R. W., *Humanistic script of the 15th and 16th centuries.* Oxford, 1960.

Flower, D. J. N., Munby, A. N. L., *English poetical autographs from Sir Thomas Wyat to Rupert Brooke.* London, 1938.

*Greg, W. W., *Dramatic documents from the Elizabethan playhouses.* 2 vols., Oxford, 1931.

English literary autographs, 1550–1650. 3 pts., Oxford, 1925–32. (4)

Facsimiles of twelve early English MSS in the library of Trinity College Cambridge. Cambridge, 1913.

Grieve, H. E. P., *Examples of English handwriting, 1150–1750.* Essex Record Office, 1954.

James, H., *Facsimiles of the national MSS of Scotland.* 3 pts., Southampton, 1867–71.

Judge, C. B., *Specimens of 16th century English handwriting.* Cambridge, Mass., 1935.

Kirchner, J., *Scriptura gothica libraria.* Munich and Vienna, 1966.

Scriptura latina libraria. Munich, 1955 (with table of alphabets).

Lieftinck, G. I., *MSS datés conservés dans les Pays-Bas, catalogue paléographique,* i, *Les MSS d'origine étrangère, 816–c. 1550.* 2 vols., Amsterdam, 1964–.

Mentz, G., *Handschriften der Reformationszeit.* Bonn, 1912.

Morton, A., *Men of letters.* P.R.O. Museum pamphlet no. 6, London, 1974.

New Palaeographical Society, Publications, ed. E. M. Thompson and others. London, 1903–30.

Palaeographical Society, Publications, ed. E. A. Bond and others. London, 1873–1901.

Skeat, W. W., *Twelve facsimiles of old English MSS*. Oxford, 1892.

Thomson, S. H., *Latin bookhands of the later Middle Ages, 1100–1500*. Cambridge, 1969.

Walley, J. I., *English handwriting, 1540–1853*. HMSO, London, 1969.

Warner, G. F., *Facsimiles of royal, historical, literary and other autographs in the British Museum*, 1st series, 2nd ed., London, 1899.

Williams, H. S., *The history of the art of writing*, portfolio 4. London and New York, 1902.

*Wright, C. E., *English vernacular hands from the 12th to the 15th centuries*. Oxford, 1960. (4)

7. Abbreviation

Bains, D., *Supplement to Notae latinae*. Cambridge, 1936.

*Cappelli, A., *Lexicon abbreviaturum*. 6th ed., Milan, 1961.

*Chassant, L. A., *Dictionnaire des abréviations latines et françaises*. Repr. Hildesheim, 1965.

Laurent, M. H., *De abbreviationibus et signis scripturae gothicae*. Rome, 1939.

*Martin, C. T., *The record interpreter*. Repr. London, 1949.

Mentz, A., *Die tironischer Noten*. Berlin, 1944.

*Pelzer, A., *Abréviations latines médiévales*. Louvain and Paris, 1964.

Schiaparelli, L., *Avviamento allo studio delle abbreviature latine nel medioevo*. Florence, 1926.

Traube, L., *Nomina sacra*. Munich, 1907.

8. Punctuation and numerals

Cawley, A. C., 'Punctuation in early versions of Trevisa', *London Mediaeval Studies*, i, 1939.

*Hill, G. F., *The development of Arabic numerals in Europe*. Oxford, 1915.

Jenkinson, H., 'Notes on the study of punctuation', *Review of English Studies*, ii, 1926.

'The use of Arabic and Roman numerals in English archives', *Antiquaries Journal*, v, 1926.

*Ong, W., 'Backgrounds to Elizabethan punctuation', *Publ. Mod. Lang. Assoc.*, lix, 1944.

Partridge, A. C., *Orthography in Shakespeare and Elizabethan drama*. London, 1964.

*Treip, M., *Milton's punctuation and changing English usage, 1582–1676*. London, 1970.

Wright, C. G. N., *The writing of Arabic numerals*. London, 1952.

9. Transcribing, editing, the detection of forgery

*Brown, T. J., 'The detection of faked literary manuscripts', *Book Collector*, ii, 1953.

Harrison, W. R., *Forgery detection: a practical guide*. London, 1964.

Suspect documents: their scientific examination. 2nd imp. and suppl., London, 1968.

*Haselden, R. B., *Scientific aids for the study of manuscripts*. Bibl. Soc., London, 1935.

Hector, L. C., *Palaeography and forgery*. St Anthony's Hall Publ., xv, London, 1959.

*Manly, J. M., Rickert, E., *The text of the Canterbury Tales*, i, description of the MSS. Chicago, 1940 (a model for describing MSS).

Marshall, R. L., *The historical criticism of documents*. SPCK helps for students of history, no. 28, London, 1920.

Mitchell, C. A., *Documents and their scientific examination*. London, 1935.

Simpson, P., *Proof-reading in the 16th, 17th and 18th centuries*. London, 1935. (8)

Thompson, E. M., 'Two pretended autographs of Shakespeare', *Library*, 3rd ser., viii, 1917.

Vinaver, E., 'Principles of textual emendation', *Studies presented to M. K. Pope*, Manchester, 1939.

Index

132